Rowena

THE
MATCHSTICK
BOY

Published by Goldcrest Books International Ltd
www.goldcrestbooks.com
publish@goldcrestbooks.com

ISBN: 978-1-913719-89-0

Author's Note and Acknowledgements

This novel is inspired by true facts. It portrays the inhabitants of a remote town in the Swiss Alps and their dependency on the local matchstick factories in the mid-19th century. The village Weissbruegg is a typical village in Frutigland, somewhere in the Kander valley between Adelboden and Spiez, in Switzerland. The reader will not find Weissbruegg on a map, it exists only in my imagination. The true village where Gretl[1] grew up is in the area, but I have changed the name to protect the privacy of its inhabitants. Likewise, all names of persons involved have been changed.

The idea of writing this book came after reading an article in a local newspaper about the opening of a new Matchstick Factory Museum in Frutigen. The opening had been delayed because of Covid 19.

Not many contemporary witnesses survive today. For that reason, we may be grateful to the Kulturstiftung Frutigland who has opened a museum "Die Zündholz Industrie" about the matchstick industry in Frutigland. Hans and Ruedi Egli have written a brochure to accompany the museum exhibition titled "die Zündholz Industrie im Frutigland." It is written in German and can be bought at

---

1. *Name changed*

regional bookshops or via mail (info@kulturgutstiftung.ch). I am particularly grateful to Ruedi Egli for imparting to me a wealth of information about the matchstick industry and the effects it had on the local population. Also to Kathi Schmidt, one surviving witness today who took time to give an interview, along with an excellent cup of coffee!

This book is dedicated to Rudolf Jungen, a living relative of Gretl.[2] I am exceptionally grateful for his open mind and the knowledge and insight into the social background he made known to me.

The terms 'mentally deficient', or 'simple-minded' or similar are politically incorrect and are no longer used today. However, at the time of the court procedures at the end of the 19th century, these terms were used. To change them in this book would be to falsify history. On no account do I wish to cause offence to any person.

There are many people that I would like to thank for helping me with the research for this book: Andreas Gyger, Pädagogisches Zentrum für Hören und Sprache, Sunneschyn Steffisburg; Lisbeth Stutz, Sachbearbeiterin Umwelt und Betriebe, Gemeindeverwaltung Frutigen.

I would especially like to thank an 'old' school friend of mine, Deborah Swift, best-selling author of historical fiction, for her beta-reading, encouragement and useful comments.

Many thanks also to Karen Ette, my fabulous proof editor, who picked out all those 'little' mistakes. Any remaining mistakes are mine.

---

2. *Name changed*

GLOSSARY

Affinage	A cave dug into the mountain for the sole purpose of maturing cheese in an ideal climate.
Alm	A middle-high pasture in the Alps.
Berchtold Haller (1492-1536)	Reformer of the city of Bern. He was in close contact with Philipp Melanchthon and Ulrich Zwingli.
Boelima	A ghost (local Swiss German).
Canton	County.
Frutigland	Name of a district.
Gehrihorn	Name of a mountain.
Gopfriedstutz!	Darn it!
Grueenmatti Innkeeper	A legendary story from the area.
Gspaltenhorn	A mountain.
Inselspital	University hospital in Bern.
Landjaeger	Double meaning: a. village policeman in Switzerland b. a certain type of smoked sausage.
League	Equivalent to 3 miles. Switzerland changed to the metric system between 1868 and 1877.
Loeli	Idiot (Swiss German).
Maeggisserenegg	Local area.

Niesen ridge	Ridge in the Bernese mountains.
Pochtenfall	Name of a waterfall.
Pot	Liquid measurement before the metric system was introduced. One pot was equivalent to 1 ½ litres.
Pouce	Old measurement equivalent to an inch.
Prost!	Cheers!
Schatz	Endearment; lit. Treasure.
Schnapps	A high-percent alcoholic drink or liqueur, usually made from fruit but also sometimes from potatoes or even garlic.
Senn	"Head" herdsman, usually responsible for looking after cows and making cheese in the summer months up in the Alps.
Spissen	A local area high up in the clefts of mountains.
Stollenwurm	A local legendary monster in the Alps.
Weissbruegg	The imaginary name of a town, typical of many in the area but non-existent.
Zibelemärit	Onion market. A traditional folks' festival which takes place on the fourth Monday every November in Bern.

The Matchstick Boy

Inspired by a true story that took place at the foot of the
Alps in the last half of the nineteenth century.

Rowena Kinread

1

OCTOBER 1849

Dusk had fallen an hour ago but still Anton was chopping wood outside their farmhouse. There was always so much work to do and never enough time. Now that Lena's time was drawing close, he had even more to do, relieving her of some of the more strenuous jobs. The wind whipped up blowing sawdust into his eyes and making them water. Anton stopped to rub them and looked into the distance. Lightning was flashing behind the Niesen mountains. He licked his forefinger and held it up in the air. Yes, the storm was coming in their direction. He stopped cutting wood and tidied his tools away quickly. He secured the shutters across the windows and made sure that nothing else was lying about, prey to the approaching gale. Then he picked up a heap of logs and pushed against the front door with his shoulder. The door banged open and a gust of cold wind and a trail of dead leaves and straw followed him indoors.

"Sorry Schatz," he said, dropping the logs hastily beside the fire and rushing back to close the door. "There's a storm brewing. We have a fair wind and I saw lightning flare behind the Niesen ridge. It's coming our way." He knelt down by the fire and started piling the logs up neatly. "Shall I put another one on?"

He smiled at his wife, his heart warming and his chest swelling with love. Lena was sitting close to the log fire, unravelling an old pullover worn beyond repair. He recognised it as one that he had inherited from his deceased uncle a year back. Several balls of brown wool lay in a basket at her feet. Lena never complained about their poverty but worked hard to make the most out of everything.

This pregnancy hadn't been so straightforward as the first two. Anton gazed at their two young boys sleeping angelically on their straw mattress in the corner of the room. Lena hadn't said anything but he saw the flashes of pain that sometimes crossed her face and he noticed her lips pressed together when she straightened up after bending down. Well, just another month to go.

"No, it's been a long day, and tomorrow will be no shorter if we have to clear up after the storm. I'm going to lie down now. Hopefully the wind will let us sleep," she answered.

"I fastened the shutters. We should be all right. What are you planning on knitting?" he asked kindly.

"Some new socks for you. I hope to get two pairs out of the wool but so much has disintegrated that it might only be enough for one. I must stop now anyway; the light is too dim and I can barely keep my eyes open."

"Why don't you knit socks for the boys, their feet are smaller?"

"Your need is greater."

"Nee, I'm fine, the little ones should have warm feet."

Lena put down the half-unravelled pullover and heaved herself up to remove her brown dress. She splashed some water over her face from a bowl and undid the bun at the nape of her neck, and then she fell down clumsily with a suppressed groan onto a straw mattress next to the boys.

Anton removed his boots, trousers and jumper. He could hear their four cows shuffling their hooves in the animal quarters in the next room, but apart from these comforting sounds, all was peaceful. He stared critically into their small oval mirror and tried to remove bits of straw from his unruly brown hair.

"Come here," Lena patted the mattress, "I'll help you."

He sat his long, lean frame down next to his wife and let her comb his hair, and then he lay down next to her, put one arm around her swollen belly, and within seconds they had both fallen into a deep sleep.

*****

Anton awoke to the cacophony of their cattle mooing in panic. He bolted upright on the mattress and listened for half a second. He shook Lena awake.

"Something is up; the cows are bellowing." Pulling on his boots on quickly, he said: "I'll go and look," and was already halfway through the door leading to the animals' quarters.

Lena pulled her own boots on and dragged herself out of bed, ignoring the sharp twinges in her belly. Anton burst back into the living room.

"Hurry!" he cried. "The hayloft is burning! Get the children out of here and bring as many buckets as you can!"

Lena shook two-year-old Jakob's shoulders and picked up one-year-old Josef.

"Quick!" she told Jakob, "the loft's burning." She opened the front door. "Run to Papa, he's near the well."

With Josef on one arm, Lena looked frantically around

for more water containers, but smoke was already drifting through the door from the byre, making her eyes sting and she started to cough. Inhaling smoke, she grabbed what she could and dashed outside. She went around their wood-built house and struggled up the mountain slope into which it was built with her child and buckets. It had only been a matter of minutes, but by the time she reached the well at the back of the house the building was in flames.

Anton was in his long johns and boots, desperately hauling water up from the well, his face streaked with grime and sweat. Little Jakob stood beside him, wide-eyed and bewildered. Thunder crashed around them and lightning bolts lit up the sky. Defeated, Anton stopped turning the handle of the well; he supported his hands on the surrounding wall and observed the flames licking up the sides of the building and devouring years of hard labour.

Lena arrived and asked: "The animals?"

Anton made a sweeping movement with his arms. "Out there somewhere. I managed to get them all out, but … oh Lena, we've lost everything else!" He broke down, gasping and crying in despair.

The wind swirled glowing, red-hot fire sparks high up into the sky towards their neighbour's farm, barely two hundred yards distant. As with most of the local buildings, the roof was tiled with wooden shingles. The fiery sparks landed on the roof, and Anton and Lena watched dumbstruck, as it too began to burn.

"It's too late for us. I'd better go and help them," Anton said, picking up their buckets. Lena bent down to put Josef onto the ground. As she tried to straighten up again, a vicious contraction ripped through her body and fluid gushed down the inside of her legs.

"Aargh!" she cried, clutching her belly and sinking to

her knees. "My waters have broken. The baby's coming early!"

"Oh no, not that as well!" Anton dropped his buckets. "I'll go and get help. Stay here," he told Jakob, "and look after your mother and brother."

Still in his underwear and boots, he bolted down the hill along the stony path, scarcely registering more burning farms. Villagers from Weissbruegg ran towards him with buckets and empty containers, eager to help their stricken neighbours. Everyone was rushing and shouting. Anton pushed past them all. He waded across a stream surging down the mountainside towards the river Kander, left the path and took a shortcut, half leaping, half skidding, down a steep-sided meadow. He vaulted over a wooden fence and pushed through a wild hedge until he finally reached his sister Margot's home. He thumped hard and urgently on the thick wooden door, and then, without waiting, he opened it.

"Hang on, we're coming." Gustl, Margot's husband, was hopping on one leg, pulling a boot on. "We've seen the fires. We were just …" he stopped mid-stream as he noticed Anton's expression. "What's up? Did the lightning strike your place too?"

"Yes, it's burned down to ashes. The baby's coming, we need help."

"Jesus, Maria and Josef!" Margot cried out, crossing herself, "Gustl, grab some blankets! Don't worry, Anton, it's not her first. We'll come with you and get you all back here."

*****

Jakob sat on the ground next to his mother, his arms around Josef who was sitting between his legs. It was dark, save for the glow of their neighbour's farm burning. He heard the crackle of fire sending red sparks into the sky and the sound of adults shouting and screaming. Already scared, when his mother let out a shriek of agonised pain, he became terrified.

"Mama!" he said, clutching her hand, "what's wrong?"

Lena bit her lip waiting for the contraction to pass, at the same time reaching out to Jakob's little fist, clenched tightly around her finger.

"Everything is fine; it's just your little brother, or sister, is coming now. Don't worry, Papa will be here soon with Aunt Margot and Uncle Gustl." She groaned as the next contraction swept through her body.

"Mama!"

"It's all right, my little treasure, it will be all right, I promise. Be brave now and look after Josef." Josef was wriggling, trying to escape Jakob's hold.

"Yes, Mama."

"Promise! If anything … does happen, look after him always. You're his big brother."

Jakob held Josef back and gave him a cuddle.

"I promise."

"Good boy," Lena answered, and passed out.

It started raining. It pelted down, soaking the boys, their mother and the ground with icy water. Jakob held Josef in a tight embrace. They were both so cold that their teeth chattered like a watermill rattling in a rushing stream. The sky was black, and their mother lay unusually silent in a dark bundle next to them. Jakob felt deserted. Why had his mother made him promise to look after Josef? Was she going somewhere? He cried, he didn't want to be left alone, he wanted to go with her.

*****

Gustl and Margot hastened after Anton, who had bolted off like a startled hare. They saw farms burning on the hillside above them and gazed at the sky hoping for rain. The first fat drops fell as they crossed the stream. A moment later the deluge came. The heavens opened and delivered a sudden torrent of rain. Small streams began trickling down the stony path towards them. Within seconds they were soaked and battling uphill against the downpour to where Anton's farm should have been standing.

Lena was lying on the ground next to the well in a foetal position. She was clutching her stomach, trembling uncontrollably. It was still dark, and if Anton hadn't known she was there, he could easily have mistaken her shape for a heap of dirty rags. Jakob sat next to her, his face white and tense, silent tears rolling down his cheeks. He was holding onto Josef firmly between his legs. As soon as they saw their father they both burst out crying loudly.

Out of breath, his lungs burning, Anton went straight to Lena. He wiped her hair gently back from her face and said, "Don't worry, we're here now."

Margot ordered Gustl: "Put a rug around her shoulders and help me get her up! We've got to get her to our place."

"No, it's too late, I can't!" Lena squealed like a wounded animal.

"No alternative!" Margot was rigorous. "Come on now, we're here to help." She took one of Lena's arms and put it around her shoulder. Gustl did likewise and together, ignoring her screams, they heaved her up. Anton wrapped rugs around both his boys and picked them up.

They set off. Lena, as pale as death, clenched her teeth together and managed to walk, supported, a few steps before the next contraction came. She bent over double.

"Something's different this time," she croaked.

Margot's demeanour was solemn but determined. "We have to get her back. She can't have it here in the middle of the road in the pouring rain."

They set off again. Lena's head tilted forward and she passed out. Margot and Gustl dragged her a few steps further.

Anton put the boys down and said, "I'll carry her. You take the boys!" He lifted Lena up into his arms and carried her all the way back to his sister's home. Kicking the door open with one foot, he entered and laid Lena gently down on the floor in front of the cold fire. Margot and Gustl came in, put the boys down and shook the rain from their clothes.

"Well, don't just stand there!" Margot ordered the men, "get the fire going. We'll be needing hot water. Gustl, find some clean rags. Anton, help me make Lena more comfortable!"

Anton put a rug under Lena's head, undid some buttons on her shift, and removed her boots. Her eyes fluttered open and focussed on him. She gripped his wrist and dug her nails into his skin.

"Don't go," she begged, "stay with me, something's not right, I can feel it!"

"I'm here," he rasped, his voice breaking. "I'm not going anywhere."

Margot knelt down between Lena's legs and pushed her shift up.

"Help me get her underwear off," she told Anton. He lifted Lena's pelvis with both hands and Margot pulled her bloodied drawers down. Lena's cervix was fully open. Margot put her hands into the birth canal and felt not a head but two feet. "It's a breech," she said. "Lena, it's too late to turn the baby, I can feel the feet. I'm going to try and help it out. Right, I've got the feet, and I'm pushing them close to the body. Now!"

Lena raised her head and back slightly and pushed with all her might, screeching out in pain. The bottom, feet and legs appeared. Margot felt the arms in the birth canal and pushed them close to the body.

"Again!" she ordered.

Lena pressed, hollering out loud. The baby was born, followed immediately by a rush of blood. Concentrating on the baby, Margot cut the umbilical cord and gave it a slap. It cried. "It's a girl!" she said, turning her attention to Lena. "She's fine."

Lena's face was the colour of pristine snow. She looked into Anton's eyes. "Look after her," she whispered, "promise!"

"Of course, I will. We both will. What are you talking about?" Still looking into her husband's eyes, Lena's head dropped sideways.

"Lena! Lena! What's wrong?" Anton shook Lena's shoulders. "Lena! Don't leave me. I need you! We all need you, Lena!"

Gustl put one hand gently on Anton's shoulder. "She's gone, Anton, I'm sorry."

Anton looked at Margot, still holding the baby. She nodded slightly. "Haemorrhage," she whispered.

"Neeein ...!" Anton cried out, sobbing, and threw himself across Lena's chest. "No, you can't go, not yet!"

Margot swaddled the baby and put some milk on the stove to warm. Then she gave Jakob and Josef a mug of warm milk and showed them their baby sister.

"Will Mama get better?" Jakob whispered.

Margot lifted him up. "No, my darling, I'm afraid not. You must be very brave now and help your papa and Josef."

"But I want Mama!"

"I know, darling, I know. Come now, drink your milk and try to rest. It's still night-time." Margot settled the boys down on the floor with a blanket. She put the baby down next to them.

"Can I help you?" Gustl asked.

"Yes, help me carry Lena into our room. We can sleep here tonight with the others."

Anton was draped, as if glued, over Lena's body. Gustl took him gently by the shoulders and guided him, like a small child, to a mattress. He pushed him down.

"Margot must prepare her now. Try to rest a while." He carried Lena onto their own bed and Margot began to wash her.

"Do you think the baby will live?" Gustl whispered.

Margot hesitated. "I lied," she answered quietly. "There's something wrong with her left foot. It's deformed. It's turned down and inwards too. But if we can find a wet nurse, she could survive. There's nothing any of us can do at the moment though. Tomorrow, you'd better try to round the livestock up with Anton. I'll take the boys to Elsa for a couple of hours and try to find a wet nurse to feed the baby, that's the main priority. I'll let the undertaker know about Lena and speak to the pastor."

"We'd better lie down for an hour then," Gustl answered.

2

OCTOBER 1849

Dawn broke. Margot got up and put a couple of logs onto the embers under the stove. She opened the door to the animals' quarters and began to milk the cows. Their farm was typical of the area. Built into the hillside, under one gabled roof, it was split into two halves combining the family's living quarters facing the sunny side and the byre facing the weather side. Above the cowshed was a hayloft. The animals spent the nights and winters in their quarters. When snow lay many feet deep on the ground, it was easy to care for them. Behind the house the entrance to the hay-barn was level. Gustl went to the outside privy first and then to the well to draw water. He filled the trough for the cows, opened the cowshed's outside door and let the animals out into their field. Then he drew more water from the well and brought it indoors. The routine needed to be done. It was good, as it saved him from thinking or worrying too much.

The earliest chores finished, Margot put a loaf of bread, butter and homemade cherry jam on the table. She started cutting thick slabs of bread – today wasn't the day to be scrimping – and sat the boys down at the table with mugs of warm milk. She risked a glance at the newborn baby. She was alive. She probably weighed about five pounds, in spite of coming early. Margot sat down herself and began to eat; it would be a long day.

Gustl came indoors with Anton. They both sat down wordlessly at the table and took a chunk of bread.

Anton was functioning automatically but his thoughts were far away. He heard voices, distant, as if through fog. When one voice became persistent and louder he broke out of his trance.

"What do you want to call her?" his sister was asking.

He didn't understand what she was talking about.

"Anton!" Margot leaned over the table and took his hands in hers. "She needs a name!" He looked up from his plate – startled – as if he had only just realised she was speaking to him. He stared at Margot, wide-eyed.

"Papa!" Jakob cried. "Are you all right? You're not going to die too, are you, Papa?"

Anton looked at his two boys, his eyes brimming with tears. He wiped them away with the cuff of his sleeve.

"No Jakob, don't worry, I'm just sad."

"Hadn't you already decided on names?" Margot asked.

"No, Lena thought it was unlucky ..." Anton swallowed. "If it had been a boy, I was thinking of Wilhelm, after our father," he said, trying to pull himself together.

"Wilhelmine then, that's a pretty name," Margot answered. "I'm going to try to find a wet nurse today. Who do you think might take her on?"

Anton considered the question. "Well, our neighbour's girl is three months old. Under normal circumstances, they would've been our best hope. Franziska's very kind – well they both are – but their farm burned down too. I don't know where they'll be staying, but their relations won't want even more people crowding them, especially strangers."

"Who else then?"

"The mayor's wife?"

"You can forget her; she won't have anything to do with our sort."

"I don't know; she seems friendly enough. She brings sandwiches and beer to the council meetings."

"Well, she has to be friendly, because of her husband. That doesn't mean to say that she would feed someone else's baby. Anyway, she's from outwards." Like most of the villagers, Margot was naturally suspicious of anyone who hadn't lived within a radius of five leagues for at least three generations.

Gustl sighed, exasperated.

"She's only from Bern, not from America! But there's always Helga …" Normally he wouldn't dare to mention his sister's name in front of his wife, but … well, these were special circumstances.

"You are joking! You can forget that two-faced bitch! She would walk over dead bodies to get what she wants." Margot was spitting venom.

"Well, she's often offered to help."

"Oh yes, she offers. Especially when she wants something from us. But whenever you actually ask her, she always has some excuse. Have you forgotten that time I was sick after losing our baby? You were on the alm and I asked her to do the milking for me. Just for one day. And do you remember her answer? She said she would if she could but she wanted to get the mail coach to Spiez that morning to buy some cloth for a new dress!"

"Well, to feed a baby is a lot to ask for, but we may have no choice, and she is family."

"Can't you think of anyone else?" The men remained silent and Margot had already racked her brains and found no solution.

"Very well then, but I'll ask your neighbour, Franziska, first. If she can't, then maybe Helga could feed her just for a day or two until we find someone else. I could ask Dr Koefeli in Frutigen if he knows of anyone. What about an undertaker? Shall I ask Schreiner Hans?"

"Yes, he won't cheat us."

"Fair enough. I'd better get the boys to Elsa and make a start then. Good luck with the livestock."

*****

Margot splashed cold water over her face and brushed her long brown hair. She parted it down the centre and carefully braided two plaits, which she then crossed over her head and fastened tightly. She removed her brown working dress and put on her black dress, which she wore only for church on Sundays and special occasions. She wrapped a shawl around her shoulders, swaddled Wilhelmine in a blanket, and went next door with the boys to Elsa. She knew she could rely on Elsa; they always helped each other out. She was the one who had milked the cows after Margot's miscarriage. She didn't flinch an eyelid, although goodness knows she had enough to do herself. She had nine children and a good-for-nothing, lazy husband. He got violent when drunk and that was often. Margot knocked at the door and Elsa opened it. She hid her surprise at seeing Margot with three children and invited her in.

"Margot, it's you! Come in out of the cold, sit down. Now, how can I help you? I'm sorry about Anton and Lena's place, I saw it had burned down. Are these her three children? I didn't know the youngest was already due."

"Yes, they're hers. The baby came early, and ... oh dear, there's no good way to say this, Lena died."

"Oh no, poor Anton! What on earth is he going to do? And the poor wee mite ... have you got someone to feed her?" As if on cue, Wilhelmine started mewing like a kitten. Nobody fed her and she mewed louder and more angrily. Her face turned beetroot and her lips trembled. Elsa stood up and took a clean rag from a drawer. She tied a knot in it, dipped it in honey and then put it into Wilhelmine's mouth, who sucked hungrily, and for the moment was pacified.

"I haven't got anyone yet, that's why I'm here. Can you look after the boys till I've settled things?"

"Of course, leave them here as long as you like. I'll make sure they come to no harm. Who are you going to ask?"

"Well, I thought I'd try Franziska first. Then it's either Helga or the mayor's wife. Unless you know of somebody else?"

Elsa thought a while. "Hmm, difficult. You can forget Franziska, I'm afraid. I was helping put the fires out last night and she told me that she'd go to her brother in Adelboden. She doesn't get on well with her sister-in-law, so it's not going to be easy. Not that they can't afford it, mind. Her brother's got eight cows. Eight! Can you imagine? He's the richest farmer in these parts. Still, the sister-in-law is a bitter old hag, always has her nostrils squeezed together as if she smells something bad. I wouldn't like to stay with that witch for a day, never mind a few months."

"Oh no, in that case I'll have to belittle myself and beg Helga."

"The mayor's wife might help; she's actually quite nice."

Margot pulled a face.

"Well, if all else fails you could always ask Dr Koefeli if he knows of anyone. You'll have to be quick though, the baby can't wait forever."

"I know, wish me luck! Oh, and afterwards I have to see the undertaker and the pastor."

Elsa nodded solemnly. "Ja, I don't envy you. Good luck then and don't worry about the boys."

*****

Margot walked down the hill towards the town centre. Wilhelmine fell asleep in her arms and Margot looked behind herself, back up the mountainside to the hill farms scattered across the landscape. She counted seven farms that had burned down. Seven! And another couple damaged, black with soot. It was lucky the rain had come before more were destroyed. She wondered what the families would do. She and Gustl would look after Anton and the boys, of course, until Anton rebuilt his farm. Hopefully, he and Gustl would retrieve all the animals today. But what about the families without relatives? They'd have to rely on the poor relief fund, she supposed.

She walked through the town centre. The lie of the land was flatter here and the houses stood upright, three storeys high to under the eaves. Many had wooden balconies, carved skilfully with ornamental motives, and several had the name of the family builder painted onto the facade in gold and black lettering along with a bible verse. The town centre wasn't large – it was just one street with half-timbered houses on both sides. There was the town hall, the school and a corner shop for everything from groceries to hardware. She went on past the Goldenen Ochsen, where the mail coach stopped, the stone water trough and the blacksmith's, and then she turned left down a road, across the bridge over the River Gungg and took a right turn along a track leading to the mill and Helga's house.

Helga, and her husband, Heinz, lived in a small, two-storey, pink-coloured house with green wooden shutters. Margot climbed the five stone steps to the entrance, knocked and then retreated back down a few treads. Helga opened the door, and seeing Margot with the baby in her arms, her jaw dropped, as if the Stollenwurm was standing there rather than her sister-in-law. She shut her mouth again quickly, pursed her lips and remained standing in the doorway, barring the entrance, her arms folded across her chest.

"Margot! What are you doing here? I heard about Lena and Anton. I'm sorry. Heinz is up there now, helping them catch the animals. I'd invite you in, but Hedwig's just fallen asleep." Helga was referring to her five-month-old daughter.

Margot held Wilhelmine up towards Helga.

"This is Lena's daughter, Wilhelmine."

Helga leaned forward and peered into the woollen bundle.

"Oh, she's tiny. I suppose she'll die now Lena's gone. At least Anton still has the boys."

"Well, actually I'm looking for a wet nurse. Didn't you say that Hedwig's onto solids now?"

"Oh yes, she's ever so good. She eats the same as us in the evening, and during the day mashed carrot or apple, whatever I give her!"

"But you still give her the breast too?"

"Oh yes, she needs her bedtime drink, and then at breakfast time and midday before her nap."

"I ... we ... well, Anton ... we all wondered whether you could ... well, we know it's a lot to ask, but could you feed Wilhelmine? She's starving."

"Me?" Helga's voice took on a high-pitched tone. Her expression was horrified, as if someone had just suggested she wash herself in cow muck. "Oh no, I couldn't! ... I mean I would if I could," she added as an afterthought, "but I can't. I've barely enough milk for Hedwig. Isn't there anyone else you could ask?"

"No. Franziska's house burned down too; she's gone to relatives in Adelboden. Please just for a day or two until I've found someone else?" Margot begged.

"What about the mayor's wife, have you asked her yet? Hari's there now, playing with Ferdinand."

"No, not yet. We thought with you being family ..." Margot's voice trailed off.

"No, I can't, I'm sorry."

Margot turned to go. "Bye then," she said, leaving.

"Bye," Helga called after her, "but if there's anything else I can do, anytime, I'll be glad to help!"

*****

Margot was fuming. Were she a bull, she would be snorting, puffs of steamy air would be exiting her nostrils and her right foot would be pawing the ground. She felt so humiliated. Helga always made her feel like that, like somebody not good enough, a second-class citizen. Her body was tense, her eyebrows knotted, as she walked back to town willing Helga all sorts of misfortune under her breath. She wished she'd never asked. She had known she wouldn't help, but Gustl had insisted. Next time he could ask himself! Helga could've at least tried though. Hari is playing with Ferdinand. Well, he was welcome to, you conceited snob.

Wilhelmine started mewing again, hungry. After that episode, Margot didn't really feel courageous enough to face Mrs Buehler, the mayor's wife, but with Wilhelmine bawling her head off, she didn't have much choice either; she felt she must ask. She could only say no. Surely words can't harm. But she wasn't too sure about that, she was still smarting sorely from the contact with her sister-in-law. Fighting back tears of despair, she nervously lifted the shiny brass knocker on the dark green lacquered door of the mayor's house, and let it drop. If Mrs Buehler didn't answer at the first knock, she'd go. She heard footsteps coming and hastily retreated two steps.

"Mrs … Piller, isn't it? Come in." Mrs Buehler stepped aside and held the door wide open for Margot to enter. "I've seen you at church with your husband. Well, don't stand out there in the cold – come in, follow me!" Mrs Buehler started walking down the entrance hall, opened a door on the left-hand side, and said, "Come and sit down in the warm."

Margot wiped her feet on the doormat, longer than necessary, and followed Mrs Buehler down the hall and into the parlour.

"Sit down wherever you like. Now what can I offer you to drink? Coffee? Tea? A small glass of wine, perhaps?"

"A coffee would be lovely," Margot answered. She had never drunk coffee before in her entire life but she definitely fancied trying it.

"Make yourself comfortable, I won't be a minute."

Mrs Buehler left the room and Margot examined her surroundings. The floor was wooden, polished and gleaming; it smelt of beeswax. A sofa, carved from dark varnished wood and upholstered with some shiny fabric, leaned against one wall. Opposite the sofa were two matching chairs. A low coffee table stood in between, upon a thick woollen rug. In one corner of the room there was a cockle stove covered in green ceramic tiles. Margot took a few steps towards it, stretched a finger out to touch it and then snatched it back quickly – it was scorching. A wooden cradle with white lacy curtains rested next to the stove. She'd never seen anything so beautiful before; it had carvings of tiny flowers and animals on. She peeked inside and saw a baby, sleeping.

Mrs Buehler entered quietly and put a tray down on the coffee table.

"That's Albert, our youngest," she said happily. "Now then, how do you like your coffee? Cream? Sugar?"

"Yes please, both. Just one sugar," Margot added hastily so as not to appear greedy. "Your boy is beautiful."

"Yes, isn't he?" Mrs Buehler flushed contentedly. "Please, sit down and drink your coffee and then you must tell me how I can help you. Is that your baby?"

"No, this is Wilhelmine, my brother's daughter. Her mother died giving birth."

"Oh no, the poor little thing, she must be starving! Shall I try to feed her?"

"Would you?"

"I can try to see if she will suck. Give her to me," Mrs Buehler said, sitting down and unbuttoning her dress. Margot gave her the baby who found the nipple immediately and started sucking noisily.

"There you are, she was hungry," Mrs Buehler said. "How did it happen? Was the birth very difficult?"

"The baby was in a breech position and it was too late to turn her. You see the fire brought labour on early and then ... well we had to get Lena home to our place and in the end ... she haemorrhaged."

"Oh, I'm so sorry. Your brother must be Anton Schneider then? Doesn't he have two boys as well?"

"Yes, Jakob and Josef, they are one and two years old."

"And his farm has burned down?"

"Yes. He managed to let the livestock out; my husband's"

helping him to gather them in at the moment. But he's lost everything else."

"And now his wife too, the poor man. I must speak to my husband about how we can help. More folk have lost their homes, I heard."

"Yes, seven houses have burned down. Anton can stay with us and Franziska Gehring has gone to her brother in Adelboden. I don't know about the others yet."

"My husband told me that no one had died in the fires."

"Not directly, no. Just Lena."

Mrs Buehler removed Wilhelmine from her breast. She protested immediately before Mrs Buehler had time to give her the other nipple. As soon as she found milk again, she stopped crying.

"Ah, she's impatient, the little one. Albert is just the same. What are you going to do about her?"

"I'm hoping to find a wet nurse. At first we thought Franziska might feed her, but she's moved away. I've just spoken to my sister-in-law but she doesn't have enough milk. I thought I could go to Frutigen tomorrow and ask Dr Koefeli if he knows of anyone. I'd go today but it's too late now and I still have to see the undertaker and the pastor. But now you've fed her, she'll be all right until tomorrow. We're very grateful, Mrs Buehler."

"Please call me Helena. I'm wondering ... well I suppose Wilhelmine wouldn't die if she didn't get fed for a day, but why don't you leave her with me? I mean, just until you find someone else. It might take a day or two until you find someone, and I'd hate to think of her crying all the time while I have milk."

"Oh, Mrs Bue ... Helena, would you do that? Have you got enough milk for both babies?"

"I'm not sure but I can try, and Albert eats a little mashed carrot already."

"I'll go to Dr Koefeli straightaway tomorrow morning. I'll be quicker without having to carry Wilhelmine."

"That's settled then. Now tell me, which undertaker are you going to use?"

"We thought Schreiner Hans."

"Ah yes, he's a good man. Fair prices. We had him last year when my father-in-law died. Mind you, he's very old. He must be approaching ninety."

"His son helps him sometimes."

"Yes, but he's no longer a young man either. I'll tell you something. Last year we had my father-in-law laid out in his coffin here on this coffee table. We didn't have the heating on. Schreiner Hans and his son came to pick the coffin up and take it to the church. Hans walked in, practically on tiptoes, and as you know, he's tall and thin and his back is crooked. With his black clothes and top hat on, he looked like an enormous black jackdaw. Anyway, he tripped over the carpet and stumbled, and for a moment I thought he was going to fall straight into the coffin himself, on top of my father-in-law!" Helena put a hand to her chest. "I nearly had a heart attack, I tell you. I was so shocked; my heart was pounding madly."

"And then?" Margot's jaw had dropped.

"His top hat fell into the coffin, but he managed to catch himself on the side of it. He apologised and I said it wasn't his fault, which of course it wasn't. But when they left … well, I had to drink a small glass of cherry schnapps to calm my nerves!"

Helena put a hand to her mouth and giggled. Margot looked at her gratefully and smiled. It was kind of Helena to try to make her feel at ease. She stood up to leave.

"I'll be on my way then, thank you very much. We really are very grateful."

"Nonsense, you would have done the same for me, I'm sure."

"I had a miscarriage last year and since then ... well, we haven't been blessed with children yet, but Lena would've helped you, if she could."

"Oh, I'm so sorry, I didn't know. But don't worry, you've plenty of time yet."

"Yes, of course. Well, I'll go to Schreiner Hans now."

Margot left Helena's home with a huge weight lifted from her chest. She felt hopeful now that Wilhelmine might survive. She entered the undertaker's office and found Schreiner Hans at his desk.

"My condolences on your loss," he said gravely. "A terrible tragedy."

Bad news travels fast, Margot realised. "Yes. Can you come to the house to collect the ... Lena?"

"Yes of course, as soon as my son returns. He should be back shortly. Have you considered what type of coffin you'd like?"

"Oh, no! I forgot to ask Anton. Nothing fancy I don't think. He will need his savings to rebuild his farm, and nothing can help Lena now."

"No. Well, this is a standard coffin," he said, standing up to show Margot a pinewood coffin with no extra adornments. "It's perfectly adequate and very reasonable – a popular choice. If you like, I could bring this one with me, and if Anton prefers a different one, we can change it."

"Yes, that's a good idea."

"Do you know when the funeral is?"

"No, not yet. I'm going to the pastor next."

"Right, well, you can tell me this evening then."

Margot was feeling drained as she walked down the road to the parsonage. She entered through the garden gate and knocked at the front door. The pastor's housekeeper let her in and showed Margot into the study. Reverend Moser was sitting at his desk, writing. He looked up when she entered.

"Ah, Mrs Piller," he said, "I was expecting your brother."

Margot tried not to feel annoyed. "He's trying to gather in the livestock," she explained.

"Yes. Well, you may tell him that I can hold the funeral on Saturday. Will he be wanting me to come to the house to pray with him this evening?"

Margot hesitated. She suddenly felt very inept.

"I think he would like that, yes."

"Tell your brother I will come at six. Good day now, I must continue my work."

Margot curtsied and left quickly without waiting for the housekeeper to show her out. She hurried back to Elsa's house, not wanting to burden her with the boys for any longer than necessary. Margot thanked her quickly and returned home; she had so much to do still. The first thing she did was to go straight to the pantry and take a bottle of her homemade plum schnapps down from the top shelf. She poured herself a small glass and drank it down in one go, telling herself that she deserved it. Then she changed into her brown working dress and started to prepare a meal.

*****

Anton and Gustl returned with two goats. They tethered them securely to a post on the hill behind the house and then came inside to see if Margot had cooked supper.

"That smells good." Gustl complimented Margot as he washed his hands.

"I've made a stew with pork sausages, potatoes and vegetables. I hope it's enough. The pastor is coming at six and his appetite has a bit of a reputation."

"Well it's good of him to come. We must be hospitable."

"Yes, of course. I've baked a fresh loaf of bread too, just to be on the safe side."

"And your plum schnapps?"

"Is already on the table," Margot replied, pointing. "Did you get all the animals back, Anton?"

"Nearly. We brought the cows back first and Stein Willi brought my sow back on a rope. He said she'd been in his vegetable patch, but he didn't complain. He just said he thought it'd be easiest to bring her back himself," Anton answered.

"That was kind of him."

"Yes, I told him I'd take him some sausages at Christmastime, after she's been slaughtered, but he said it wasn't necessary."

"You will though?"

"Yes, of course."

"Well, I saw you both returning with the goats, so it can only be the hens left. Did you see Heinz by the way? Helga told me he'd gone to help you."

"Heinz? He was there, yes. But he said he'd left his hen coop open by mistake and his hens had got out. Said he was up there catching them."

"Huh? They live half a league away!"

"Yes I wondered about that, because I thought one of the hens under his arm was one of mine, but it could be possible, I suppose. I didn't want to argue. He's family after all."

"So, he just stole one of your hens!" Margot cried out.

"I don't know that. Anyway, we rounded the other nine up so we didn't do badly. A fox could've got the last one. What about Wilhelmine, can Helga help?"

"No, if she had I would've given her one of my own

hens gladly! She said she didn't have enough milk. But don't worry, Mrs Buehler is going to feed her until we find somebody else."

"Mrs Buehler?" Anton looked up astonished. "Everyone is being so kind," he said. "Don't be harsh with Helga, Margot. She probably really doesn't have enough milk."

"Well, I'm happy to give her the benefit of the doubt. We have enough other problems to deal with." She'd have to tell him about Wilhelmine's foot soon, Margot thought. Out loud she said, "Now get cleaned up. Schreiner Hans will be here soon, and then the pastor will be arriving."

3

MAY 1850

Anton hammered a long nail into the rectangular block of wood. Save for a little masonry under the stove and fire, the entire farmhouse was built from wood. The front of the house looked south-east across the valley and towards the Gehrihorn. He had finished the steps that led up from the vegetable garden to a loggia, which accessed the entrance door, but he needed glass for the windowpanes still. The ground floor was otherwise complete.

For the second floor, he needed more wood. Luckily, he had plenty of that. Like nearly every hill farmer round these parts, he owned a small portion of forest. Wood was an essential part of their income, and that way the forest was looked after and tended to.

Anton was pleased with his progress, but he frowned thinking of the cost of the nails and paint, and everything else he needed. He had already sold one cow but he would need to sell another.

He hit his thumb with the hammer and was shocked out of his day dreams. He would have to stop soon, dusk had already fallen and he could hardly distinguish the nail from the wood. He managed the next three nails and then gave up, defeated. It wasn't just the lack of light; the rain was still pouring down incessantly and his muscles were aching all over.

He tidied the tools away and began to walk back to Margot's farm. The mud squelched under his boots as he strode down the mountain slope. The numerous streams, normally just brooklets trickling down the mountainside in picturesque rivulets, were gushing frantically down the Alpine peaks, the water splashing and spluttering out of their rocky beds and flooding the fields each side, waterlogging the soft ground.

The people of the Kander valley were used to flooding. The River Kander and its main tributaries, the Oeschibach and the Engstlige, all began in the Alps. Every spring, when the temperatures rose and the snow began to melt atop the mountain peaks, millions of pots of clear icy water cascaded down the inclines towards Lake Thun. This year the water wasn't clear though. In addition to the snow melt, it had rained much more than usual. The downpours had scoured the soft ground and carried earth, mud and stones into the rivers.

The wooden footbridge that crossed the Heiti brook still stood steadfast. Anton began to cross it, stopping in the middle to gaze over the edge at the muddy brown water, bubbling angrily just a hand-breadth below his feet as it rushed eastwards towards the River Kander on the valley floor. He hoped it would stop raining soon, before more damage was done; the farmers in the lowlands were already complaining about ruined crops. Suddenly, the bridge shuddered, jolting Anton and nearly knocking him over. He grabbed the railing instinctively, his heart racing with shock, as a further boulder, swept along by the force and swell of the water, hit the bridge. There was a loud crack and a slow creaking as the bridge was ripped away from its anchorage.

Anton was plunged backwards, arms flailing, into the frenzied water. The back of his head hit a rock and the wooden bridge swept over him, slashing the skin on his cheeks and hands. The river hurled itself at him with all its force, and Anton was pushed down under the water and jostled downstream, along with rocks, stones, logs and other debris. His lungs burning, he thrashed about frantically, trying to break the surface. He hit air, took a gulp, but was forced immediately back down underwater again with the next swell. He floundered with his arms desperately and managed to throw first one, then the other, over a floating tree trunk. He gasped for air as he was swept further downriver. Stones hit him again and again as he tried to swim nearer to the riverbank. He could make out trees and overhanging branches. Waiting for the right split second, he removed his left hand from the tree trunk and tried to grab an overhanging branch, but it slipped through his fingers. With almighty effort, he managed to get his left hand back onto the trunk, as he continued to be catapulted downstream. Powerless, he was bumped along, rocks hitting him repeatedly. *Again*, he thought, *try again.* Ignoring pain, he found unknown strength and began to swim nearer to the shore. Now! He pushed himself up to grab a branch and this time managed to hold on to it. He slowly heaved himself half over the branch as the river tore at his legs, now floating horizontally behind him. Little by little, he pulled himself along the branch until he felt ground beneath his knees, and then he let go and crawled to the shore and safety.

Anton collapsed on the ground. Choking for air, he spluttered and threw up. He trembled uncontrollably. He tried to sit up. His vision spun and everything went black.

*****

Anton regained consciousness to rain beating down on him and wondered where he was, before he remembered. He tried to get onto all fours. Dizziness and nausea overcame him and he threw up anew. He remained on all fours. Instinct told him to find shelter and he lifted his head slightly to look around. His head throbbed violently and felt too large for its skull. He knew that he couldn't stay immobile. He dragged himself further inland and uphill into the forest until he saw a rocky overhang. He wriggled himself underneath it and then, at least, he was protected from the rain.

He turned onto his back and pushed himself up onto his elbows. Blood was running down his right arm and he could also taste blood in his mouth. He looked to see why his left leg hurt so much; his torn trousers revealed a long, deep gash along his thigh and his ankle was turned inwards and was swollen. He fell back onto the ground and tried to think. Where could he be? He had got out of the river before it flowed into the Kander, so in spite of thinking he'd been in the river for a lifetime, he couldn't have gone that far, probably less than half a league. His heart lifted a little. He wasn't far from settlements; maybe he could get help. He considered yodelling. It was the locals' usual call for help, but how far would his voice carry in the forest? He didn't have any other option. He couldn't walk on his leg and he wouldn't get far on all fours.

Anton pushed himself up into a sitting position. He took a few deep breaths, gasping at the pain in his ribs.

"Ho lo-di ri-di jo ho-la djo di-ri di-a-di ri-di jo," he yodelled, miserably. He waited a couple of seconds but heard no echo. The leafy forest muffled his voice. Suddenly, a deafening screeching and shrieking came his way. Anton held his breath. A rush of wind, a thundering of hooves and a sounder of wild boar raced past him, squealing. He let out a sigh of relief. Just boar. He must have disturbed them with his call – so it did travel then. He should try to crawl out of the forest. No one would hear him here with the trees swallowing his voice.

*****

Bartli Gerber had finished all his chores and eaten with his family.

"I'll be off then," he told them.

"Isn't it a bit late to be visiting Maria?" his mother protested. "And it's pouring down outside."

"Leave the lad alone." His father came to his rescue. "He's old enough to know what he's doing."

"I won't be long; I'll just say hello." Bartl left quickly before his mother thought of any more objections. He was twenty-two and she still liked to decide what he could and couldn't do. Maria was his betrothed, they'd been engaged for four years now. Four years! Much too long, but he couldn't afford to buy his own farm and his parents didn't have enough money to help him. He wished he could find work somewhere. He'd asked around as far as Spiez, but nobody had work for an unqualified labourer, and his only experience was farm work. He held his lantern up to peer through the rain and strode out determinedly. If he arrived too late, Maria's parents wouldn't let her out.

*****

"Anton's never been this late before," Margot said to Gustl. "It's been dark for well over an hour now."

"You're right," Gustl acknowledged, picking up the lantern. "I'll go outside and see if I can see him coming."

Gustl returned a couple of minutes later.

"I can't see him, but it's streaming down outside. He's probably taking shelter with a neighbour somewhere."

"He wouldn't stay this long though. He knows we're waiting with dinner for him."

"Tell you what then, you eat with the boys and I'll walk back along his route just to make sure he hasn't slipped or anything. Give me a bottle of your good schnapps, the one from forty-six, just to be on the safe side. He might need it to warm up."

"Don't you want to eat?"

"I'll eat with Anton when we get back."

Gustl hurried away from the house before Margot changed her mind. He'd been waiting ages for an excuse to get his hands on that bottle of '46 schnapps; she guarded it like the Stollenwurm. He ran uphill along the path, around the corner and out of sight, before stopping. He took the bottle from his pocket, unscrewed the top and took a slug.

"Booarr!" He shook himself as the fiery schnapps burned his throat and warmed his insides. "Mmmn." It was even better than he remembered. He took another slug, looked at the bottle a little sorrowfully, and then, screwing the lid back on, returned it to his pocket. Finally he took the time to fasten his jacket properly, tie his scarf around his neck and pull his hat down over his ears. He looked at the rain, hesitated, retrieved the bottle from his pocket and took another big gulp. He did a short jig and put it away again. Cheerfully, he continued his way towards the Heiti bridge.

*****

Anton crawled tortuously on all fours out of the forest. It hadn't been far, maybe just six hundred feet, but he was covered in sweat and gasping for breath. He turned into a sitting position and waited for the intense pain to decrease. Rain beat down upon his battered body. He tried to recognise something, anything, to give him a clue to his whereabouts, but visibility was down to a few feet and all he could see was grass. He tried to sit up straighter, took a few deep breaths, and yodelled: "Ho lo-di ri-di jo ho-la djo di-ri di-a-di ri-di jo."

Nothing. Everyone would be indoors on a night like this, he thought. If only a few hunters were out and about. He tried again, waited and yodelled anew.

Bartli stopped in his tracks. Was that someone yodelling? No, he must have imagined it. He continued on his way. Again?

"Ho-la djo di-ri-di-o di-ri-di-djo." He returned the call just in case and kept still to listen.

"Hola ra-di-ri di-ro di-ri-di-o."

There! Someone was calling from the direction of the forest. He lifted his lantern up higher and headed across the meadows to where he thought he had heard the call. A hundred feet from the forest he stopped and called loudly: "I'm coming but I can't see you. Shout if you hear me!"

"Here, over here!" Anton could see a pinpoint of light bobbing up and down; it was coming in his direction. "Here!" he yelled as powerfully as he could.

Bartli saw a figure sitting with its back against a tree and ran. He held his lantern high and gulped.

"Mr ... Schneider, is it you? What on earth happened? You look as if a bear chewed you up and spat you out again!"

"Not a bear, just the Heiti." Anton smiled weakly. "You're one of the Gerber boys, aren't you?"

"Yes, Bartolomaeus ... Bartli."

"How far ...?"

"To our farm? About a half a league. I'll run back quickly and get help. My pa and my brothers are at home."

"I can try to walk if you help me."

"I don't think so, Mr Schneider, your leg doesn't look good. I won't be long."

Bartli placed his lantern on the ground next to Anton, and then removed his jacket and draped it over Anton's shoulders. He ran off through the darkness, across the meadow.

Help on its way, shock set in. Anton lay on the ground, curled up and shook like the bell around the neck of a galloping cow.

*****

Bartli burst through the door.

"There's been an accident ... near the forest ... Mr Schneider ... he's in a bad way." He bent over to catch his breath, supporting his hands on his thighs.

"Right. Düri, Jörg, get the sledge from the barn and some rope. Wife, blankets and schnapps!" Mr. Gerber barked his orders, not wasting any time to ask questions. "Bert, you'd better go and fetch the doctor from Frutigen. Tell him to ride straight to Piller's farm. We'll take Mr Schneider there!"

"What can I do?" Edeltraud asked.

Mr Gerber looked at his sixteen-year-old daughter.

"Best you stay here and look after your ma," he said.

"Shouldn't I go to Piller's and let them know you've found him? They'll be worried."

Mr Gerber looked at his wife who nodded slightly.

"All right then, but stick to the paths, we don't want any more accidents, and put your cloak on! Bartli, put another jacket on! Are we all ready? We'd better hurry."

*****

Gustl arrived at the point where the Heiti bridge should've been. Ah, that explained it, Anton would have taken a detour to the upper bridge. He patted his pocket, and after just a short moment's hesitation, removed the bottle and took a slug. Miserable weather, he thought, giving himself an excuse to drink. Oh well, he'd better carry on to meet Anton. If he came back without him, Margot would wonder why the bottle was half empty.

*****

Edeltraud arrived at Piller's farm and told Margot that they'd found Anton, injured, and were on their way.

"Oh my God! How bad is it?" Margot put a hand to her chest.

"I don't know. Bert's gone to get the doctor," Edeltraud answered. The door to the loft opened and Jakob and Josef peered down the steps.

"Where's Papa?" Jakob asked. "Is he hurt?"

"A little bit, but he'll be fine. He's coming home now and the doctor is on his way. Go back to sleep, it's late."

Margot started to clear the table.

"Can I help you?" Edeltraud asked.

Margot tried to think. "You could put a few logs on the fire. I'll heat some water." When they'd finished their preparations, Margot paced up and down the room.

"Sit down, Mrs Piller, they'll be a while yet. Where's your husband?"

"Who? Oh Gustl! I'd forgotten all about him. He's out looking for Anton. He wanted to go up to his house."

"Ah, he'll be back soon then."

*****

The Gerbers found Anton, and Mr Gerber poured some schnapps down his throat.

"That will warm you up a bit," he said.

"Th-th-thank you." Anton's teeth were chattering. He spluttered, the liquid ran down the corners of his mouth and his eyes watered. He snatched the bottle for another swig.

"Let's get you onto the sledge, we'll carry you home." The four men took an arm and a leg each and lifted Anton carefully on to their long wooden sleigh. Bartli covered him with a blanket and they set off, each man carrying one corner of the sledge. Arriving at Piller's farm, they set the sledge down and carried Anton indoors.

"Oh my God! What happened to you? On the table!" Margot told the Gerbers.

They laid him down carefully and everyone stared at him. Mr Gerber poured some more schnapps down his throat.

"Thank you," Margot said to the Gerbers. "Thank goodness you found him! My God, Anton, you've taken a battering! Edeltraud, help me undress him please. Men, go and warm yourselves up by the fire."

Tears streamed down Margot's cheeks as she and Edeltraud carefully removed Anton's badly torn clothes. His whole body was covered in cuts and bruises. When Margot began to gently clean his wounds, he smiled crookedly at her, grimaced and passed out. She heard a horse trotting up the path and sighed with relief as Dr Koefeli opened the door.

"What have we got here?" he said as a welcome, going

straight to the table and feeling Anton's pulse. "Has he been unconscious all the time?" he asked, at the same time examining the back of Anton's head.

"No, he could speak a little when we found him," Mr Gerber said.

"He has a substantial bump," the doctor said, showing Margot, "but it's bleeding, which is a good sign." He prodded Anton all over and listened to his heart. He tutted at the deep gashes. "Bring me a candle and hold him still," he said. "I'll stitch these." Dr Koefeli placed his needle in the candle flame and when it was hot he stitched the worst gashes on Anton's arms, legs and cheeks.

"My head," Anton moaned.

"Yes, you'll feel that for a few days, you've got concussion. You've cracked a couple of ribs too. Let's hope you don't get pneumonia," the doctor said. "You'd better stay in bed for the next couple of days and let your sister spoil you. Let's look at your ankle." He felt it all over. "Well, it's swollen badly, so I'm not sure, but I don't think it's broken. Keep him warm," he told Margot, "and let me know if he develops a temperature."

"Oh thank you, doctor, thank you so much! Now, Mr Gerber, if you and your lads would be so kind as to help me get Anton onto my bed, then I'll make some supper for everyone."

Margot began to fry sausages and set the table with a loaf of bread and her last bottle of the '46 schnapps.

By the time everyone had gone, it was well past midnight. Margot went to Anton.

"Sorry," he mumbled.

She felt his forehead. It was hot but not burning.

"What on earth were you doing? How often have I told you to be more careful?"

45

"Stupid, sorry ...." He closed his eyes, heavy with exhaustion, and Margot left the room. She laid a mattress down in front of the fire for herself to sleep on. On second thoughts, angry that Gustl still hadn't showed up, she put an enamel bowl full of pig slop in the middle of the floor before she lay down to rest.

*****

Gustl walked all the way up to Anton's half-rebuilt house without meeting a single soul. He walked round the house once, to make sure Anton hadn't fallen and was lying wounded somewhere, and then wondered what to do. He walked back down the path, past the partly rebuilt and partly charcoaled remains of the seven farms and came to Stein Willi's home. He saw light through the window and knocked.

Willi opened the door.

"For heaven's sake, you're soaking! What are you doing out there, come inside!"

Gustl explained that Anton hadn't come home.

"Well, he isn't here I'm afraid. Just a second, I'll come and help you look for him."

He put his boots and jacket on, hesitated, and then went into the pantry and took a bottle of Vreni's mirabelle schnapps down from the shelf. He placed two glasses on the table, poured a generous measure in each and said: "Prost!" They both tipped their glasses up and Willi strode over to the bed chamber. He opened the door a crack.

"Anton's missing," he told his wife, Vreni. "I'm going out with Gustl to help look for him." He slipped the mirabelle schnapps into his pocket and they left the house.

They hadn't gone a hundred feet when they saw light behind Saddler Eric's windows.

"Maybe he took shelter there," Willi said. He knocked at the door.

It was several hours later as a band of intoxicated men, with lanterns in their hands and schnapps in their pockets, staggered their way down the steep inclines, singing at the top of their voices. Six more neighbours had joined Gustl, Stein Willi and Saddler Eric on their erratic journey along the river.

"Hola-ra-di-di!" Gustl sang. "Can you hear us, Anton, are you there?" A terrified roe deer sprang deeper into the forest.

An hour had passed without any sign of Anton and they were back at Gustl's farm. The house lay in darkness.

"Psst!" Gustl whispered loudly to the group of helpful neighbours. "I'll see if he's home yet. Sssh, you'll wake Margot!"

Margot had heard them coming from two hundred feet away. It didn't matter, she hadn't slept, adrenalin was still racing through her blood. She turned on her side with her back to the door, pretending to sleep. Gustl was trying to be quiet, she had to give him that, but he opened the creaking door so slowly that she wished he'd just come in and get it over and done with.

Gustl entered the pitch-black room and took his boots off. He tiptoed towards the bed chamber, intending to ask Margot about Anton, and tripped straight over the bowl of slop.

"What the devil? Aaagh!" He slipped on the slop, and thrusting his arms out to break the fall, landed on all fours as the enamel bowl clattered noisily upside down.

Margot sat upright on her mattress and Gustl looked straight into her eyes.

"Aaargh!" he screamed, putting his hand to his chest.

"For God's sake Margot, you scared the life out of me. What in heaven's name are you doing there? Is Anton back yet?"

"Yes, the Gerbers brought him. He's injured and lying on our bed. That's why I'm here."

"I'll tell the men outside then. Where am I supposed to sleep?"

"On the floor. You can get your own blanket; and clean up the slop before you lie down!"

4

EARLY JUNE 1850

"Tomorrow, I must to go up to the forest and fell more trees. I can take the boys with me if you like, so that you can have some peace." Anton's bruises were fading and he was eager to get his house finished; it wasn't fair to inconvenience his sister any longer than necessary.

"Well, Jakob maybe, if you're sure he won't be in your way," Margot replied. "Josef is too small; he'd hold you up. Besides it's not safe for him."

"He has to learn some time."

"Yes, but not yet."

"Very well then. Are you bringing Wilhelmine home tomorrow? Is there enough money left to pay the wet nurse?"

"Yes, everyone was very generous after the funeral and there's still some left from the cow you sold."

"I'll have to sell another one. I've plenty of wood but there's so much else I need. Nails, windowpanes, door handles … paint. I'm doing my best to be thrifty, but even without any extras, so much still has to be bought. Without you both, lending me tools, feeding and looking after us, well I don't know where we'd be."

"We're family, you'd do the same for us. And just look at how all the villagers rallied around after the fires. They brought clothes, and pots and pans, and all sorts, not to mention money donations."

"Yes, I'll never forget their generosity. Even from people who have nothing themselves."

"Especially from people who have nothing themselves, they know what it's like. We all look after each other. Why most of us have lived here for generations, it's not as if we were strangers."

"I could come with you tomorrow, if you'd like." Gustl offered.

"Really? Aren't you needed on the building site?"

"No, the foreman has laid us all off for at least a week. The ground water is rising and he's getting experts in from Bern to see what can be done about it. Otherwise, the owners are going to have their cellars flooded every spring."

"Didn't he make any drainage channels?"

"Yes, of course he did, but he didn't reckon on this amount of rainfall."

"Oh," Margot said and sighed, "you won't be earning then."

"No, sorry love. There just aren't any jobs available."

"Well in that case I'm lucky!" Anton said. "Thank you Gustl, I'll be much quicker with your help."

*****

The next morning, Anton and Gustl packed everything they needed: saws, axes, hammers and other tools, into two rucksacks. They put on their heavy boots and took extra jackets with them. In Weissbruegg it was spring, but high up on the forest slopes it could feel like winter. They set off uphill, along a trail that meandered between towering pine trees, dense bushes and boulders covered in moss. They stepped over tree roots and crossed small bridges, stopping to look at the water thundering down into the valley. Anton held onto Jakob's hand tightly. Although they were only three thousand feet above sea level there was still snow lying in the shade, and the track was partially covered with ice. They gradually gained more height until after eight miles they reached Anton's section of forest.

The whole parcel of his forest was on an extremely steep mountain slope. Telling Jakob to sit down and stay put, Anton and Gustl tied ropes around their waists and secured them to a tree trunk. Then they walked downhill sideways, wedging one boot carefully into the moist forest floor before taking another step, until they were below a suitable fir. They picked up a two-handled saw and began sawing the trunk until they were almost halfway through. Taking a few steps upwards again, they began to saw from the other side. The tree creaked. Anton and Gustl stepped aside quickly as there was a deafening crack and the tree crashed down, plunging forwards onto the forest floor. Picking up their one-handled saws and axes, Anton and Gustl freed the main stem from its branches. They rolled the long trunk, now bare of obstructions, sideways to a channel in the forest floor. Generation after generation had harvested the trees in the same manner. Over hundreds of years channels had formed in the ground, making the passage for the trees swifter and easier. With sheer gravity it sped down the mountainside to the valley floor.

They went back to Jakob.

"Can I help you with the next one Papa?"

"Not until it's fallen, then I'll come and help you downhill and you can help us break some twigs off. But wait until I come, all right?"

"Uh-huh."

Together, they chopped down two more trees and then they packed their things together to go home. Walking down the mountain was harder than going up. Anton's knees felt the strain and his ankle throbbed, but the view compensated for any discomfort. The sun, on its descent, glowed like a burning fire of gold and damask upon the virgin snow of the mighty peaks of the Alps. They looked as if they were ablaze.

"Who did you ask to collect the tree trunks?" Gustl asked.

"Stein Willi. He's going to pick them up first thing tomorrow morning with his horse. Said he wouldn't charge. I'm meeting him at the crossroads and we'll go together to his brother-in-law's sawmill. Willi said he'd ask him to give me a good price."

"Oh, that's decent of him! I'll come with you to help, it might save some time."

"Good, thank you."

*****

Margot walked along the road to Reichenbach. It was only two leagues but she hurried because she wanted to call in at Helena's on her way home. The news that Gustl had been laid off work had hit her much harder than she had showed. The cost of flour had shot up recently. Floods were hitting the whole of Europe. Switzerland imported grain but at horrendous prices, and by the time it was on the market … well … it was becoming a luxury! But she needed flour to bake bread.

Margot had recently made a lace collar and cuffs as a present for Helena. She had saved Wilhelmine's life with her kindness. Helena was really pleased with her present. She came originally from Bern from a well-to-do family. On a visit home she had worn a dress with the lace collar and cuffs and received many compliments from her friends. They had enquired who had made them and admired the fine workmanship. Helena passed the compliments on to Margot and asked if she would be interested in making more, for payment. Margot was thrilled and Helena had said that she would buy thread for her. She could pay her back when the lacework was sold. So today Margot was hoping that Helena already had the thread and some orders. What with the weather and four more mouths to feed and the wet nurse to pay, they were already running on their iron reserves.

Margot was so busy deliberating over her troubles and possible solutions that she was surprised to find herself already entering the small town of Reichenbach. With its two and a half thousand inhabitants it was about the same size as Weissbruegg. Going along the main street she was passed by a bedraggled-looking woman with six children, all holding their hands out, begging. They were dirty, barefoot and unkempt. They looked painfully thin. Shocked, Margot stopped the mother.

"Where have you come from?" she asked. The mother answered in a foreign tongue that Margot didn't understand. Margot took the woman's hand and led her to the town hall. She entered, still holding the woman's hand and with the band of children in tow. Margot went to the mayor's secretary, knocked on the door and upon hearing a bark, stepped inside, the family standing humbly behind her.

"This family needs help," Margot told the secretary. "I found them on the street, they're starving!"

The secretary was a woman of uncertain age. She had a pale complexion and greying coiffed hair, but smooth skin void of wrinkles. She looked at the heap of misery behind Margot and wrinkled her nose up as if she'd smelt rotting cabbage.

"Well, you can't bring them here, we have enough to do looking after our own people!" she answered.

Margot looked at her badge, which said she was Ursula Huber.

"Mrs Huber, they are obviously starving, can't you spare something at least for the children?" Margot glared purposefully at Mrs Huber's ample stomach and a full paper bag on the windowsill. A torturous aroma of freshly baked bread wafted across the room. Margot's mouth watered.

"No, if they're not from here, and they aren't, they must move on."

"Do you at least have a soup kitchen in Reichenbach?"

"You can try at the parsonage, but get them out of here now, immediately, or I shall call the guard."

"What? Whatever for? They are hardly a threat!"

"Look, Mrs Do-Goodbody! We've had at least three hundred beggars passing through our streets in the last two weeks. We can't feed them all, nor is it our duty to do so. You're causing an obstruction, please leave, this is the last time I ask politely!"

"Mrs Do- ... what a cheek! You've no right to talk to me like that, I'll—" Margot stopped mid-stream as she heard Mrs Huber ring a bell. A guard came hurrying along the corridor. Margot held her hands up in disbelief. "It's all right, we're going," she told the guard. "But you haven't heard the last of this!" she shouted back over her shoulder to Mrs Huber.

Margot exited the town hall indignantly. Where was

the parsonage? That self-righteous, pompous old bat had knocked the sense right out of her. Ah yes, of course.

"Come on," she said, grabbing the mother's hand again. "Follow me, we won't give up yet." She led the family to the rectory and took them round to the back entrance. She knocked loudly on the kitchen window. The pastor's housekeeper, deep in concentration on her chores, jumped in surprise nearly dropping the pan in her hand. She put it down and dried her hands quickly on her apron, before opening the door.

"Good day," Margot said politely. "These people need help. Do you have some bread or soup to spare?"

Margot could not help noticing a look of dismay flash across the housekeeper's face. She answered kindly, however.

"Yes, I can give them some bread now and soup in half an hour, but that's all I can do I'm afraid. After the soup they must move on."

"What will happen to them?"

"They'll probably end up in a workhouse in one of the large towns."

"Oh, oh I see. Well thank you for your help, I must get on myself now."

Margot took a deep breath to calm herself and then walked back up the road, took a right turn and then a left until she arrived at Barbara Urban's house, the wet nurse.

"You're late, I've been waiting for you," Barbara greeted Margot impatiently.

"Yes I'm sorry, I got held up. How is Wilhelmine?"

"She's fine. She's still a little small though."

"Yes, she'll need a while to catch up. Is she ready?"

"Yes, I'll go and get her."

Barbara Urban brought Wilhelmine in a small carry basket covered with a rough blanket.

"Thank you for caring for her," Margot said, paying Barbara.

"I'll miss her." Barbara stroked the baby's cheek.

"You can visit anytime you like," Margot offered. "I must go to Dr Koefeli now; we have an appointment about her foot."

*****

Dr Koefeli examined Wilhelmine's left foot. It was still rotated inwards and downwards, as at birth. He measured both legs.

"Well," he concluded "I'm afraid there's nothing that can be done about it. It is called a clubfoot and occurs sometimes. It is a rare condition but not unknown. Luckily, it's just one foot and at the moment both legs are the same length."

"Will she be able to walk?" Margot dreaded the answer.

"Oh yes. She will probably walk on the side of her foot and have a limp. She may need a special shoe when she's older, but otherwise she can grow up normally."

Margot was so relieved and happy that she felt like kissing the doctor.

"Oh, thank you doctor, thank you so much, thank you!" She took his hand and shook it up and down enthusiastically, not letting go of it.

Dr Koefeli extricated his hand carefully from Margot's and smiled.

"Yes, no need to worry. Give your brother my best wishes."

"Oh thank you, yes I will, thank you so much, goodbye."

Margot left the surgery with a broad smile on her face. It did her well to hear some good news for a change. She walked back to Weissbruegg in high spirits. She had spent eight months worrying herself sick about poor little Wilhelmine, or rather Mina, as they called her. Now, they would all be reunited at home, like a proper family. She wished that Anton's family could stay forever, it made up a bit for her failure to conceive. As she strode out hastily, the rain set in again. What had been a permanent drizzle turned into a heavy downpour. Looking towards the sky, and cursing under her breath but at the same time praying to God that Helena had the thread and some orders, she started to run. She arrived at Helena's house dripping wet and knocked at the door.

"Oh goodness, just look at you! Come in quickly." Helena held the door wide open and stood aside.

"No I can't, I'll drip all over your carpet, I just wanted to ask if you had the thread yet?"

"Yes, come in, you look as if you could do with a small schnapps to warm you up."

"Are you sure, I'm very wet?"

"Yes, for goodness' sake, come in and warm up by the cockle stove. It's just an old carpet. I'll go and get the thread and something to drink. Do you drink schnapps or would you prefer a coffee?"

"A small schnapps would be lovely."

"Right then, take your shawl off and hang it over the stove to dry, I'll be straight back."

Helena returned with two glasses and a bottle of cherry schnapps.

"Is cherry all right, I made it myself?"

"Yes, thank you."

Helena peeped at Mina, sleeping peacefully in her basket.

"Today's the big day then?"

"Yes, this bundle of joy will cheer us all up."

"How's Anton?"

"A lot better, thank you. Looking forward to getting Mina home."

"Good. Well, here is the thread I brought back from Bern for you." Helena opened a pretty box and revealed six large spools of fine white thread.

"Oh, it's silk!" Margot exclaimed, removing one spool and feeling it. "It's so soft!"

"It's all right then? I asked at the haberdashery and they said it was suitable."

"It's wonderful! It will be a pleasure to make lace with this!"

"I've written down some orders for you. My relations were very enthusiastic!"

"The thread must've been terribly expensive."

"Don't worry, I'll get it back later. Your work is so exquisite; it deserves the best thread."

Margot blushed modestly. A little embarrassed, she changed the subject.

"In Reichenbach there was a family of beggars in the street. I took them to the town hall and there ..." Margot hesitated about using an appropriate word for Mrs Huber in front of Helena, "I spoke to the mayor's secretary and she was ... unfriendly."

"You spoke to Mrs Huber? That old witch? I'm surprised she didn't set the guards on you!"

"Well, she did actually!"

The two women looked at each other straight-faced and then burst out laughing. Helena held onto her stomach and bent over double, shaking with laughter. Tears ran down her face. Margot grinned foolishly. Finally composing herself, Helena poured them both a second glass of schnapps.

"Tell me everything!" she demanded. "I want to hear every single word."

5

JUNE 20TH 1850

The snow had melted on the middle-high alpine pastures and the farmers prepared to move their livestock, as they did every year, from the lowlands up the mountain slopes to sweeter grass. The big reddish-brown Simmental cows, with white markings, wore huge bronze cow bells around their necks, with wide leather collars. The clapper of the bells was deafening as the farmers moved them along the road towards upper pastures.

Gustl was the Senn – the head-herdsman and responsible for making cheese up on the alm. He would stay on the alm throughout the whole summer and walked now at the front, leading the long procession. The villagers accompanied him with their own cows. Once settled, they would leave them in Gustl's care in return for looking after his farm during his absence, and a portion of the cheese when he returned in September. Goats followed the cows and a couple of pigs followed the goats. Anton took up the rear with a long wooden stick in his hand, to ensure that no animal was left behind.

Although the temperatures were still cold, the sun was shining. The rock-strewn path led them steadily upwards through meadows abundant with colourful wild flowers, along surging mountain streams, through leafy forests and past rumbling waterfalls. The path became steeper and narrower, the cows walked in single file. As they progressed, the track hugged one side of the mountain and fell steeply down on the other side. The ground was covered with loose pebbles. Men and livestock alike, trod with care. Merely a flimsy rope, attached loosely to short wooden stakes, separated the path from a dizzying, sheer drop hundreds of feet to the valley below. It was a six-hour march to their destination.

A mountain valley, carved by glaciers millions of years ago, appeared before them. The cattle began to run excitedly towards the fresh green grass, emitting a cacophony of sonorous cow bells echoing back and forth between the mountains surrounding them. Not until they had all settled down, happily chewing the grass, did the noise reduce to a peaceful clank-clanking in the valley. The herdsmen walked on until they reached a mountain hut with overhanging eaves, on a hill overlooking the alpine pasture. Next to the wooden chalet was a cheese dairy.

Gustl laid down his tools and a few provisions in the hut and then joined the other men outside to eat the food that they had brought with them. The villagers sat outside in a circle, drinking beer and eating bread and cheese, smoked ham or sausage. Emil, the youngster responsible for the goats this year, had fetched logs from the side of the hut and placed a couple inside a ring of stones between the men. He fiddled with his flintstone and a piece of metal until a flicker of flame kindled some dry grass in his hand and he slowly got a fire burning. Stein Willi, Franziska's husband Linus, and a couple of others, stuffed tobacco in their pipes and began to smoke. Peter Zaehler, Willi's brother-in-law who owned a sawmill, tapped some snuff from a small tin onto the back of his hand, took a deep sniff and then offered the tin around.

There was a pleasurable silence, the men all waiting patiently for Eddie to start speaking. Eddie was the oldest amongst them, over eighty years old. Although he had never asked for the honour, he was habitually the first to open the conversation. For at least the last seven years he had been saying that the respective year would be his last on the alm. He took a puff on his pipe and cleared his throat.

"Ah, it's so beautiful up here," he enthused. "I'm going to miss it next year."

"Get on with you!" Emil, his beloved grandson, seventy years his junior, could speak freely with his grandfather. "You'll still be coming up here every year, long after I'm dead and buried."

Eddie took off his hat, revealing his near bald head, and cuffed his grandson with it playfully.

"Did you hear that?" he guffawed. "Cheeky youngsters these days! If I'd spoken to my grandfather like that, he'd have taken his stick out."

"You'd have to catch me first," Emil retorted. Eddie shook his head in mock exasperation. He took a swig of schnapps from a bottle and then passed it on to the next man.

"Well, at least you're here lad, I'm glad about that. Did you all hear about Xaver's two boys down at Muelenen?"

"Xaver Bentele, the owner of the slate quarry?" Willi asked.

"Yes. Both his sons, Albrecht and Friedrich, have gone off to America."

"What? No!" Consternation spread around the circle of men as they inched in a little closer to make sure they didn't miss anything.

"But what will he do?" Willi asked. "They were supposed to take over the quarry after him, weren't they?"

"Yes, not only that, they were doing most of the heavy work already. Xaver can't do much after his back injury," Eddie replied.

"What on earth do they want in America?" Peter asked. "They already had a good future ahead of them here."

"Well, I'm not so sure about that. Xaver told me that the cheap competition from abroad is crippling, and the dust inside the mines isn't good for the lungs either."

"That still doesn't explain what they want in America though. They can't just leave their whole family alone here, surely?"

"Their poor mother sat at the window waving them goodbye and weeping that she'd never see her boys again. But the youths today," Eddie continued, "are young and optimistic. The lads have cousins in Schaffhausen who went to America last year. They wrote home very enthusiastically, said how farmers could stake out good fertile land in the West, and after seven years working the land, it was given to them, for nothing! And now Bentele's lads want to do the same."

"Is it true that you can find gold in the rivers in America?" Emil addressed his teacher, Karl Stettler. He was a close acquaintance of the mayor, who always gave him his newspapers to read when he was finished with them. Barely in his mid-twenties, Karl was respected by the villagers as the most learnt amongst them. They now turned their faces to him, eager to hear his answer.

"Some gold has been found, yes. Hundreds of thousands

of men from all over the world are rushing to America, hoping to find it. About a third of them die from disease on their voyage over there. In America, even more die from yellow fever or snake bites. The lure of gold entices all sorts of men thither: ruffians, criminals, outlaws, there is no law and order. The men carry guns and knives and can murder anyone without fear of punishment. You'd be better off staying here and learning a trade, Emil."

"Oh, I wouldn't go." Emil, who had been glued to his teacher's tale, brushed off any idea of himself leaving the area. A sigh of relief encompassed the men.

The subject of America exhausted, the conversation turned to the weather.

"I heard that the floods aren't just here but all over Switzerland," Peter said.

"Not just Switzerland but other parts of Europe too," Karl the teacher replied. "The headline in the Bernese Times last week was: 'The Year With No Summer'!"

"It's only the middle of June," Eddie protested. "I can remember a year 'bout forty-five years ago. Was just the same as this year, then come July we had brilliant sunshine right through till September. Saved the harvest, luckily."

"Well, I hope the rain stops soon," Karl said. "I've read some very disturbing accounts about potato blight in Ireland. A million have starved to death and more than another million have emigrated."

"Do you think potato blight will come here?" Anton asked, looking worried.

"I'm afraid it's already in France." Karl answered. "It's just a matter of time before it gets here."

Gustl looked dismayed. "Will you check my crops, Anton?"

"Yes, first thing, as soon as I get back tomorrow.

Gopfriedstutz, darn it, that's the last thing we need now. Mine were all right two days ago though, when did you last check yours?"

"Not long ago, Monday I think it was."

"Karl, what does the mayor intend doing about the poor?" Linus asked. Several of the men present were town councillors, but Karl was the mayor's representative. Faces turned towards him.

"The folks from here will be looked after. Outsiders will have to move on."

"My wife's cousin in St Gallen said the town was paying for tickets for families willing to emigrate!"

"Yes, there are several towns offering families a one-way ticket to Russia or America, Mayor Buehler isn't going to do that, not yet anyway."

"Isn't it expensive? Some people save for ages to buy a ticket and now the lazy sods are just getting tickets given to them, that's not right!" Heinz butted in.

"The mayor thought that some of the men might think like you, Heinz. Fact is, in the long run it's cheaper to buy the poor a ticket rather than have them rely on poor relief for years on end. And despite what you may think, laziness is rarely the reason for poverty. Besides, Reverend Moser would tell us it's our Christian duty to help those less fortunate than ourselves."

"I work fourteen hours a day at the sawmill, six days a week, and at home there's plenty more work. We've still barely enough to live on and nobody ever gives us something for nothing!" Heinz nearly spat his words out.

A couple of men nodded in agreement, most, however, stared at the ground in silence. The silence hung in the air and the sound of the cow bells seemed louder.

Gustl was embarrassed for his brother-in-law. "Time to

milk the cows," he said, standing up. The men took this as a signal to stand up also.

"Yes, time to get a move on." Anton sighed with relief.

*****

The men got up at the break of dawn.

"I've not slept a wink," Gustl told Anton. "I tossed and turned all night worrying about the potatoes."

"There's no point worrying, either they have it or they don't, we can't alter it. I'll look at them carefully and do whatever's necessary."

"You're right, we can't change things, but if they're all right will you let me know? It'll save me worrying."

"Yes, I'll do that. If you don't hear anything then you'll know they've got it. I'll sell another cow and the calves; we will survive. You concentrate on those cheeses now."

"Yes I will. See you hopefully soon then. Don't say anything to Margot, not until it's certain."

The men took leave from Gustl and began to hike back down the mountain slopes. The loose stones beneath their feet were wet from the permanent rain. Mist hung beneath the trees. A chill was in the air. Nobody talked much, the men just stuck their long, sturdy walking sticks into the ground before them, concentrating on the steep, slippy track, hugging the mountainside.

Peter touched Anton's elbow. "Can I have a word?" he asked. "In private, drop back a bit."

"Of course," Anton said. "Is something wrong?"

"No, no. Well, I'm a bit embarrassed to ask but the mill isn't doing too well at the moment, and the invoice I sent you, well I know you've been through rough times, but when do you think you'll be able to pay it?"

"The bill? For cutting my wood? Well yes I got it but I

thought it was a mistake. You see I paid immediately, when we brought the tree trunks."

"Huh? But I always send an invoice."

"Yes, but because you gave me a good price Heinz asked for it and said he'd pass it on, maybe he forgot. Gustl was with me, and Willi, ask Willi, he'll tell you!"

"Oh, I'm sorry, there's been a misunderstanding, Heinz must've forgotten to give it to me. Look, do me a favour, Anton? Don't mention this to anyone, forget that we've spoken."

"Of course." Anton was a little irked. He hoped that Heinz hadn't cheated him and that now he must pay twice. Luckily, Willi and Gustl had been with him. Surely Peter would believe his own brother-in-law?

Descending into the valley, Anton felt depressed. He could tell that his companions were downcast too. No one was joking or fooling around. No doubt they were all worrying about their dismal situation and were anxious about their potatoes. The rainclouds hanging low between the trees in the forests did nothing to cheer him up. To the contrary, he knew that cold, wet weather promoted potato blight. There wasn't a single inhabitant of Weissbruegg, or the whole of the surrounding area, that wasn't negatively affected by the enduring cool, moist summer. Even those who weren't farmers were hit by the price increases for groceries. Anyone who could, worked two, or even three, jobs. But there were hardly any jobs available.

Anton went straight home to Margot. Having completed her morning chores, she was sitting down with the boys to breakfast.

"Smelt the bacon, did you?" she greeted him.

"Yes, smelt it a league back, best bacon in the Kander valley," he answered, smiling. "Didn't the hens lay any eggs today?"

"No, the cock's lost his charm."

Anton gave his children a kiss and then sat down with them.

"Tell me all the gossip," Margot demanded.

"Gossip? What gossip?"

"Oh get away with you. Twenty men together up on the alm? It must've been worse than the fishwives down at Thun!"

"No, we men don't go in for idle chat."

"Nonsense. Now tell me everything, word for word, or you can get your own supper tonight!"

"I've got something urgent to do now, I just stopped by for a spade, but I'll try to recall our discussions tonight if you make me one of your sausage casseroles."

"What do you mean urgent? What's going on?" Margot called to Anton's back, already retreating hastily outdoors.

6

JUNE 21ST 1850

Anton went to Gustl's potato field first. It was close to the Gungg brook, partially shaded by a small forest of firs in the west, just a mile from their farmhouse. From a distance the foliage looked fine and Anton's hopes began to rise. Even when he arrived at the field and started walking around the perimeter, nothing seemed out of order. But as Anton walked along the furrows through the middle of the field, his hopes were dashed to the ground. He saw brown freckles on the potato leaves, a sure sign of potato blight. He thrust his spade into the soil under one plant, raising the tubers to the surface. Immediately, a foul smell hit his nose and dark patches on the tubers were clearly visible.

Anton went to the brook to clean his spade and then walked towards the foot bridge. He met the Saddler Eric, who like most villagers, in addition to his trade, also had livestock and a field or two.

"Morning, Anton," Eric greeted him. "You've heard then? How's Gustl's crop? Affected yet?"

"Yes, Karl told us yesterday up on the alm. Not good

I'm afraid, the tubers are already rotting. What about your crop?"

"Mine too, we'll have to dig them all out and burn them; try to stop the spread."

"Mmmn, I'm going to check my own field first. It's a bit sunnier on the other side of the Heiti."

"Well, good luck, if the tubers are all right, maybe you can still save the potatoes."

"I hope so, maybe if I cut off all the foliage above soil level and burn it."

"Have you got anyone to help you?"

"No, Gustl is on the alm."

"Of course. When we've burned my crop, I'll send my two boys to help you if you want?"

"That would be good, thank you. I can't pay them much though."

"Just give them something to eat, they'll be satisfied with that. They're always hungry those two."

Anton crossed the bridge and walked to his own potato field. He couldn't see any infection on the leaves and the tubers looked all right too. He decided that it would be best to cut off the foliage and burn it. Maybe he could save the crop before it was infected. It would mean harvesting the potatoes early, and he wouldn't get a heavy crop, but it would be better than nothing.

He decided that saving his crop had priority over digging up Gustl's field to burn; he only had one pair of hands after all. He set about cutting off all the green potato leaves above soil level and bringing them to a corner of the field. His back was burning with pain, and the midges swarming low, by the time he finally finished the last row of plants. He struck his flintstone on metal and after four attempts got a bonfire burning. He straightened his back, swiped at the midges settling on his sweaty head, and looked down into the valley and across to the mountain slopes on the other side of the Kander. Spotted all across the hillsides, between the trees and houses, were tell-tale puffs of smoke rising in spirals, sending messages of heartbroken woe to heaven.

Anton could tell that almost everyone was affected. What were they going to do? he thought desolately. They'd all starve. He gathered up his tools and strode out purposefully, intent on getting back to his temporary home, sister and children.

"Stop! Wait!"

He heard someone out of breath calling behind him. It was Mayor Buehler, climbing hastily up the hill. He was panting. Anton waited until he caught up.

"I was just coming to see you. My goodness, you can't half move on those long legs of yours!" The mayor, red in the face, pulled a handkerchief out of his pocket to wipe his brow.

"Sorry, I didn't see you."

"That's all right. I just wanted to tell you that I'm holding an emergency council meeting tomorrow evening."

"Ah right, I'll be there. Gustl can't come, of course."

"No, of course not. Look, do you think you could let Willi and Linus know? I've still got eight others to inform."

"No problem, do you want to come in for a drink?"

"No, no. I must get on, till tomorrow then."

"Yes, till tomorrow."

Anton continued on his way, wondering what the mayor was going to suggest. What if there weren't any solutions? Would he offer one-way tickets to America too? Well, he wasn't leaving the valley that was for sure. He'd been born here and would only leave in a coffin.

*****

All evening, and the next day, Anton met curious chatter and speculation. The extraordinary meeting had been called in for eight o'clock in the evening. The first councillors arrived at the town hall shortly after seven. Anton arrived just before eight. He noticed a nervous young man, lurking in a corner, half-behind a tall green plant. He held his cap in his fist and was wringing it anxiously in his hands. Anton recognised Bartli, and shaking hands, said a quick hello before entering the meeting room. He looked at the large clock on the wall, saw he had ten minutes left and hurried to Helena Buehler's platter of famous sandwiches. He picked up the last one and bit into it quickly before someone else snatched it. Helena usually made enough for everyone and a couple of men were still arriving, so somebody must have been digging in. He looked around surreptitiously to see if he could find the culprit.

At that moment, the mayor arrived and sat down at the head of the long rectangular table. The councillors hurried to take their places, eating on the way. The mayor looked solemn.

"Thank you for coming," he said. "I haven't called you here to discuss the potato blight, although I deeply sympathise with those of you affected."

"All of us then," Eric butted in.

"Yes. Now, you all know that my wife comes from Bern and her family has, well how should I express myself, some connections with ... influential people. For the past two months, since the fires and the floods, I've been putting my feelers out and trying to entice some sort of industry to Weissbruegg."

"Industry? What type of industry?" Erwin Klopfenstein, the landlord of the Goldenen Ochsen, wanted to know.

"Shut up, let him carry on." Peter Zaehler nudged Erwin to keep quiet.

"Well, any industry actually, anything that would bring employment to our town. We already have over eight hundred inhabitants relying on poor relief, and to be honest, the pot is emptying rapidly. A few businessmen were interested to hear exactly where we were and asked about the sort of wages they'd have to pay. At present, matchstick factories are opening up all over the place. I told the gentlemen that we had plenty of land for them to build on. I offered them a very reasonable price for building land and ensured them that we had plenty of wood and able-bodied men and women looking for jobs. Now, I wanted to let you know because yesterday I received a letter informing me that four gentlemen will be arriving with the mail coach tomorrow to have a look around."

The councillors all started talking and asking questions at once. Mayor Buehler could answer hardly any of the queries.

"The talks are at early stages yet. I just wanted a quick vote and heads-up from you to continue negotiations."

The men voted unanimously and complimented Mr Buehler on his efforts to save their community.

"Good, good," he said. "Now, there's just one more small matter to be dealt with before we all go home. Some of you may have noticed Bartolomaeus Gerber on your way in here. He's made an application to the council; he wants permission to get married."

"Gerber you say? Aren't they on poor relief?" Erwin Klopfenstein asked.

"Yes, they are, otherwise he wouldn't need permission to get married." Mayor Buehler stated the obvious.

"But it's clear then, he can't get married and start his own family, getting more and more people reliant on relief."

"It's complicated, I'm afraid. You see he's engaged to Maria Wiederkehr and she's already expecting a child."

The councillors sucked their breath in and let it out again noisily. A few were concerned, everyone knew that unmarried mothers were sent to a workhouse or even sentenced to prison; the baby would be taken off her.

"That's a fine pickle!" Saddler Eric said. "Didn't he think of that beforehand?"

"Let's not pretend that we were never hot-headed youngsters," the mayor said. "I could've said no straight-away without consulting you all first, but in fact they were engaged before the family hit bad times. He's a hard-working lad and swears he'll pay back every centime he receives from our community before he has another child. They can live with his parents and he'll do any job he gets. He pleaded with me and I found him believable and trustworthy. Don't you think we could make an exception?"

"Rules are rules," Erwin said. "Make one exception and they'll all start breeding like rabbits."

"I know the Gerbers, they're a decent family," Anton said. "Why, if my sister and brother-in-law weren't helping me out, well, I'd need poor relief too. As soon as work's available he'll be after it, I'm sure of that."

"Along with a hundred other men," Erwin argued.

"You're absolutely right, we can't make exceptions," Saddler Eric agreed.

"It's very hard on his betrothed; Maria is a decent girl," Karl the teacher said. "And the baby will be taken off her."

"She should have thought of that before she let him push her skirt up," Erwin shouted back.

"Gentlemen, gentlemen, stop!" The mayor cried. "Please, let's keep this civil! Master Gerber is waiting outside. We can either invite him in and you can listen to what he has to say, or we can take a vote here and now."

"Listening to his excuses won't help, we might as well vote," Peter said.

"All right then. Those in favour of the marriage raise your hands!" The mayor counted eight hands.

"And those against?"

Seven hands went up. Four councillors were not present. The mayor added his own vote to make it nine to seven.

"I'll let him know," he said.

*****

"Have you heard?" Margot asked Anton at breakfast.

"What? Do you mean about the River Kander?"

"No, well yes, that too; forty people died in the flash floods in Reichenbach, but I didn't mean that. Heinz has lost his job!"

"He'll find another job. Bad business, those houses getting swept away, I'm glad we don't live so close to the Kander."

"You don't seem very surprised about Heinz. Did you already know?"

"No, but I'd heard that the sawmill's struggling."

"Still, Heinz was the foreman, why him? He won't get another job so well paid. Maybe he can't even send Hari to boarding school anymore!"

"It's a few years until then. I don't know why he was aiming so high anyway; none of the children round here go to boarding school."

"The mayor's boys will."

"For goodness' sake, Margot! Mrs Buehler is from a respectable family in Bern – that's different. What is it to you, anyway? You never have a good word to say about them."

"I was just telling you, that's all."

"Well, I'm off now, I've no time for your gossip."

7

MARCH 1852

"I need a wife," Anton announced at supper. "The house is finished, I've moved the animals and the vegetable garden is in order. But we can't live from that, I need a job, and when I'm working I need someone to look after the children. I can't leave them here indefinitely, it's not fair on you two."

Margot looked up from buttering her bread.

"I don't mind, they're good, even little Mina."

"But you're doing so well with your lace, you could devote more time to that."

"Have you got someone in mind?"

"No, I thought I could put a notice in the Frutiger Parish Weekly. It's not expensive."

"You've already asked then?"

"No, Willi told me. Well, he suggested it actually."

"It's mainly widows with children who write those personal advertisements. You'll end up with more mouths to feed."

"One child would be all right, I suppose. I mean, she'll

have to cook and wash, look after the animals and the vegetable patch, so it'd only be fair."

"I think it's a good idea," Gustl butted in. "Lena's been gone two years now; it's time Anton finds some happiness again."

"I'll never find a second Lena, but some companionship maybe. I'm really grateful for all you've done for us, Margot, but it's time we go home."

"Fair enough, but we'll always be here for you, you know that. What will you write then?"

"I haven't thought about that yet; will you help me?"

"Just stick to the truth, that's always best."

The following week, Anton's notice appeared in the personal column of the Frutiger Parish Weekly.

Widower, 34 years old, 3 children.

Farmer with own house and no debts,

is looking for a hard-working wife.

8

REGINA, 1827 – 1852

When Regina Ruf was seventeen years old, her parents sent her to distant relatives in Basel, ostensibly to see how a higher household was led, in order to promote her chances of a good marriage. In fact, she was treated like a servant and expected to work hard. Regina didn't mind. The house was large and beautifully furnished, and Basel was an exciting city. The main appeal, however, was their eighteen-year-old son, Heinrich, who obviously found her attractive. For the first time in her life, Regina fell head-over-heels in love.

Whenever they met in one of the corridors of the house and thought no one was watching, Heinrich would touch her, and on a couple of occasions even sneaked a kiss. This went on for several weeks until they started to meet secretly in the park on her half-days off. He said he loved her and asked her to marry him. She imagined living with the man she loved, in a grand house in the city, with children and servants. She was ecstatic and said yes.

Heinrich asked to speak with his parents. Regina

waited at the top of the stairs. She heard loud shouting and arguing penetrate through the closed doors. Heinrich exited the room with a red face; he strode to the front door, opened it and went out, slamming the door behind him. Regina caught her breath and ran upstairs to the servants' quarters. She threw herself onto her bed and sobbed her heart out.

The door burst open.

"You ungrateful little bitch! Is that how you thank us for taking you in from your cow-shit village? Pack your things, my husband will take you to the post carriage personally and make sure you get on it!"

Heinrich's mother, Mrs Urwyler, pulled Regina's arm up forcefully to get her off the bed.

"But we love each other!" Regina's cheeks were wet with tears and her hair, usually tied back neatly in a bun, was hanging in streaks around her face.

"If you don't pack, you can go without your things, but you are leaving the house now. This minute." Mrs Urwyler's face was set like strawberry jelly in a mould. She had her arms crossed in front of her ample chest and she didn't budge a dot from her stand. Regina quickly opened a drawer and bundled her few possessions into the small carpet bag that she had brought with her.

"Right, out – now!" Mrs Urwyler held the door open and pointed the way down the stairs.

*****

"Oh Regina! What on earth were you thinking?" Her father spoke in a slightly admonishing tone.

"She wasn't! You stupid girl, you've come away in shame and brought disgrace upon our family. What are we going to do with you now?" Her mother was harsher.

"She can stay with us surely?" Mr Ruf replied. "She can help you. You're always complaining about your workload."

"Well, she'll have to I suppose. No decent family will take her on now, not without references. Oh you stupid girl, you've ruined all your chances."

*****

Regina stayed at home. She pined for Heinrich and dreamt that he would turn up one day and marry her without his parents' permission. She went to the post office twice weekly in hope of receiving a letter, but none came. After six months of drudgery at home, helping her mother with the cooking, baking and washing, the tables turned, but not for the better.

Her mother, who hadn't been feeling well for a while, was diagnosed with a growth in her abdomen. Regina cared for her and for her father. She milked the cows and goats and tended the kitchen garden. She washed her bedridden mother, fed her and pushed the bedpan under her backside. She mopped up the sick and ran to her whenever she called, day and night. Her mother died and her father was heartbroken. His health took a rapid fall downhill.

Regina's older brother returned home, with his own family, to take over the farm – his inheritance. He let Regina stay to look after their father and to continue working. His wife couldn't do everything alone, so Regina showed her sister-in-law how to make cheese and preserve fruit and vegetables for the winter. She tended to her bedridden father, changed his soiled sheets until one day, two years later, he too died. Regina's brother asked her to leave, his family was growing and there was no room for her. She could stay, of course, until she found something else. Why didn't she look for a proper job or get married?

Regina was twenty-two, practically an old maid. She didn't know any eligible single men. She had no social life. She had almost given up hope of hearing from Heinrich. Her father's second cousin from Basel, Mr Urwyler, came to the funeral to pay his last respects. He assiduously avoided looking at Regina. He spoke to her brother in short, serious sentences before taking his leave.

"What did Mr Urwyler say to you?" Regina asked her brother later.

"He told me of your misdeeds. You took advantage of their trust and kindness. I must admit I was surprised, sister. I had no idea."

Regina pressed her lips together.

"What about Heinrich? Did he tell you what he's doing now?"

"Heinrich? Oh yes, he's overseas somewhere. He has a sugar plantation and married an English countess. He quickly recovered from your allures, sister."

Regina thought her heart had stopped beating and expected to fall down and die. But she didn't. She realised that she was rooted to the spot like some statue and felt smutted in pigeon shit too. A switch clicked inside her, turning off any warmth she had left in her heart. She whirled around and left the room without speaking.

The next morning there was a knock on the front door; it was her Aunt Theresia from Reichenbach.

"Hello, my dear," she greeted Regina who opened the door to her. "I heard that you're looking for somewhere to live and I've come with a proposition."

They sat down at the table together and her aunt invited Regina to come and live with her. "I'm not getting any younger," she told Regina, "and my son doesn't visit very often. He lives with his family in Basel and it's too far for him to travel with his children. I could do with some help. My house is not very large but it has two sleeping chambers so you can have your own room. There's a garden and I have some chickens and a goat. I'm afraid of dying on my own. If you look after me in my old age, I will bequeath my house to you."

"What about your son?" Regina asked. "Won't he be wanting the house?"

"He has a large house in Basel. What would he want with a small cottage in the countryside? Anyway, I can leave the house to whomever I want."

"Well if you're sure, thank you, I will accept your offer."

Regina packed her work dress and a few other belongings into her carpet bag and left her family home, together with Aunt Theresia, the same day. She liked the idea of inheriting a house of her own and being independent.

Her aunt became old and frail. Her aunt became bedridden. But she didn't die. Regina was glad at first – she had grown fond of her aunt – but the last few years were very hard. Her aunt could no longer speak or articulate and she soiled her sheets several times daily. She cried out in the night and Regina couldn't sleep. Her son didn't visit once. She lived twenty years.

The son came to the funeral.

"Thank you for looking after my mother," he said. "There's no need for you to vacate the house immediately, you can stay until you find something else."

"No, you're mistaken," Regina corrected him. "Your mother left the house to me, for looking after her."

"I know nothing about that, did she write a new will? I'll go to her lawyer in the morning and ask."

A wriggle of uncertainty lodged itself in Regina's abdomen. Surely, she would have ... she searched her memory back twenty years, trying to think if her aunt had ever visited her lawyer. Regina had taken everything at face value. She'd simply trusted her, presumed she'd left the house to her, as promised.

Certainty came the next day when her aunt's lawyer arrived at the doorstep with her aunt's son, her cousin. They were quite friendly and her cousin was even regretful that his mother had given Regina false hopes. But the house was in his father's name and the will couldn't have been changed even if his aunt had wanted to. He wasn't so sympathetic that he said Regina could continue to live there indefinitely, but instead he gave her twelve months to find something else.

Regina was forty-two and penniless. She had one brown workday dress and one plain black dress for Sundays. Her hair was streaked with grey, her face lined and haggard. Her body was thin, bony and unfulfilled. She picked up the Frutiger Parish Weekly and turned to the personal advertisements on the back page.

9

APRIL 1852

Anton received only one answer to his notice in the parish magazine.

Dear Mr Schneider,

I read your advertisement in the Frutiger Parish Weekly with interest. I am single with no children. After caring for my deceased aunt in her old age, I find myself now without a home. I am used to hard work in the house, garden and around animals.

Yours sincerely,

Regina Ruf

Anton met Regina on two occasions. They got on reasonably well with each other and agreed that a marriage could work for both parties. They spoke with Reverend Moser and two months later they were married at St Martin's church in Weissbruegg.

In spite of it being a marriage of convenience, Regina told Anton that she wanted it to be consummated.

"Are you sure?" he asked.

"Yes."

Regina lay on her back as cold and rigid as an iron gate. Anton tried foreplay but she wasn't in for that.

"Just get on with it!" she told him. So he did.

The next morning, Regina removed the bed sheet, folded it up carefully and tidied it away in the bottom of a wooden chest.

"What are you doing?" Anton asked.

"I've been cheated out of my inheritance once already. It won't happen again. This is proof that we were properly married, should you die before me," she added.

"But—"

"No, don't worry, you won't need to repeat last night's performance, I have all I need now."

"But—"

"There is only one reason for cohabitation and I'm too old for children. Anyway, it'll be hard enough feeding your three. I'm going to milk the cows, what about you?"

Anton took a deep breath.

"Well, now you're here to look after the children, I'll go and look for paid work."

*****

In the last year, matchstick factories had sprung up all over the Kander valley. After the first one in Weissbruegg, a further four had opened nearby. Matchsticks had found an excellent market because it was so simple to strike a flame with them, especially in comparison to the cumbersome messing around with a flintstone and metal. The factories rose and prospered quickly, particularly here in this remote valley where there were few other jobs.

Anton knew that the factory in Weissbruegg had no vacancies. It was in town on the first floor of a gabled house next to the baker. Three men worked there, six women and twenty children. He had heard that it was very cramped with barely enough space for the workers. Still, it was a pity because it would've been nearby; just a ten-minute walk.

The factory in Kandermatt was new. It hadn't opened yet; they were looking for a workforce. Anton hoped to get the position of dipper. The dipper was the best-paid job; he could earn two to three francs a day. It was also the most dangerous job, and unhealthy. The dipper was exposed all day long to poisonous phosphor steam. That bothered neither Anton nor any other men. Packers only earned half that amount for the same hours, so he might as well do the better-paid job, if he got it. He strode out quickly to Kandermatt, sending a prayer to heaven that the position hadn't already been taken.

After a fifty-minute, hurried march he arrived at the new factory. It was only six o'clock in the morning but word of work had spread quickly and already a line of men, women and children were waiting patiently for the factory director to arrive. Anton took his place in the queue and gazed at the wooden building in front of him. It was smaller than he had expected. Rectangular, maybe forty feet long and twenty wide. He saw only three small windows. Next to the factory there was a well and a small stream was not far away. Less than a three hundred feet away, a grand villa, newly built for the factory director, stood proudly, three storeys high. It was set in beautiful gardens with a gatehouse and surrounded by a stone wall. Even the stables looked more inviting than the factory building before them. More people joined the queue. Everyone greeted each other, eyed one another up, and calculated their own chances of getting a job. They wished each other luck, at the same time hoping the jobs wouldn't all be gone before it was their turn to step forwards.

At seven-thirty, a horse-drawn carriage left the villa and pulled up at the entrance to the factory. The coachman got down from his coach box and opened the carriage door. Two gentlemen, both in three-piece suits and top hats, stepped out. The prospective applicants removed their caps respectfully and stood to one side to let the two gentlemen pass. They went inside, closing the door behind them, and the labourers continued to wait patiently. A quarter of an hour later, the shorter of the two men reappeared.

"My name is Mr Haeberlin," he told them. "I am the supervisor. The director, Mr Carl Lauber, wants to see the dippers first. All applicants for dipper, please step forwards."

Anton stepped forwards along with seven further adult males and two adolescents.

"Right, follow me!" he said leading them inside the building. Mr Haeberlin took them upstairs to his office, sat down at a wooden desk and wrote down the names and addresses of the applicants, any previous experience and their wage expectation.

Anton heard his fellow applicants dither and hesitate. Most asked for two-and-a-half francs per day, probably thinking that it was about average and not too greedy. Anton slipped back to the rear of the line.

"Name?" Mr Haeberlin asked.

"Anton Schneider, sir."

"Experience?"

"None, sir."

"Wage expectation?"

"Two francs, sir."

Mr Haeberlin gathered the application sheets together.

"Wait here!" he ordered the men, and went to the director's office at the end of the building.

The men gazed intently in the direction of the office, straining their ears to pick up any conversation. Mr. Haeberlin returned almost immediately.

"Dipper Bartolomaeus Gerber, dipper assistant Anton Schneider. Be here tomorrow, six sharp. Right, out with you all. Those not accepted can apply as packagers if they wish."

The men trooped out. Anton shook hands with Bartli.

"Congratulations, you'll be earning a bit more now. How's Maria and your little boy?"

"They are both well, thank you. Yes, up till now I wasn't earning much at Slaters, but I was only assistant dipper there. I hope you don't mind being my assistant, Mr Schneider, with you being twice my age."

"No, not at all, I'll learn from you and apply for dipper at the next factory that opens."

"Do you think more will open?"

"Probably, yes. Just look at the fine houses the factory directors are building, they must be making considerable profits. I heard that they're even employing maids and cooks so that their wives have nothing to do all day!"

"Well, they could pay us better then. Up at Slaters the owner was complaining all the time about the costs."

"Ah, I wouldn't take that too seriously. What about you, have you finished paying your debts back to the council yet?"

"Nearly. Now I've got this job it shouldn't take much longer."

"Well done, that'll keep some loudmouths quiet. See you tomorrow then."

"Yes, till tomorrow then. I'm looking forward to working with you, Mr Schneider."

*****

"And? Did you get the job?" Regina asked.

Anton couldn't help thinking that Lena had always greeted him with a hello and a kiss. He quickly pushed sentimental feelings aside.

"Dipper assistant, I've no experience."

"Good. How much? Two francs a day?"

"One and a half."

"What? They only pay one and a half? Well that's a dampener. Maybe I should get a job too."

"You can't. Who'd look after the children?"

"Children work in the factories too, as you well know."

"But Wilhelmine is only two, she can't!"

"Well Margot has offered to look after her often enough."

"But that's why we married, so that she's not burdened and you look after the children."

"It wouldn't be forever. I want to build a dairy next to the farm so that I can make cheese to sell at the market. We can't go on living in poverty forever. Don't you want your children to be able to get an apprenticeship and improve themselves?"

"Well, yes, but the factory isn't very nice inside. It's dark and smells."

"I'm not demanding from anyone anything I won't be doing myself. Jakob and Josef can fill the dipping frames and Wilhelmine can stay with me in the packaging room. She can sit under the table."

"Oh, Regina, I don't know. Can't we wait until they go to school?"

"I haven't got a job yet, let's wait and see. If I get one, they come with me. If not, I'll stay at home with them for a while longer. Agreed?"

Anton nodded reluctantly.

*****

Jakob tried to remember his own mother. He was unhappy that he could no longer picture her clearly, but he remembered her voice, singing a lullaby to him at night, and he remembered feeling her love, her warmth and her softness. Josef and Wilhelmine couldn't remember their mother at all, but they missed their Aunt Margot. Jakob tried to make things up for them by humming a lullaby to them, the one that his mother used to sing, when they lay down to sleep at night. Anton heard Jakob humming through the thin partition to the bed chamber. He felt desperately sad. Tears ran down his cheeks and soaked his pillow, his heart heaved.

*****

Regina got up at four in the morning, milked the cows and goats, and lit the stove. She woke Jakob and told him to collect the eggs while she dressed Wilhelmine and warmed milk on the stove. Josef put plates and knives on the table. They ate breakfast and packed potatoes in their lunch packs along with a bottle of water. Regina gave everyone an apple too, to soften their first day at work. By five o'clock they were on their way, Anton carrying Wilhelmine.

In the factory, work began at six in the morning. Anton went to the dipper room, nicknamed the devil's kitchen, on the ground floor. Together with Bartli, he began to prepare the dipping process where frames, filled with short, thin wooden sticks, were dipped into the sticky, poisonous, combustible substance necessary for matchsticks to ignite.

The kitchen was cramped and dark. There was just one tiny window and the air was stale. The men began by melting sulphur in pans over the fire.

"Careful," Bartli told Anton, "the molten sulphur is over two hundred and twelve degrees, and it's flammable."

"It stinks like goat's fart," Anton answered. "I'd heard it stank, but I didn't think it would be this bad."

Bartli laughed and said, "You'll get used to it, it might spoil your appetite for a day or two though."

"Oh, it's not that bad."

They weighed the paste and other ingredients and put them in a bowl with water. Then the mixture was heated carefully to a hundred and thirteen degrees. They added saltpetre and chalk and then, little by little, under continuous stirring, yellow phosphor. This required deep attention because the yellow phosphor was not only poisonous but also began to burn immediately if exposed to air, and that was why it was always kept under water. The yellow phosphor was delivered in solid bars, a few fingers thick, in metal canisters filled with water.

When the combustive mixture had a thick syrupy consistence, Bartli poured it into a flat tin tray. He turned a wooden roller over the mixture, Anton passed him a frame filled with wooden sticks over which Bartli passed the roller. This procedure was repeated several times until the sticks had a head thick enough to ignite. Then he handed the frame to Anton who placed it on a trolley and then gave Bartli the next frame to be dipped. When the trolley was full of frames, Anton rolled it to the drying room.

They worked for the next fourteen hours with just a short break at lunch time to eat whatever they had brought with them.

*****

Regina brought Jakob and Josef to the first floor and sat them down at a table with an untidy heap of wooden sticks in the centre. Vreni, wife of their neighbour Willi Stein, sat there with six other children, supervising them filling frames with wooden sticks from the pile in the middle.

"Sit down there!" Regina told the boys, "and do what Vreni tells you. I'll see you at the lunch break."

Vreni gave each of the boys an empty frame, showed them how to insert the tiny wooden sticks into it, row for row, and then continued filling her own.

Regina went to the packaging room, Wilhelmine on her hip. She placed the baby girl under the table and told her to stay put. She then took up her own position, standing at the table, filling exactly fifty matches into one oval box and putting the lid on. It didn't last long until, like the other packagers, she no longer needed to count the sticks separately but took one handful of matches, and placing them quickly into a box, pushed the lid on. There were always exactly fifty matches in the box.

The work was monotonous, the air was stale and stuffy, the light dim. The workers were paid according to performance. The wage for filling one thousand boxes was thirty centimes. A practised and diligent worker might manage three thousand boxes in a fourteen-hour day, for ninety centimes. A two-pound loaf of bread cost thirty-five centimes, two pounds of potatoes seven centimes and two pounds of the cheapest cheese seventy centimes. Regina added her wages in her head to those of Anton, and worked out how much they could save.

At twelve o'clock, after six hours of concentrated work, she was lagging and longing for the one o'clock lunch break. She looked under the table for Wilhelmine and saw her six feet away, playing with another toddler her age, in the dirt and rubbish on the floor. The floor was untidy with broken matches and matchstick boxes and all other kinds of waste and debris.

Regina glanced at the young woman working next to her. She was roughly seventeen years old and wore a filthy apron over a brown dress. Her blonde hair had probably been tied back neatly that morning, but now, six hours on, greasy strands had worked themselves free and hung loosely around her face. She saw Regina looking.

"Anneli ..." she introduced herself briefly, removing her hand from the pile of matchsticks and offering it to Regina. "... Ebner. I'm the oldest of Elsa and Fridolin. You'll have seen Chasper, Buolf and Berta upstairs. The others work at Slaters, except my father, of course, he works at the slate factory."

"Regina Schneider," she answered, giving the hand a quick shake, before continuing to work.

When the lunch bell finally rang, Regina sighed with relief. She looked at her hands, soiled with phosphor from the matchstick heads, and searched for somewhere to wash. But she couldn't see any basins.

"Where can we wash?" she asked Anneli.

"There's a well outdoors, or you can go to the stream."

Regina picked up Wilhelmine from the floor and collected Jakob and Josef from the filling room.

"Were they good?" she asked Vreni.

"Yes, they behaved, Josef is a little young though, he had difficulty keeping up."

"Did Mr Haeberlin complain?"

"No, no, nothing like that. He did his best but the others are all a bit older."

"Well, if no one complained he can stay here, it doesn't matter if he earns a little less. Come on then boys, we only have twenty minutes."

Jakob took Josef's hand and trotted quickly after Regina. Once outside they ran urgently behind a bush to pee and then Jakob led Josef back to Regina. He was so hungry, he felt sick. Regina gave him a boiled potato in its skin. It was cold but he ate it ravenously.

"Can I have my apple now, please?" Jakob asked Regina.

"Wait until four o'clock when we have the next break, otherwise you won't have anything left to eat."

"But I'm still hungry."

"If you wait a while the hunger will get better. Now, look after your brother and sister, I must go to relieve myself."

Regina looked around for some bushes to hunker down behind. She chose one, went behind it and saw Anneli crouching down behind the next one. Regina pulled her skirt up and weed next to her.

"What are we supposed to do in winter?" Regina complained.

"There is a curtained-off corner indoors," Anneli answered. "There's a bucket behind it, but the men use it too. I prefer it out here, if possible."

Regina humphed. "I'd better go and collect the boys and bring them back to their workplaces before Mr Haeberlin says anything. We don't want to be late on our first day."

She went to where she'd put the children and found them all still sitting apathetically in exactly the same place she'd left them. She winced.

"Come on then, get up!" she said with forced cheerfulness. "Just a couple more hours until you all get an apple."

*****

Jakob took Josef's hand and brought him back to the table. He sat down next to him. On his other side was Berta, one of Elsa's daughters and just a year older than him. Two of her older brothers were also there.

It was the children's job to lay the sticks, from the middle of the table, individually onto long, narrow, grooved wooden plates inserted in a wooden frame. One frame held 2,500 sticks. Jakob transferred one stick after another from the pile. When one row was finished, the next wooden plate came on top until the whole frame was full.

The only light came from small dim oil lamps, which emitted more smoke than illumination. The room was warm, the air musty. Jakob nudged Josef, whose head was drooping nearer and nearer to the table.

"Pssst, you can't go to sleep, Josef, wake up," he whispered.

Chasper, Berta's older brother, heard him whispering. He threw a handful of wooden sticks towards Josef.

"Hey, baby, wake up!" he cackled.

Josef jerked his head up just as Chasper threw the sticks. They hit his face full on. It didn't hurt, nor did he cry, but Chasper laughed.

"Leave my brother alone!" Jakob shouted.

"Pssst, stop it, all of you!" Vreni intervened. "Carry on working now before Mr Haeberlin comes to see what the fuss is about."

Jakob scowled at Chasper who stuck his tongue out.

Josef tugged Jakob's sleeve.

"Forget it," Jakob whispered, "or we'll get into trouble." Glowering, he continued putting sticks onto wooden plates. It was so tedious that every minute seemed like an hour. As soon as the bell for the four o'clock break rang, he jumped up, grabbed Josef's hand and pulled him outside.

*****

Regina didn't get on well that afternoon either. Picking up a handful of matchsticks, she rubbed them unintentionally together, causing sparks to fly and a small fire broke out. She screamed and leapt back from the table, grabbing Wilhelmine from under her feet.

Anneli ran to a corner where a bucket half-full of water stood and emptied it onto the flames.

"Don't worry!" she told Regina, who was trembling with shock. "That happens quite often, just look at my fingers!" She smiled, showing Regina her fingertips. They were red and blistered. "Nobody goes home without burned fingers," she told Regina.

The fellow workers at the long trestle table laughed kindly and waved their fingers in the air to show her.

Regina looked at her own fingers. They were red from the burn but it wasn't serious.

Anneli swept the pile of wet matches and boxes in front of Regina onto the floor with her hands.

"You'll get used to it," she tried to reassure Regina. "The fires are seldom serious."

She continued to work.

*****

At four o'clock, Regina took Wilhelmine's hand and led her outside. She saw the boys and gave them both their apple. She noticed that Jakob was sulking but she put it down to hunger. She dipped her sore fingers into the cool stream and then hurried to eat her own apple.

Jakob and Josef had already finished theirs; as always, they had eaten everything, even the core and just the stalk remained. She did likewise.

"We'll work until seven," she told Jakob. "Not much longer now."

"Seven?" Jakob was alarmed. "Papa said six."

"Yes, we'll work one hour longer today, and on Saturday we'll go home early."

Jakob knew it was pointless to argue.

"Yes, Mother," he replied meekly. Taking Josef's hand, he went back to their table.

Berta and her brothers were already sitting there, working.

"Didn't you eat anything?" Jakob asked Berta.

"No, my mother couldn't buy any groceries. My little sister Millie can't stop coughing. Mama took her to Dr Koefeli and he gave her some medicine but it cost five francs. That was all she had."

"Is Millie better now?"

"No, the medicine didn't help. This morning she coughed blood and Mama is afraid she might die." Berta began to cry and Mistress Vreni looked at Jakob severely.

"Stop chattering, Jakob, you're upsetting Berta, get on working now!"

"Sorry, mistress," Jakob said, genuinely sorry. "Don't cry, I'll ask Mother if I can bring you something to eat tomorrow," he whispered to Berta.

*****

Trudging home that evening, they were all exhausted. Anton carried Wilhelmine most of the way. It wasn't that they weren't used to hard work, but not such dreary, tedious work in dark dank rooms. Regina cooked eggs, potatoes and mangold from the garden. She stopped Anton and the children from eating all the potatoes saying that she had cooked more so that they had some for the next day at work.

"Mother, please can I take some food for Berta too, tomorrow?" Jakob asked. "Her sister's ill and her mother had to pay the doctor, so they don't have enough to eat."

"Is that her sister, Millie?" Anton asked. "Has she still got that cough?"

"Yes. Berta says she might die."

Anton and Regina both crossed themselves.

"The poor girl; Margot said she was very sick," Anton confirmed.

"We must all pray for her tonight," Regina suggested. "I'm sure we can spare something to eat," she told Jakob, "for her brothers too."

"We shall visit Elsa after Church on Sunday," Anton said. "Regina, you must prepare a basket of food for them. Elsa helped us after Lena died. Better you prepare two baskets on Sunday, then after we have visited her, we shall go on a picnic with the children."

"Oh yes!" Jakob and Josef cried as if from one mouth.

"Me too!" Wilhelmine pleaded.

"All of us!" Anton agreed. "We've worked hard and Sunday is a day of rest."

*****

Jakob hated working at the matchstick factory. As soon as his stepmother sat him down at a table with other children, boredom kicked in, paralysing his head and arms and making the work even more monotonous. His arms felt heavy, his fingers clumsy and the frame in front of him refused to get full. He looked around, watching the other children at his table. He would like to chat with them and ask questions, but the one adult present, Vreni their neighbour, whispered urgently to him that talking wasn't allowed.

One day, Chasper stood up from the table, telling Vreni he had to pee, then walking behind Jakob, pushed him so violently that Jakob's head hit the table sending two frames and a pile of matches scattering to the floor. Utz, the loeli, laughed out aloud. Jakob was so surprised that by the time he'd caught his breath and shouted at Chasper, the latter had already run down the stairs.

The tumult brought the supervisor, Herr Häberlin, running. He had just been rolling a full trolley of frames to the devil's kitchen. Herr Häberlin's forehead was bald and the rest of his hair was cut extremely short. He had a tidy moustache and small round glasses with a metal frame. He looked like someone military. Seeing the chaos on the floor, he marched over quickly, snatching a cane from his workplace on his way.

"Utz, pick those frames up and pray to God they're not broken!" he yelled at the grinning child. "You!" he shouted at Jakob, "hands on the table!"

"But sir, that's not fair, it was Chasper—"

Herr Häberlin grabbed Jakob by his unruly brown hair and slammed his hands onto the table. Holding his arms tight with one hand, with the other he began to beat the back of Jakob's hands with his cane. The supervisor was red in the face and out of control with anger. The other children stopped working and looked on with horror. Jakob screamed in pain and terror. To his shame, he wet himself and tears rolled down his cheeks. Red, bloody cuts crisscrossed the backs of his hands. Vreni stood up alarmed and put her hand down firmly on Herr Häberlin's wrist to hinder him beating Jakob further. She looked the supervisor firmly in his eyes and said: "It's enough!" Everyone held their breath. Herr Häberlin looked at the table of children and said: "This morning's work will be annulled, no payment! And now step to it!" Then he marched back to his desk.

Jakob's hands were bleeding. The skin had been torn open and they were red and swollen. Vreni put her arms around him gently and muttered, "Come with me, I'll bring you to your father."

She went to Anton in the dipping room and spoke quietly in his ear. Anton stopped working, thanked her, and picking Jakob up in his arms, carried him home. There he put some salve on Jakob's hands and bandaged them. He gave him a cup of warmed milk and told him to lie down and rest.

Anton watched Jakob sleeping. He sat down at the table, buried his head in his arms and cried.

Vreni told Regina what had happened.

"Well, if Anton's gone home with him, there's nothing more I can do. I'll stay here and work until it's time to go home with Josef and Mina," Regina answered.

Jakob woke up to his parents arguing. His Papa wanted Regina to stay at home with the children but she refused.

"It was just one incident." He heard his stepmother argue.

"He's four, he's far too young to be there. He'll carry the scars for life!" his Papa retorted.

"Others are younger. I'll stay home till they heal, but then we're all going back to work!"

For Regina the matter was settled.

10

MARCH 1853

During Sunday service, Reverend Moser scrutinised the congregation before him. The men were on his left, women and children to the right of the centre aisle. The well-to-do sat on the front pews, the poorer population at the back. There were no written rules where to sit, but the inhabitants themselves chose their own places. The poor were a humble folk. He had been told when he was sent to this remote parish, five years ago, that the people were extremely pious, and in truth, the church was always full. The children on the back pews, coughing, pale and apathetic, worried him. He knew that they worked in the matchstick factories, some of them up to fourteen hours a day, and some were only three years old. He must find a way to change this, he thought, without plunging his congregation into even more poverty.

After the service, he stood at the door shaking hands with the heads of the families. He knew most and tried to remember the names of those he didn't, and place in his mind where they lived. The parish of Weissbruegg wasn't large from the number of inhabitants, but it stretched over an area of 7,000 hectares and reached from the valley floor at 2,000 feet above sea level to over 10,000 feet. The well-to-do citizens lived in the town on the valley floor. From there, houses and hill farms were scattered up the mountain slopes. Generally, the higher up you lived, the poorer you were. The poorest families lived at roughly 5,000 feet in the Spissen. They couldn't come to church often, it was a strenuous journey across jagged mountain ridges and crooked crevices, but Reverend Moser wanted to make it his business to visit them at least twice a year.

On Monday morning the weather looked fair. Reverend Moser got up at five, washed and combed his mousy brown hair, parting it on the left-hand side. It was a little longer than usual on the top of his head, but he had shaved the sides over his ears. He dressed in trousers and a shirt and pullover over his white clerical collar. Instead of wearing his normal shoes, he laced up a pair of robust walking boots. His housekeeper hadn't arrived, so he packed some bread and cheese and a bottle of water in his knapsack, removed his sturdy hiking stick from its stand, and left the parsonage.

Consulting his paper map, he began to walk along a narrow forest path on the left flank of a tree-lined gorge. The path went steadily uphill and was riddled with tree roots. He felt completely secluded, meeting not a single soul on his way, hearing just the Otter Brook gushing its way along the gorge twenty-five feet below him, and the birds, startled by his presence, fluttering away to the safety of higher branches.

The path led him through the width of the middle-high forest until he emerged onto an uneven terraced ridge with marshy meadows. Ahead, he saw a steep rugged mountainside adorned with a waterfall cascading down the rocks towards the Otter Brook. Above a wood of alders and maples, followed naked scree. When rain fell heavily, the loose pebbles were in constant danger of rolling and sliding down the hillside. Reverend Moser removed his knapsack from his back, found his bottle of water and thirstily drank nearly all of it. He loosened his collar, hesitated a little and then removed it completely and put it in his pocket. He could always put it back on later.

He studied the vertical mountain in front of him, consulted his map, and strode out across the meadow to circumnavigate the impassable obstacle. The earth was soft and his boots were soon heavy with clods of soil. He continued walking around the mountain until he reached a deep gorge with rocky sides. Further away, he sighted the sunny side of the creviced mountain. The reverend examined his map again; he couldn't be far away but he couldn't see any dwellings. There was a thick fir forest, one of the narrowest he'd ever seen, but dwellings might be hidden behind it. He hitched his knapsack higher up his back, gripped his hiking stick tightly in his fist and began to climb down the rocky chasm to the bottom of the gorge. The brook trickling along the base looked harmless. It was hard to believe that when the snow melted in early summer, this brook had swollen up to twenty-five feet high and swept mud, rocks and boulders, like flimsy toys, down into the valley. Nature was not as innocent as it looked, he mused. He refilled his water bottle and ate some bread and cheese to regain some strength before tackling the steep path in front of him. At first he had to climb, scrambling up the rocks using his hands and arms to heave himself up. Then the path zigzagged across a sandstone scrag. Eaten up nearly every year by mud or rockslides, the holes in the path had been filled provisionally with fir branches. One wrong step and he could easily plunge to his death. Reverend Moser concentrated on every move. By the time he reached comparative safety, he was exhausted. Scary, even in daylight. He shuddered and sent a little prayer to heaven that he wouldn't have to cross it at night or during bad weather.

Finally, he sighted the dwelling that he had been seeking. Even from a distance it looked more dilapidated than he had been expecting and he wondered if the family was really still living there, completely isolated from its environment. Even as he thought this, he heard voices and approached with trepidation.

The two windows had broken panes and were so dirty that he couldn't peer inside; the roof was fallen-in and had holes. He knocked at the door. The head-of-the-house, a Mr Schmidt, opened it and stood aside. He wore trousers tied around the waist with string, but no shirt. He showed no surprise at seeing the reverend and bade him indoors. The family sat at the table eating lunch. The children moved closer together on a bench to make room for him to sit down with them. They were eating boiled potatoes in a broth of nettles. The youngest child stood on the bench and could just reach a bowl placed in front of it, in which a potato had been crushed in nettle broth. The child was scrawny and pinched. She tried to fish the tiny chunks of potato out of the broth into her mouth. Her hands were almost translucent. Reverend Moser had never seen such a pitiable child. He knew that he would never forget the sight as long as he lived.

Nine of the children were supposedly over fourteen years old, but they were all much too small and bony for their age. In the room next door, the reverend could see open

103

sky. An untanned sheepskin was roughly sewn together
with a goat skin and served as a sleeping place, which was
supposed to protect the children in their sleep from rain,
snow and cold. The floor was covered in a thin layer of
hay. Every surface was thick with dust and ancient spider
webs stretched across the ceilings, walls and windows.
There was scarcely a difference between their house and a
goat's shed.

Reverend Moser prayed with the family and then left
to visit more families in these isolated heights. It was a year
of hunger worse than he had ever encountered before. The
potato harvest had been meagre and groceries overpriced.
He met families who were even poorer than family
Schmidt. Their last potatoes eaten long ago, they had been
living from nettle broth for the last six weeks. Many males
wandered about their tiny properties half-naked, without
even a shirt on their back.

When Reverend Moser arrived home it was late evening.
He was physically and mentally exhausted. He sat down
and ate the meat and vegetable stew that his housekeeper
had prepared for him, at the same time having a terrible
conscience picturing the small starving children before his
eyes. He prayed and soothed his moral scruples by telling
himself that he must stay strong in order to help the weak.

He sat down at his desk and wrote to his fellow
clergymen at Frutigen, Kandergrund and Reichenbach.
Something must be done to help the poor and put an end
to child labour, and together they had a better chance of
being listened to. He knew though, that until any action
was taken, even on a communal level, months would pass,
if not years. While he was waiting for answers, he would
speak to some of the families and try to persuade them to
leave at least the smallest children at home.

11

APRIL 1853

On the Sunday after Easter, Reverend Moser visited Anton and his family at their home. Anton sent the children outside to play, but they crept into the hayloft from the back entrance, hunkered down behind the hay bales, and as quiet as mice, tried to listen. Jakob couldn't make out all the words but he could hear the reverend speaking heatedly with his stepmother. He determined his father's voice, deep, quiet and reasonable; then his stepmother again, raising her voice in protest.

After the reverend had left, his father opened the door to the byre.

"You can come down now," he told them. Jakob's cheeks flushed red at being caught out. He followed his brother and sister down the rickety wooden steps from the loft to the animals' quarters. They sat down at the table without a whisper. Jakob did not dare to look into his stepmother's eyes; he concentrated on his father. He wondered why his father didn't hold his gaze.

"Your mother and I have decided that Mina and Josef

are too young for the factory," Anton told them. "They will stay at home and make matchstick boxes, here at this table instead."

Jakob's jaw fell. "And me?" He asked.

"You are the eldest, you can come to the factory with me. We need your earnings."

Jakob felt as if a rock had just dropped in his belly. The thought of working in the stinking factory filled him with horror. Why him? He blamed Regina. Why hadn't his father stood up for him more? His face blackened.

"Just until June," his father comforted him, "then I'll ask Uncle Gustl if you can spend the summer with him up on the alm. You'd like that wouldn't you?"

"Oh yes please, Papa."

"You can keep half of the money you earn and save it up to pay for an apprenticeship when you're older; we'll find a tin and put your name on it. After this summer you'll be old enough to start school, then you won't be working all day."

"Thank you, Papa." Jakob looked at him gratefully and beamed at Josef and Mina.

*****

It was still dark outside. There had been a severe frost in the night and the ground crunched under the wooden soles of Jakob's boots. He was wearing trousers, a jacket and a woolly cap, all passed down from someone he didn't know. A glacial wind hit him head on and pierced through his inadequate clothing. His father held on to his hand and they marched quickly towards the factory, but despite the brisk movement, he trembled with cold. When they arrived, his father said a quick goodbye and hastened to the devil's kitchen.

Jakob ran upstairs and sat down at his place at the worktable. For once he wasn't bothered about the stuffy air, at least it was warm. His fingers were numb and useless. He rubbed his hands together vigorously until the pain of warmth ripped through them. He waited until the burning sensation lessened and then pulled a pile of sticks from the centre of the table to his place and began to fill the empty frame in front of him. He was motivated and worked quickly. The knowledge that he could keep some of his earnings pleased him extraordinarily. He wondered whether his stepmother or father would notice if he removed five centimes from his tin. He would really like to buy one of those big colourful lollipops that Mr Brotz, the owner of the corner shop, displayed in a jar in his store window. The children of well-to-do families were always going around licking them, making a show of it and goading the children of poorer families. He would share his lollipop with Josef and Mina of course. He glanced at Berta sitting next to him and decided that she could have a few licks too. She looked sad today. He would like to ask her how her sister Millie was, but they weren't allowed to speak. Mistress Vreni had to be strict because otherwise Mr Haeberlin would come to the table and punish them all. At eight-thirty a bell rang and the school children jumped up to go to school. Chasper and Buolf were the first to barge their way down the stairs. Berta, a year older than Jakob, followed her brothers, but before she disappeared, she turned around and gave Jakob a small wave.

Jakob continued laying wooden sticks into their grooves as quickly as he could. His father had told him that for every finished frame, Jakob was paid two centimes. Whenever he finished one, he jumped up and took it to the supervisor who put a mark against Jakob's name. Three thousand sticks fitted into one frame. Jakob couldn't count that high, but Mistress Vreni had told him. When the bell rang for the lunchbreak at one o'clock, Vreni commented on how well he had done that morning.

He ran outside and was surprised to see the sun shining. He had to blink his eyes several times to get used to the bright light. He looked into his lunch pack and found a piece of bread, a small lump of cheese and a boiled potato. He ate the bread and cheese quickly and looked at the potato longingly. He knew if he ate it now he would have nothing at four o'clock. He drank some water instead and went to the stream behind the factory to have a pee into the bushes there. On the other side of the stream he saw Ramun, the ten-year-old son of the factory director. He was dressed elegantly in long pressed trousers, a white shirt and a smart blue jacket. He went to boarding school in Bern and the blue jacket belonged to his school uniform. It was very dapper and made Ramun easily recognisable, even from a distance. He was scuffing his shoes on the shingle and throwing stones into the stream. He looked bored. When he saw Jakob, he tried to throw a stone further, to hit him. He missed. Jakob buttoned his trousers up quickly and turned back to the factory.

He sat down at his workplace and began to fill the frames with wooden sticks again. He tried to work as quickly as that morning, but he couldn't. The air was too suffocating, the light too dim and the work too monotonous. He filled one frame but only managed to half-fill the second before the bell for the four o' clock break rang. He went outside and devoured his potato in two bites. He watched the older children returning from school and followed them back into the factory. When he sat down at his place, he saw an empty frame instead of his half-full one. He looked around the table and saw Chasper in front of a half-full frame. An impossible feat for the half-minute he had been there.

"Hey, you've taken my frame!" Jakob yelled, stretching himself across the table to snatch it back.

"Finders, keepers," Chasper smirked, holding onto the frame tightly. Mistress Vreni returned to the table just as a tug-of-war started.

"Stop it, both of you!" She spoke angrily but under her breath, while glancing around to see where Mr Haeberlin was. Chasper let go of the frame and Jakob flew backwards. The sticks fell out and the frame clattered onto the table. It fell apart. Vreni picked it up quickly and tried to piece it together again, but Mr Haeberlin was already at the table. He demanded to know who had broken the frame. The boys both pointed at each other accusingly. He looked at Vreni. She hesitated before answering: "It was both of them."

Mr Haeberlin picked up the broken frame.

"The price of a new one will be deducted from your earnings, half each."

"That's not fair! He stole my—" Jakob began to protest, but seeing Mr Haeberlin's expression, he shut up.

"Get back to work, now!" Mr Haeberlin ordered, "or shall I get my cane out?"

The children continued working. About an hour later, when everyone had settled down again, Berta pushed her finished frame over to Jakob and slid his half-finished frame in front of her place. Jakob looked at her and then around the table. Nobody was paying them any attention.

"Thank you," he whispered.

At long last it was seven o'clock. Jakob and Berta stood up and went outside.

"Thank you," Jakob said again, "but you shouldn't help, you need your earnings yourself."

"You have to pay for the frame out of your earnings. It costs two francs. That means you will have to pay one franc. It's not fair, it was Chasper's fault."

"Two francs? Oh," Jakob said and sighed. "There won't be much money left then. My stepmother will be livid."

"Will you get a beating?"

"No, my parents don't beat us. But I'll probably go without supper when she finds out."

"Don't tell her until Sunday then, after you've visited your Aunt Margot. Didn't you say she baked cake for you on Sundays?"

Jakob grinned and said, "That's a great idea, Berta. And if she ever gives me food for Chasper again, I won't give it to him, I'll eat it myself! How's Millie?"

"She's very poorly. Mama says she will die. She's saving our earnings so that she can pay for a coffin. My father hardly gives her anything towards housekeeping. But she can't be buried in a pauper's grave, she needs a proper one." Berta's eyes swelled with tears.

At that moment, Anton came out of the factory. He said hello to Berta and then started walking home with Jakob. He hadn't failed to notice the tears.

"What was all that about?" he asked Jakob.

"Millie is dying and Berta is worried that they won't have enough money for a coffin. She said her father is stingy with his wages."

"That man is a drunken piece of shit!" The angry words just slipped out of Anton's mouth. He suddenly realised what he'd just said.

"Oh sorry, Jakob, I shouldn't have said that. Look, just forget I said anything, all right?"

"Yes, Papa, but don't worry. Berta doesn't actually say much but I'd already gathered that he's not a nice person."

When they arrived home every surface in the house was full of pieces of matchstick boxes. The floor, the table, the chairs, the chest of drawers, everywhere. Regina made room on the table so that they could sit down to eat. There was vegetable soup and a thin slice of bread each. After supper, Regina cleared the plates away quickly and they all started gluing pieces of shaving wood together with homemade paste made from flour, water and vinegar. At ten o'clock the children were allowed to go to bed. They took their boots off and laid down on their shared straw mattress in the living room. Anton and Regina worked a further hour.

"We're not going to get rich doing this," Regina complained. "One franc for a thousand boxes and it's even our own wood!"

"No, but as long as we've a roof over our heads, and we're not starving, we must be grateful. I'm going to bed now."

"Yes," Regina agreed, "I'm coming too."

*****

Gradually, the days became longer and the temperatures milder. Jakob looked forward to going to the alm with his Uncle Gustl. It was just another couple of weeks until the annual procession to the middle-high pastures.

He arrived at the factory and saw that Berta had been crying. Her eyes were red and swollen and dried-up tears had left dirty streaks down her cheeks. He thought that Millie must've died, but he couldn't speak to Berta until she returned from school later that afternoon. He touched her arm and asked if Millie had gone.

Berta began to cry. "Yes, but it's even worse! My father stole the money for her coffin. She'll have to go into a pauper's grave now and can't go to heaven!" Her chest heaved.

Jakob was shocked.

"How? He stole the money?"

"He came home from work last night and saw us all praying around her mattress. He didn't join us, he didn't say sorry or anything, he just said that he was going to the pub for a drink. He demanded money from my mother. She said she needed it for the coffin. And ... and, can you imagine what he answered?"

Berta stopped sobbing and shook with wrath. She didn't wait for Jakob to answer.

"He said that a coffin wouldn't help her now and he needed the money more to get a drink! My mother refused to give him anything and he started shouting and swearing at her. When she still didn't give him anything, he hit her, really hard across her cheek. She lost her balance and fell over and then ... then he started kicking her. When she stopped defending herself, he knocked everything down from the shelves and emptied tins. He made a terrible mess. He found the money, we don't have many hiding places. As soon as he had it, he pocketed it all and left us alone, slamming the door behind him."

Jakob didn't know what to say, he thought that maybe Regina wasn't so bad after all. Berta hadn't finished.

"In the middle of the night he came home stone drunk. He couldn't walk properly, he banged into the table, swore loudly and then fell onto his mattress. We all woke up but my mother put a finger to her lips to signal to us to keep quiet. My father started snoring. I watched my mother search all his pockets. She started crying and I got frightened because my mother never cries. She frantically searched his underwear and everything, but not a single coin was left. That was over eighty francs, she told us. It's impossible to drink that much.

As soon as it was daylight she went down to the Goldenen Ochsen. Mr Klopfenstein was cross at being woken up. He told her that my father had been playing cards. My mother came home and said Millie will have to go into a pauper's grave now. We can't afford a coffin anymore. I hate my father!" Berta proclaimed angrily, "Millie's body will be put in a sack, and she'll be put in a communal grave with other paupers! And everyone knows that without a proper burial, you can't go to heaven. I wish it was my father dead and not Millie." Berta was inconsolable.

Jakob rubbed Berta's arm to comfort her. He mulled over the situation. He had an idea, deliberated shortly, and then decided.

"Don't worry, Berta. I've got some money saved up. I'll buy a coffin for Millie."

"But how?" Berta asked. She stopped crying and looked at him. "Your mother and father would never allow it."

"No it's my money. It's supposed to be for an apprenticeship when I'm older, but I've got plenty of time to save up for that yet. I'll bring the money to the factory tomorrow and then we can sneak away and go to Schreiner Hans."

"Are you sure?" Berta asked.

"Yes, of course."

That night at home, Jakob waited until everyone was asleep, then he quietly wrapped all the coins from his tin into his handkerchief, so that they didn't jingle, and put the hanky in his trouser pocket.

The next day, when Berta returned from school, she and Jakob hid behind a bush until everyone else had re-entered the factory building. When all was quiet, they rushed hotfooted to Weissbruegg. They ran down a road parallel to the main street, hoping that nobody would notice them and crouching close to the funeral home, slipped around the corner and opened the entrance door. A little bell tinkled and Jakob jumped. He grinned at Berta foolishly. The undertaker rose from his desk to get a better view of the children.

"Good afternoon, Master Jakob, isn't it? And Mistress ... there are so many of you ... are you Berta?"

"Yes," Berta answered.

"Ah," Schreiner Hans said, "well I'm very sorry to hear about your sister, Berta."

"That's why we're here," Jakob said. "We would like to buy a coffin."

"A coffin?" Schreiner Hans had to repeat Jakob's words, he was so dumbfounded.

"Yes. You see, Berta's father spent the money that her mother had saved up for a coffin, so I'm going to buy one instead, so that Millie doesn't have to go into a pauper's grave. How much does a coffin cost?" Jakob hoped he had enough.

Schreiner Hans stroked his chin. He looked at the two pairs of dark brown eyes gazing up at him.

"Ah, well, it depends on which coffin you choose. Why don't I show you a few?"

The children nodded solemnly and followed Schreiner Hans into a side room. The curtains were drawn and the only light came from two burning candles. Berta stood on the spot and looked around. Noticing one, she walked straight over to a small coffin, lacquered with white paint. She stroked the lid. Schreiner Hans walked over to her.

"You have very good taste, Mistress Berta. This is our best coffin. We can write your sister's name with pink lettering on it, if you'd like that."

"Mmmn, that would be lovely. Can you paint a flower on it too?"

"Yes, it would be my pleasure. Now then, what type of handles would you like? How about these nice shiny brass ones?"

Jakob went hot and cold. He was anxious that he didn't have enough money.

"Do I have enough money?" he asked.

"Let us see," the undertaker answered. Jakob put his handkerchief on the counter and undid the knot. They counted the money together.

"Six francs, eighty," Schreiner Hans said. "That's a lot of money, you've worked very hard for that."

"Since Easter, yes."

"And you haven't spent anything for yourself?"

"No. I wanted to buy a lollipop. I would've shared it with Josef and Mina of course." He looked at Berta. "I would've given you a lick too. But I didn't buy one. I was too scared what my stepmother would do if she found out."

Schreiner Hans wrote something on a piece of paper. "The coffin costs exactly six francs eighty," he said. "Are you sure you want to buy it just like this? I could put different handles on."

"No, it's lovely as it is," he said, pushing the coins towards the undertaker. "Millie deserves a nice coffin; she didn't have a very nice life."

Berta looked at him gratefully and he squeezed her hand.

"In that case, I'll come to your house tonight to measure Millie. Will that be all right with you, Mistress Berta?"

"Yes," Berta said happily.

Jakob became anxious again. "Please don't tell Berta's mother that it's from me," he said. "Can you say it was paid for by an anonymous person. If my mother and father find out that I've spent my apprenticeship money they will be furious. They don't need to know, do they?"

Schreiner Hans stroked his chin again, pondering.

"Erm … I can tell her it was an anonymous well-wisher, if you want. It's been an honour doing business with you, Master Jakob, Mistress Berta."

He opened the door for them and gave a little bow. The children giggled and ran back to the factory as fast as they could.

They had been missing for over two hours. Vreni looked at them sternly. "Where have you been?" she asked.

"Berta felt sick, she kept throwing up and felt faint. I stayed with her to make sure she was all right," Jakob lied. He and Berta had agreed on this story beforehand but he still felt uncomfortable about it.

"Are you feeling better now, Berta?"

"Yes Mistress Vreni, thank you."

"All right then, get on with your work."

Jakob's heart was thumping so loudly that he was sure everyone could hear it and it would give him away, but the whole table was concentrating on working in silence. Time to get on, he thought, and start saving again.

*****

The undertaker's son emerged from the back room where he'd been doing the accounts.

"Six francs eighty? That coffin is worth a hundred francs. If you carry on like this, we'll be starving ourselves soon."

Schreiner Hans looked at his son.

"I know, boy, but as you also know, I've only done it twice before. We're not starving yet. We all heard about Fridolin at the Goldenen Ochsen last night. It's an absolute disgrace, that's what it is! Erwin should've stopped him.

Elsa must've spent ages scraping that money together, and he beat her terribly by all accounts. It's not right. The poor children looked so pitiful."

"Oh you're a big soft heart, but I wouldn't have done differently. Still, I don't like the idea that we're supporting Fridolin's drinking and gambling addiction. Erwin won't stop him as long as he's making money with his beverages. Who was he playing cards with? Any chance they might get a bad conscience and give the money back to Elsa?"

"Fat chance of that! The usual crowd, Ernst, Noldi and now Heinz, from what I've heard. I can just hear their answer before anyone even asks!"

"Heinz? What's he doing playing cards? I heard he wasn't earning so much now he's at the slate factory."

"Aye, a lesser position. None of our business."

"You're right. Strange though, I wonder why Peter sacked him? And now best buddies with Fridolin? That's a right pair!"

"Peter will have had a reason; he doesn't act on whims."

"Ah well then, I'd better get on."

12

JUNE 1853

Millie was buried, and although there was gossip about the coffin – everyone soon knew that Fridolin had wasted the money – after a couple of weeks with all sorts of speculation, the subject dried up and the villagers turned their attention to the approaching annual procession to the alm.

Jakob was excited about staying with his uncle. His father gave him a shepherd's crook and Regina had sewn a traditional outfit for him – black leather shorts with braces over a white shirt and a short-sleeved black suede jacket. White edelweiss flowers were embroidered on the lapels of his jacket and a black felt hat completed his outfit. He was so proud and happy, he thought he would burst. He hugged Regina for the first time ever and despite her reserve, a small smile slid over her lips.

Regina had packed a knapsack full of food for him and they all set off together, as a family, to Aunt Margot and Uncle Gustl. His aunt gave him a pocket knife and a whole cake for his knapsack. His uncle came from the barn with a goat on a piece of rope.

"She's called Maisie and she's for you." Gustl passed Jakob the rope. "Look after her well, and if she bears a kid in spring, you can sell it for pocket money."

Jakob was staggered. "Thank you, oh thank you!" he cried, and gave his surprised uncle an enthusiastic hug.

"All right, calm down now," Gustl said, more severely than he intended. He smiled to take the sting from his words. Mina raced up to Jakob with a bunch of wild flowers to pin to the band around his hat.

"Thank you, Mina." He crouched down to hug her too. He looked at all the faces surrounding him with love. Confounded and at a loss for words, he simply stroked Maisie. Ready to set off, he gave Josef a last hug and whispered that he'd miss him.

Jakob marched at the front of the line beside his uncle and holding onto Maisie. A huge grin stretched across his cheeks as he shyly waved to the villagers bordering the way. They waved back, calling his name and wishing him luck. Everyone knew Jakob and was happy for him.

Just one family looked on morosely. Jakob noticed Hari's sullen face, but it couldn't wipe the joy of this moment from his heart.

*****

Helga was fuming. She stormed off back home, dragging Hari and Hedwig behind her.

"Did you see that?" she complained to Heinz. "My own brother gave Jakob a goat. Just like that! They're not even properly related!"

"Jakob's his nephew," Heinz replied. He hadn't accompanied the herdsmen to the alm this year, he had sold his last cow. He didn't dare tell Helga that he'd been playing cards and needed the money to pay his debts, concocting some other story of misfortune.

"On Margot's side. Hari is of his own blood and he's never given him such a valuable present." Helga didn't let go of the subject.

"Well, Jakob's spending the summer working on the alm with Hans. No doubt he'll have to earn the goat. At least Hari isn't forced to work and can spend the holidays playing with Ferdinand and the other respectable children."

"Hmmn," Helga replied, slightly mollified. "That's true. Will we still be able to save enough for Hari to go to boarding school when he's ten?"

"I'm doing my best, dear. If I get a better-paid job, we should manage."

Heinz left the house to work outdoors. He'd have to get things sorted out.

*****

Jakob and Gustl settled down in their wooden hut on the Griesalp in the Kien Valley. There was just one room with a small wooden table and two chairs, a bed for Gustl and a straw mattress on the floor for Jakob. They had made themselves comfortable before a small cosy fire. Gustl smoked his pipe.

"Would you like me to tell you the legend of the Grueenmatti Innkeeper?" Gustl asked.

"Oh, yes please!" Jakob had only ever heard stories from the Bible before. He listened intently, trying to remember everything so that he could retell the story to Josef and Mina. He fought to keep his eyes open but he soon fell fast asleep.

The next morning Gustl showed Jakob his tasks. His main task would be to watch the goats. Cows were selective eaters; their special diet of natural meadow grasses produced a high-quality aromatic milk, called hay milk. Gustl made it into local cheese specialities using traditional methods. Gustl's father, and his father before him, had been the Senn. Gustl had learnt their craft and secret recipes as soon as he was old enough to accompany them to the alm.

The goats were kept to eat the rest – shrubs and bushes that the cows didn't touch. They jumped up rocks to places that the cows couldn't reach, and sometimes, a young high-spirited goat would go too far and get stuck. Jakob was there to keep the goats in order, or to rescue them if necessary.

He also milked the goats and helped with small, everyday routine jobs. The pigs were kept in a pen close to the hut. When Gustl stirred the milk to make cheese, whey was an unavoidable by-product. Nothing was wasted. Jakob scooped the whey up and emptied it into the pig's slop. Gustl showed Jakob which herbs he used and where they grew. He took his time and explained everything patiently, letting Jakob smell the different aromas. When the time was ripe, Jakob harvested the herbs and hung them up to dry.

Jakob enjoyed his days on the alm. His uncle was complacent, and although they worked from dawn till dusk, there was still time to enjoy the scenery and wildlife. There were roe deer, red deer, ibex, chamois and marmots. Jakob soon learnt where to find them. He tried imitating the marmots' whistle but they always disappeared quickly down their burrows, as soon as they noticed him. Gustl pointed out a pair of golden eagles, showing Jakob roughly where their nest was. Jakob lay on his back in the meadow, watching them soar in circles above him, against the backdrop of a cobalt blue sky and brilliant white mountain tops. His skin became tanned and his muscles toned.

Jakob didn't feel lonely but he missed Josef. Every two or three weeks someone from Weissbruegg would visit them on the alm, bringing provisions for them and making sure all was well. Anton was too busy working at the factory to visit, but one day his future teacher, Mr Stettler, came, bringing Josef with him. They stayed for two days letting Jakob show them everything.

All too soon the days began to shorten and early mornings had a nip in the air. One Saturday, in the middle of September, the hill farmers who had stayed during the summer in the valley, climbed up the alm to help Gustl return the livestock to their winter quarters, now stocked full of fresh hay.

They were a curious sight to the unexperienced eye. Men and women alike, were dressed up in their traditional clothing, worn only on important festive occasions. The men wore clean white shirts and short-sleeved black suede jackets with bronze buttons, the lapels embroidered with white edelweiss flowers. The women wore white blouses underneath dark blue dresses with a tight corsage, black aprons, black bonnets and knee-length white socks to complete their outfits.

The poorer farmers wore costumes that had been passed down from one generation to the next. Many were ill-fitting: too tight, too short or too long, but everyone did their best to look festive.

Up on the alm, the accompanying women decorated the cows with garlands of wild flowers, and ribbons attached between their horns. Then they marched back to Weissbruegg, where the villagers had left their houses to line the paths and watch the parade. The hill farmers lifted their hats chivalrously to pretty women bordering the way and cheering them on.

When the cattle were settled, everyone made their way to the square in front of the town hall. Lampions were strung up between the trees bordering the plaza. A wooden platform had been built for a brass band with plenty of space for dancing. One half of the square was filled with long rows of trestle tables, decorated with wild flowers. Sucklings were turning on a spit, their aroma tantalising the nostrils of anyone passing. There were fresh loaves of bread and sweetmeats, piles of apples and pears, cheeses and three very large barrels of beer. Jakob's eyes were as big as the apples there for the taking. The beer flowed and everyone celebrated happily and noisily. Some men played the alphorn. A group of men demonstrated swinging flags. There was traditional dancing with many a coy look and flirting. It was the most joyful day of the whole year.

13

AUTUMN 1853

After summer Jakob started school. The children, aged from six to thirteen, all sat together in one classroom, the youngest at the front and the oldest at the back. When the bell rang for lessons to start, Hari and Ferdinand quickly sat next to each other at one desk, leaving Jakob to sit next to Utz Schmidt, one of the boys who lived in the Spissen.

Utz's clothes were not only in rags but they were also filthy. They had presumably never been washed for fear that they might fall apart completely. Utz had a dirty face and hands and he smelt like a cesspit about to overflow. He scratched his head and arms continually.

Mr Stettler read the children's names from his register and the respective child stood up and answered: "Yes, sir". When it came to Utz's turn, the boy stood up hesitantly and stammered: "Y-y-yes, s-sir". The teacher looked him up and down.

"Utz, go and stand by the door," he said kindly, "I'll be with you presently."

Mr Stettler gave the older children some maths tasks to do and asked Berta to write the alphabet on the blackboard.

The new children were to copy the letters onto their slates. Then he told the oldest boy, Rolf, one of Saddler Eric's boys, to come to the front of the classroom and keep an eye on his school comrades.

"If anyone disobeys you, then write their name down and I will deal with them when I return. I won't be long, I'm just going to take Utz to Dr Koefeli. Come on now Utz, follow me."

Karl saw the doctor looking out from his surgery window. He waved and signalled to Dr Koefeli to meet him outdoors. It wasn't the first time that the two of them had had to deal with children from the Spissen and Karl knew that the doctor wished to avoid contamination of his indoor rooms.

"Hello, Lukas," he greeted the doctor. "This is Utz, I think he'll need the full treatment."

"Well, I'll shave his head first to get rid of the lice, and my assistant can help me bathe him. We can make him clean and I will put some salve on the scabies, so they itch less. I can give him some clean clothes and burn his old ones. That will deal with the fleas. But the moment he goes home, he will be prey for a whole new bunch of vermin."

Karl Stettler heard the frustration in the doctor's voice. It was understandable. Together, in the past, they had both spent a lot of time and energy trying to improve the situation for the children who lived in the Spissen. They had even helped to clean the houses where they lived and brought clean blankets. But inevitably, as soon as a few weeks passed, everything was back to its neglected mess.

The people weren't lazy, to the contrary, they worked from morning till night making chipwood boxes for the matchsticks. A family with four children might manage to make eight to ten thousand boxes in a week, which brought them a weekly income of about ten francs. Although the earnings were so meagre, they were vitally important for the poverty-stricken families. It was too far and the path too perilous for them to walk to the valley bottom daily and get a better paid job at one of the factories. There was no time for luxuries like cleaning.

"There's nothing that we can do about the malnutrition," Karl Stettler answered. "I'll speak to the mayor again though, about free school milk and an apple, at least for the paupers. There's nothing we can do about the state of their housing either. But you know me, the first thing the children from the Spissen learn from me is to wash their hands properly, at least twice daily. There are plenty of streams around."

"Yes, well, leave him here and go back to school before the classroom erupts. I'll bring him back when we're done. Who sits next to him?"

"Jakob."

"Ah, I'd better warn his mother in that case."

"Yes, I can't send Utz home. The Spissen children come irregularly enough to school as it is."

"That's all right. Mrs Schneider is a sensible woman, not like some others I could name."

"Goodbye then."

*****

Mr Stettler entered the classroom just as Buolf threw a piece of chalk from his place at the back of the room towards the front. Mr Stettler caught it with one hand and beckoned Buolf with his finger to come to the blackboard.

"I was hoping your behaviour might improve now Chasper has left school," he said. "In vain, apparently. Write on the blackboard I must not throw chalk in the classroom."

Buolf cramped his fingers around the chalk. He began to write; the tip of his tongue hung out from the side of his mouth and his forehead creased in concentration. He rubbed letters out and corrected his writing many times.

Mr Stettler waited until Buolf had finished writing. He took so long that some children began to snigger. Mr Stettler sighed.

"Berta, come here please and correct your brother's spelling mistakes."

Berta went forwards, and rubbing out Buolf's mistakes, corrected them in her neat writing.

"Thank you, you may return to your seat. Now, Buolf, write the sentence again, correctly this time, and then repeat it a hundred times."

At three-thirty the bell rang to signal the end of school for the day. The children filed out in an orderly fashion and Buolf made to follow them.

"Not you, Buolf, you haven't finished your hundred lines yet."

"But sir, I'll be late for work!"

"I'll give you a note for your supervisor."

Buolf started writing quickly. It wasn't Mr Haeberlin he was worried about; rather the beating his father would give him when he noticed the reduction in his earnings at the end of the week.

*****

The new school year had brought changes in the factory. Bartli had gone to work for Ramberts, a new matchstick factory that had opened in Wengi. They hadn't been able to find a dipper with experience and so they had offered Bartli a considerable pay rise if he would come to work for them. Bartli accepted immediately. He even saved a quarter of an hour walking distance to work.

Mr Lauber offered Anton Bartli's old position as dipper. At first, Anton was thrilled; it meant a pay rise too, and then he learnt that Chasper was to be his assistant.

Chasper had already made himself unpopular in the packaging room, where his work was irresponsible at the least. He thought it funny to rub the matches together on purpose in order to start a small fire. Once he set some boxes on fire intentionally and then threw them onto the floor next to the toddlers who were playing there. The mothers nearly lynched him. They marched him off in high dudgeon to Director Lauber's office and reported his offence. Ten minutes later, Chasper returned to his workplace, smirking. Nobody understood why he hadn't been sacked on the spot. Lesser offences had ended up with losing the job.

"And now I've been ditched with him," Anton told Regina at home. "He's an absolute loeli and that in the devil's kitchen. It's an accident waiting to happen!"

Regina considered what Anton had told her but couldn't think of a satisfactory solution.

"There's no point speaking to Mr Lauber, I suppose. Threaten to resign?"

"Hardly! He won't give me a different position either. In fact, I wouldn't put it past him to make sure I didn't get work anywhere else, like he did with Fechtig, Bert."

"It's unfair, you've been waiting ages for that position."

"I know, but it's dangerous and I won't be able to watch Chasper all the time."

"Why on earth wasn't he sacked? He must have some kind of hold over Lauber. I did hear rumours of him being a skirt hunter, maybe Chasper witnessed something."

"Whatever the reason, it doesn't help me. Hopefully, another new factory will open soon and be looking for a dipper."

*****

Anton started every day telling Chasper the safety rules and making him repeat them.

"It's nothing to laugh about," Anton said for the umpteenth time. "You could die or worse still, spend the rest of your life seriously injured."

Chasper, fourteen years old and at a loss in his life, promised to be careful and at first he seemed to take Anton's warnings seriously. Anton relaxed a little and started thinking about saving for a cow.

Regina worked in the packaging station again and Josef at the filling frames. She and Anton agreed that she finish work daily at four and go home with Josef. She had enough work to do there, making her cheeses, seeing to the vegetable garden and preserving food for the winter. Josef could help her at home, it was preferable to the factory. Just Thursdays were different. On Thursdays Regina sold her cheeses at the weekly market and then worked at the factory with Josef from one till seven.

Mina stayed with Margot. Margot had requested to look after her. She hadn't conceived again after her miscarriage and told Anton that Mina brightened up her days.

"Just until she starts school," Margot pleaded. "I'll teach her how to sew."

"If you're really sure," Anton answered. "Regina can pick her up at four thirty on her way home."

*****

The mountain peaks were obscured from view and a forceful wind swept wild flurries of snowflakes down the hillside from the west. Regina battled to close the barn door, putting all her weight behind it. She trembled with the effort of slotting the heavy wooden latch into position, the wind tearing through every crack in the wood, determined to blast the door open again. Finally successful and satisfied that the livestock were all indoors in safety, she went downstairs and put another log on the fire. The wind whistled down the chimney sending stray sparks into the living quarters. She hastened to attach the fireguard.

She looked at Mina and Josef cracking walnuts at the table and hoped that Jakob and Anton would get home soon. Although she would never admit it, not even to herself, she had grown fond of her new family.

They arrived home together, late and covered in snow. They shook it off their clothes in the porch and entered the living quarters, dashing straight to the fire. Regina put a pot of steaming stew onto the table.

"Come on then," she said in her habitual harsh voice. "Sit down and eat, the stew will warm you up."

The next morning the snow had stopped and the wind died down. Jakob set off with his father to the factory.

"If we had a sledge like Ferdinand, we'd get to work much quicker," Jakob commented.

"Do you want to work more?" Anton asked.

"No! But we could sleep longer."

"What about pulling the sledge back uphill after work?"

"I wouldn't mind," Jakob maintained.

*****

The factory bell rang at eight thirty and the school-aged children jumped up and ran outside. It was sometimes a hectic dash up and down the hills to get to school on time at nine o'clock. A straight line to school would show a distance of scarcely two leagues, but because of a deep rift in between, they needed a good thirty minutes. When snow lay on the ground like today, and they had to wade through drifts partly up to their thighs, the route took much longer.

The children could avoid this steep rift and go over the lower rift instead. It was much easier to pass but imperilled by avalanches. For that reason, parents forbade their children to cross the lower rift in winter, even if it meant arriving late for school.

Jakob and Berta stuck to the upper rift, but knowing they had a good excuse for arriving late, had a snowball fight on the way to school. These sneaked ten minutes were often the only playtime that they ever had.

Jakob was tired. Mr Stettler tapped his cane on Jakob's desk and admonished him.

"Sit up, Jakob, and pay attention!"

Jakob sat up, wondering for a moment where he was. He noticed that Utz wasn't sitting next to him, again. He was almost jealous of Utz living in the Spissen, he hardly ever came to school in winter. He wondered dreamily what he would do if he didn't have to go to school and realised with dread that he'd just have to work longer at the matchstick factory. That made him sit up straighter and pay attention. The last thing he wanted to do as an adult was to work at the factory.

School finished and Jakob, Berta and the other factory children walked back to Kandermatt. The remaining children laughed happily, playing on their way home. The sun had come out and the trees dripped snowmelt steadily from their branches. Buolf ran on ahead, hid behind a tree, and waited until his sister Berta came along unsuspecting with Jakob. He shook the tree and they shrieked as an icy shower drenched them from top to bottom.

"Buolf! Just you wait, that was not funny," Berta yelled at him. She pelted after his disappearing figure.

"What a twerp!" Jakob muttered to himself and followed them.

*****

Rowena Kinread

After, from his point of view, a tiring and pretty rotten day, Jakob was glad that it was finally seven o'clock. He just wanted to go home, eat and sleep. He went to look for his father.

"I'm running late ... again. Everything seems to take twice as long these days," Anton told Jakob, glaring meaningfully at Chasper. "Go on without me. Take the lantern and tell your mother I'll be along shortly."

Jakob took the lantern and went outside where Berta was waiting. Jakob looked at her questioningly.

"I'm waiting for Buolf; he has the lantern," Berta explained.

"Well he's not inside, nobody's there now, just Papa and Chasper."

"Oh!" Berta stamped her foot. "He must have gone home without me. He's a sick bastard! He knows he's supposed to accompany me home with the light."

Jakob raised his eyebrows; he'd never heard Berta using such language. She was right though, Buolf was a pea-brained muttonhead, thicker than the trunk of a 500-year-old oak.

"Well, we can go together," Jakob offered, "Papa gave me the lantern."

"But it'll be a detour for you."

"Not far, besides I have a headache, I could do with some fresh air."

The full moon reflected white dazzling jewels glistening on the ivory snow. The air was crisp, freezing all below it, and Jakob and Berta crunched with their boots through the frosted terrain. All else was silent.

"Look!" Berta laughed, pointing at her breath that glowed green, luminescent in the dark. Jakob giggled and copied her. They both tried to conjure up figures with their green, luminous breath.

"That's Buolf!" Berta cried, pointing to a formless creation of hers that floated towards the sky before disintegrating.

"And that's Mr Haeberlin," Jakob countered, exhaling short puffs of air and chasing them up the hill.

The factories worked with vast quantities of highly poisonous white phosphorous. The workers inhaled air saturated with phosphorous vapour; their clothes were permeated with the poison; their breath was luminous in the dark.

Jakob brought Berta home and then retraced his steps until the turn-off to his own house. His bad mood had flown away and his headache had disappeared. Arriving back, he was surprised to see his father pacing up and down the porch. As soon as Anton saw Jakob he raced down the steps and seizing his arm pulled him forcefully towards the house.

"Where in God's name have you been? I told you to come straight home, we've been worried sick!"

Jakob was frightened. His father had never shouted at him like this before.

"W-why? I brought Berta home, Buolf took the lantern without her; I'm not that late. I thought you were working late." Jakob broke down, crying. It was just too much for him after the rotten day. His headache returned with a piercing throb.

Anton felt suddenly ashamed of himself. He knelt down to Jakob and hugged him.

"I'm sorry, lad, I'm sorry. I was so worried. Mr Haeberlin came to the factory to send us home. There's been an avalanche by the lower rift, people are missing. I came straight home and when you weren't here, then …"

"You must've passed me when I took Berta back."

"I thought you might've taken the short cut by the lower rift."

"You told us not to go that way."

"Yes, I know. I'm sorry."

"It's all right, Papa. Can we go indoors now, I'm hungry?"

"Yes, yes of course, let's go indoors."

They ate and Jakob asked to be excused from further work that evening.

"May I go to bed, please? I'm so tired." He asked Regina.

Regina looked to Anton, who nodded.

"Yes, let's all retire early tonight, we've had enough excitement for one day."

They had scarcely lain down when there was a loud knocking at the door. Anton opened it to Linus Gehring, their neighbour.

"I'm sorry to disturb you," he said, "but I thought you should know, he's your neighbour as well as ours. It's Saddler Eric, his boy Rolf, they've retrieved his body from the avalanche, he's dead."

Jakob sat up on his mattress.

"Rolf? It can't be, I saw him at school this morning!"

"I know, lad, I'm sorry. That's why I came to tell you rather than you hearing it from the other schoolchildren tomorrow."

"But ... he wanted to go sledging with Ferdinand ... and anyway, he wouldn't cross the lower rift ... he's sensible. That's why he's head boy!"

"I'm afraid it's true, Jakob. His younger brother, Urs, was with him. They got him out alive, though both his legs are broken. Dr Koefeli's at their home now."

Jakob stood up. "I don't understand," he said. "Rolf

was perfectly all right this morning. What about Ferdinand? And Hari? Hari wanted to go sledging too."

"They are both safe at home," Linus assured him. "No one else is missing."

Nobody could sleep and the next morning Anton told Jakob he needn't work that day in the factory. He still had to go to school though. In the classroom everyone spoke in hushed whispers and a few children were crying. Mr Stettler led the class to church where Reverend Moser held a service for Rolf and they prayed for Urs too; he had a high fever and it wasn't certain that he would recover. After the service, Mr Stettler sent the children home. He held Jakob back.

"You live nearest to Urs," he said, "take this book and read to him, it will distract him if nothing else."

"Yes, sir," Jakob answered obediently, and took the book. It was titled The Three Musketeers by Alexandre Dumas. He wondered whether his parents would excuse him from making matchstick boxes after supper for the next few weeks, otherwise he could only visit Urs on Sunday afternoons, he had no other spare time. He called in on his way home and brought the book. Urs lay in bed delirious and his mother was weeping. Jakob left quickly and said he would visit again.

Urs's fever raged for five whole days. Dr Koefeli didn't know whether he would survive or not and Reverend Moser was called. On the fifth day the zenith passed and Urs lived. Pale as a winter morning and sapped like a wrung out dish cloth, he lay flat on his back, both legs in splints up to his groin. He was to stay flat in his bed for three weeks the doctor said. He even had to use a bed pan to relieve himself. After three weeks he would be allowed a pillow to prop himself up a bit, if the legs healed well, then he must stay at least a further three weeks in bed.

Worse than the physical damage was the loss of his brother. There were just the two of them in the family and they had been not just siblings but also best friends. Jakob wasn't really Urs's friend, he was nearly four years younger than him, but nobody else came more than once or twice and the book was really exciting. Urs's mother couldn't read and his father had shut himself away in his working shed since Rolf had died, so he looked forward to Jakob's visits. His reading wasn't very accomplished, but at least he didn't ask stupid questions all the time and while he was there, he managed to forget the accident for a while.

Ferdinand visited once, his mother said he had to, it was the decent thing to do. Hari went with him but they had both left again almost immediately. They had felt awkward with the invalid, and the bed pan smelt bad. Jakob came in the evening of the same day, his father had excused him from after-supper duties until Urs recovered. He was happy because the book was a cliffhanger and he couldn't wait to continue reading it. Urs was in a black mood.

"It was all their fault!" He declared upon Jakob's arrival.

"Whose fault and about what?" Jakob asked.

"Ferdinand and Hari's'... well, more Hari's. The accident! Ferdinand went home and Hari persuaded him to lend us his sledge so we could continue playing. Rolf said 'just one more time' because it was getting dark, but in the end it was three times and already dark. Rolf was worried about getting home and Hari persuaded him to take the short cut. He said the danger was exaggerated. You know the rest."

"But do you mean Hari was with you in the lower rift?"

"Yes, of course!"

"But nobody said that! He didn't get help, it was Mr Brotz who raised alarm. Regula saw the avalanche happening and went running home to tell him."

"Doesn't make any difference now," Urs said sulkily.

Jakob saw that he was about to cry and quickly started reading.

At home, Jakob told Anton and Regina what Urs had told him.

"After a terrible loss like that, it's natural the boy wants someone to blame." Anton answered, "but even if the story's true, they could've said no. Hari couldn't force them to take the shortcut."

"But he could've got help!" Jakob was outraged. Having read the first chapters of The Three Musketeers he was now an expert on injustices and honourable behaviour.

"It wouldn't have made any difference," Anton replied, "the avalanche couldn't be stopped and the damage was already done."

The next day, after work and on their way to school, Jakob told Berta everything. He had already been telling her all about the book in detail.

"Let's form a band, like musketeers, and avenge victims of wrongdoing," Berta suggested.

"That's a good idea!" Jakob replied. "I'll suggest it to Urs tonight."

Urs got better. He was young and his bones healed quickly. When Dr Koefeli removed his splints, Urs looked at his scrawny legs. He didn't recognise them, they were so thin and gangly. He tried to stand up and fierce pain shot right through him. It went black before his eyes. He toppled over forwards and might have broken his nose had not the doctor and his mother been there to catch him. But he tried again and again and again, untiringly. After a further six weeks his muscles had strengthened and he was nearly back to normal. He asked his father to make four wooden swords from his splints and his father was so happy to see him recovered, that he did so.

It was the week before Christmas as the four new friends,
Urs, Jakob, Berta and Josef, now armed with four blunt
wooden swords, swore allegiance to one another. They
raised their new swords and crossing them, pledged eternal
friendship. They all spoke together. "All for one and one
for all, united we stand divided we fall."

Now they just needed to wait for a suitable adventure.

14

1854

One day in January Mr Lauber strolled around the packaging station. Regina had the impression he was looking the women up and down but she wasn't certain. Not until he stopped at Anneli's workplace.

"Come up to my office, Mistress... Ebner, I believe."

Anneli wiped her hands hurriedly on her apron, "Yes, Sir." She hastened after him, glancing back to Regina just once with a shrug of her shoulders.

She returned ten minutes later, her face flushed, and took up her position again.

"His wife's away," she whispered to Regina. "He asked if I would take over the housekeeping until she returns."

"What did you answer?"

"Yes, of course! The pay's better. I'm to start tomorrow."

"Well watch out for yourself, you know what they say."

"Yes, don't worry. I'm nineteen! Anyway, the cook's still there and the maid."

"What are you supposed to do then?"

"Some cleaning, he said. Can't be too bad, Ramun's at boarding school."

"Good luck then."

Regina hadn't expected to see Anneli for a few weeks but two days later she was back at work again. She was taciturn and avoided looking at Regina. At the one o'clock break, they ate their lunch together and Regina decided it was better not to ask. Anneli would tell her what happened when she was ready.

She didn't have to wait long. After ten minutes chewing on their food silently, Anneli checked no one was watching, then pulled back the long sleeves of her dress to reveal a deep purple-black bruise on each of her wrists.

Regina gasped and nearly let a scream out. Anneli put a hand over Regina's mouth to stifle it just in time. "Sssh!" Anneli said. "He said if I told anyone then he'd sack me and make sure I didn't get work anywhere else either."

"Oh my God!" Unusual for her, Regina swore vehemently. "What did he do? Did he... I mean ..."

"No!" Anneli replied fiercely. "Although he-he tried to." She let out a sob and their fellow colleagues looked over to them. "I'll tell you later," Anneli said and hurried back to her working place.

At four o'clock, Regina collected Josef and walked home with him. She was convinced that the director had taken advantage of poor Anneli and was indignant on her behalf. The poor girl was too ashamed to talk about it, she thought, as if it was her fault! Picking up Mina, she would have liked to talk to Margot about the injustice of it all, but she didn't want to break Anneli's confidence. If something had happened, she wouldn't want everyone knowing about it.

*****

February came and Jakob's nanny-goat, Maisie, surprised everyone with two kids. One was female and Jakob decided to keep her. The well-to-do gentlefolk in Switzerland, especially in the cities, traditionally ate roast goat on Easter Sunday. The week before Easter, Jakob went with Regina to the weekly market and sold the male kid for seven francs. He was exuberant.

He went straight to Mr. Brotz's corner shop, the coins jingling in his pocket. He gazed at the lollipops in the window and admired the sign written over the door in large black and gold lettering: BROTZ COLONIAL WARES. Then, for the first time in his life, he opened the door and stepped inside the dark interior.

Mr Brotz's eldest daughter, Magdelena, was standing behind the counter serving Mrs Siebold, the wife of the district administrator. Gertrud and Regula, the two younger daughters, who Jakob knew from school, weren't to be seen. His wife, Johanna was at a separate counter for post deliveries and telegrams. While Mrs Siebold bought her groceries, he waited patiently, gazing at all the brightly coloured tins piled high on shelves right up to the ceiling. Unfamiliar exotic aromas tickled his nostrils, and he stood in awe.

Mrs Siebold left and Jakob bought five lollipops, one for each musketeer and one for Mina, who they considered too young to be a member of their group. He chose five different flavours so that they could all taste each other's and paid Magdelena 25 centimes. She put the lollies in a brown paper bag and he hurried to school so as to arrive before nine.

He just made it before the bell rang and sat down quickly. He put the brown paper bag on the floor next to his bench and placed his slate on his desk, determined to concentrate that day. He imagined what it would be like to have a well-paid job like Mr Siebold, and to be able to buy as many lollipops as he wanted, and maybe even cocoa powder too!

Mr Stettler called Jakob to the blackboard and made him do some sums. He got them all right and basked in the teacher's praise as he returned to his seat. At the midday break the children were queueing up waiting for a small bottle of free milk and an apple, when Jakob noticed that his brown paper bag was missing. He let out a cry of shock.

"Jakob, behave yourself! What's got into you?" Mr Stettler reprimanded him.

"But sir! I had a bag by my seat, someone's stolen it!"

"That's a very serious accusation, Jakob. Nobody's left this room, we shall look if you have misplaced your bag." Mr Stettler stopped distributing the milk and asked the children to look for a paper bag. Regula recognised the bag immediately. It was on the floor at the back of the classroom, battered and crumpled as if someone had stamped on it. She picked it up and handed it to Mr Stettler. Mr Stettler gave it to Jakob.

"Is this yours?" he asked.

Jakob opened the bag to look inside and had to blink tears back. The lollipops were broken into lots of fragments, not one had remained whole.

"Yes sir," he stammered.

"Well be careful with accusations in future."

"But sir, the bag didn't walk by itself from my place to the back of the room!" Jakob protested and the children giggled.

"Enough! Come to the blackboard and write I shall not answer back twenty times. You can do without your apple and milk today."

*****

Helga nagged Heinz constantly about their lack of money.

"How are we going to afford to send Hari to boarding school when we don't even have enough to buy him a smart winter jacket like all the other boys have?"

"Not all of the boys are dressed smartly, in fact only a few."

"But you don't want Hari wandering around like the riff-raff here. Next thing I know you'll be demanding that I work, like a common fishwife!"

Heinz had decided to stay honest after the episode at the sawmill and the fiasco at the Goldenen Ochsen. But Helga's nagging left him no peace. He began selling slate at the quarry and 'forgetting' to write it down in the books.

Xaver, the owner, had a bad back but a sound mind. He wondered why the turnover was so small but the usual amount of slate was taken from the inventory. He paid close attention and soon discovered what Heinz was doing. He sacked him on the spot.

Fridolin told his drinking mates at the Goldenen Ochsen that Heinz had been caught stealing. If the rumours after losing his job at the sawmill had been met with scepticism, these additional rumours destroyed Heinz's reputation.

People started avoiding Heinz. Hari suffered, especially when Ferdinand made excuses not to play with him. Nobody spoke openly about the thefts but Hari heard the whispering behind his back and burned with shame. He started hanging around with Buolf, Chasper and Utz from the Spissen.

*****

When the first factories opened in the Kander valley, the matchsticks had a good market. The demand was large, the supply still small. This changed with the growing number of rivalling factories. The manufacturers underbid each other and the selling price scarcely covered the production costs. For this reason, some factories were repeatedly temporarily closed. Most factories could only just keep their heads above water and many had to file for bankruptcy. There was a frequent change of owners or leaseholders due to a debt overload of the previous owner.

This was dire for the workers who relied on their job and had no earnings during closure. It was a catastrophe for people who continually lived on the edge of misery.

*****

On Sunday afternoon, three days after buying the lollipops, Jakob and Josef met Urs outside his house. Berta was already there. Jakob opened his bag of broken lollipops to show them and they all took a piece of hard sugar to suck.

"Wasn't fair you got punished," Urs commiserated with him.

"It must've been taken when you were doing the sums. I bet it was Hari!" Berta added.

"Did you see him?" Jakob asked hopefully.

"No, I wasn't looking. Sorry."

"Hari gets plenty of sweets," Josef said. "He's always flaunting them in front of us."

"He could've thrown the bag to Buolf though, when no one was looking."

"Hmmn. But why break them?"

"To spoil it for me maybe," Jakob said.

"Well, they still taste really good, thank you," Urs said.

"Yes, thank you," Berta and Josef repeated.

They were walking uphill along the banks of the Heitibach, swashing their swords against long grasses.

"What shall we do today?" Urs asked. "We can't avenge Jakob if we don't know who did it."

"Let's walk across the meadow to the River Schlumpach. Who knows, we might find an adventure on our way?" Berta suggested. Nobody had an alternative idea so they started walking across the meadow above the new matchstick factory Rambert where Bartli worked.

"Look, there!" Berta cried out dramatically "On your stomachs, hide!"

The boys dived to the ground and whispered to Berta "Where? What have you seen?"

"Sssh, over there, look! What's Ramun doing there?"

The children saw Ramun crouching in the grass and creeping around the factory.

Urs laughed. "That guy is bored!" he said. "He doesn't have any friends here, they're all at his posh boarding school."

"Wait!" Berta ordered. "He's up to something. You don't creep about like that normally. Look, there! He's checking to see if anyone's watching."

The children peeped between the long grass.

"You're right," Jakob agreed. "It does look suspicious."

They continued to watch. Ramun was putting small bundles of what looked like hay around the building. Then he lit a match and ran around the factory lighting the bundles. Within seconds flames licked up the walls and Ramun sprinted off in the direction of Kandermatt.

The children looked at each other horrified and momentarily stunned. Berta recovered quickest.

"Is anyone in the building?" she asked.

"No, it's Sunday," Jakob answered. "No one will be there."

The flames were already high and black smoke drifted into the sky.

"Quick, we must run to the Koenig's, they are the nearest, they'll know what to do."

The children raced down the hill and hammered at the Koenig's door. Mrs Koenig bade them inside and she and her husband listened as they cried hastily all at once: "Fire! Ramberts!"

The Koenig's owned a factory for making boxes, specifically for the matchsticks. It was a long way outside of town and the packaging material for the processing of plywood boxes made it susceptible to fire. For that reason, Mr Koenig owned a hunting horn for beckoning the fire brigade, if necessary. He took it now from its hook on the wall, went outside and blew on it several times. It was so loud that the walls of their house shook.

Within minutes, the first fire engine came into sight, with several men pushing and pulling it up the hill. They put the fire hose into the Schlumpach and started pumping water onto the burning factory building. Jakob heard Mr Koenig warn the fire brigade about the phosphorous. No one knew whether it would explode or not.

More volunteers came running along the road from both directions and more fire brigades arrived too. One came all the way from Rybruegg. The fire looked nearly distinguished as suddenly there was a large explosion from inside the building. Wood and metal flew high into the sky in all directions. The firefighting team ran backwards but one man got knocked over by a long metal pole. Someone pulled him out of the danger zone and someone else ran to fetch the doctor.

The children looked silently on, in awe, from the safety of the Koenig's garden. Not even the combined efforts of several fire brigades could save Rambert's factory from burning to the ground. They did, however, manage to contain the fire so that it didn't spread and no other buildings were affected. When the doctor announced that the injured fireman was not seriously wounded, the manoeuvre was declared a success and people started going home.

Mrs Koenig told the children to come indoors and gave them mugs of warm cocoa and cake.

"If you get into trouble with your parents for coming home late," she told them, "tell them I'll come to visit them tomorrow. You did well; without your early warning more buildings might have burned down."

The children walked home together. Only then did it occur to them that they hadn't mentioned Ramun to anyone.

"What shall we do?" Berta asked. "We can't just let him get away with it!"

"We could tell August at school tomorrow." Urs suggested. "Ask him if he thinks we should report it to his father or not."

The children agreed.

August Struenzli was the son of the Weissbruegg's only gendarme. Neither father nor son were the brightest sparks in town but they were good natured and wanted to be liked by their fellow villagers rather than renowned for harshness. August's father was amicably known as Sausage.

During the school break Jakob, Berta and Urs went up to August. He was standing alone in the play area eating a sandwich and was visibly pleased to receive their attention. After they had told him the events of the day before, he pulled back his nine-year-old shoulders importantly.

"This is a very serious matter." His voice took on the tone of an adult. "I shall report it to my father as soon as I get home and I'm sure he'll want a statement from all of you."

"Berta and I work at the factory in Kandermatt, Josef too," Jakob told August, although it was certain he knew this already. "Can your father visit us at home after eight o'clock?"

"I'm sure that can be arranged," August answered seriously.

Constable Struenzli came and conscientiously took statements from all the children. He wrote everything down on a piece of lined notebook paper with a blunt pencil and let them sign the statement with the date.

"Will Mr Lauber find out that our boys have made a statement?" Anton asked worriedly. "We can't afford to lose our jobs."

Constable Struenzli chewed the end of his pencil thoughtfully. "Normally the accused have a right to know who's made a statement," he said.

Anton and Regina looked worried. They didn't want Ramun to get away with it, but they couldn't lose their jobs either.

"Then, as Jakob and Josef's father, I'm afraid I must withdraw their statements," Anton said. He looked apologetically to his boys. "I'm sorry lads."

Elsa, Berta's mother, didn't allow her to make a formal statement either, although she confirmed the boys' statements to Constable Struenzli.

Constable Struenzli knew a wrongdoing had taken place but his hands were tied. All the same, he still visited Director Lauber, albeit solely with Urs' statement. Mr Lauber invited the constable indoors and offered him a small schnapps. He introduced his wife and son and only then asked how he could help him.

Constable Struenzli laid the case out before Mr Lauber and showed him Urs' statement.

"Hmmn, Urs, the son of Saddler Eric, I believe. Terrible business with the avalanche, killed his brother and Urs was badly injured himself, if I remember rightly. Terrible matter indeed. Well, I'm afraid this must be a case of mistaken identity. You see Ramun was at home all that day."

"All Sunday, are you sure?"

"Well, apart from church, yes. Do you doubt my word?"

"No, sir, but Urs has no reason to lie. Ramun can you confirm that you were indoors all day?"

"All afternoon, yes sir, I had homework to do."

"There you are then; I hope you're satisfied!"

"I'm just doing my duty, sir."

"Yes. Well, I must get on myself now, so if there's nothing else?"

Constable Struenzli took his leave. With just Urs' word against the well-connected family Lauber, there would be no chance of a court hearing. He'd better let the children know. Sometimes his job was dissatisfying.

*****

"What on earth were you thinking of?" Mr Lauber raised his arm to strike his son but Ramun dodged out of the way. His mother let out a small scream.

"I just wanted to help!" Ramun protested. "You complained that Ramberts were underbidding you and ruining the business."

Mr Lauber let his arm drop. "The first rule in business is, that if you feel compelled to break the rules then make sure you don't get caught. You could've ruined your future if more people had seen you. Off now, go to your room, I must think."

*****

Family Schneider weren't feeling happy. Regina felt as if she had been oppressed all her life. She had no solution

149

other than to continue saving for a proper dairy, but when she saw Anneli at work, she determined to at least try to help her. Anneli had neglected her appearance entirely. Her work had become careless; Regina had to jump in and help more and more often. The worst thing, that caused Regina the most worry, was Anneli's mental state. She was no longer the carefree, good-humoured lass from before the attempted rape. Her eyes were dull and she was dithery all the time.

At first Regina hoped that time would heal, but to the contrary, the matter worsened. Yet again a small fire started at Anneli's workplace. It wasn't serious and Regina was there to help in a matter of seconds, but this time Anneli broke down completely.

"I'll go outside with her for a few minutes," Regina told her workmate to the left. "Cover up for us if anyone comes."

Regina led Anneli down to the stream and sat her down. She let her cry and gave her a clean handkerchief.

"S-sorry," Anneli sobbed. "I'm sorry."

"There's no need to apologise," Regina said. "I just wish I could help you."

"Nobody can!" Anneli cried louder.

Regina waited till the crying began to ebb.

"I can't sleep," Anneli told her. "I keep waking up and seeing his hands with the missing thumbnails."

"Missing thumbnails?" Regina asked. "You never mentioned that before."

"He took his gloves off, the ones he always wears. He has no thumbnails and some fingernails are missing too."

"Ah."

"When I'm at work, I'm terrified of seeing him. I can't concentrate, I worry so much."

Regina's blood boiled when she thought of the damage men who raped women did to their victims. Even if it was only attempted rape.

"What you need is a fresh start, a new job somewhere else," Regina said.

"As if I had any choice!" Anneli cried. "I'm useless, he said so! And I've no qualifications."

"That's not true! As the oldest of your siblings, you've had plenty of experience looking after children and helping your mother with the household."

Anneli looked up. "Do you think so?"

"I know so,' Regina reassured her. 'I read in the Frutiger Parish Weekly that a new hotel is opening in Thun. They are looking for honest, Christian chamber maids and offer accommodation, cost and a small salary. Wouldn't that be something for you?"

"I can't. I've got nothing respectable to wear and my only reference would be from the matchstick factory. Then they'll know I want to leave."

"Don't give up so easily. If you give me permission to tell my sister-in-law, then I'm sure Margot could come up with a decent dress for you. And you could ask Reverend Moser for a reference, and Karl Stettler, maybe even the mayor."

"Oh no, I couldn't possibly … if they found out … well, I would rather die."

"Nobody needs to know, Anneli. Just tell them that you'd like to apply for the job."

Anneli looked at Regina. There was a streak of hope in her face.

"We'd better get back to work," she said.

15

1855

Heinz had difficulty finding employment within the vicinity of his home, his ill repute being widely known. The matchstick factory in Kandermatt was looking for a timberman. The director knew all about Heinz's dishonesty, but there was no possibility of stealing from them, and Heinz's dire situation enabled the director to pay him even less than customary.

Heinz started work half an hour before everyone else at 5.30 a.m. First he lit the kiln so that it had time to reach the correct temperature for drying wood. It was situated a small distance from the factory in an open barn, where the preparation of the tree trunks also took place. Then he sliced thin strips of fir wood from roughly cut planks. The rods had to measure exactly two feet in length and were the same thickness as matchsticks. They looked like extra-long spaghetti. When he had enough to fill the kiln, he put them inside it to dry.

Next, Heinz collected a large portion of pre-dried wooden rods, and taking his place inside the factory at the chopper's stool, began to push a sharp blade up and down to cut the rods into the exact length of the matchsticks. It was necessary to work very quickly, pushing the blade back and forth rapidly in rhythm, to process all the wood. It was dangerous work, requiring concentration. The job was disliked as it was not unusual to lose a finger or two under the blade.

Also, part of his work was preparing ultra-thin slices of wood shavings for the production of matchstick boxes. Although the Koenig family owned one box factory, and the deaconry had opened another, most of the boxes were made in people's homes as a cottage industry and supplement to their meagre income. Some families thus converted three tree trunks a year to matchstick boxes. Others who owned no forest of their own, could get the wood shavings already pre-cut, from the factory. However, when they brought the completed boxes back to the factory, they received half the money that the families who used their own wood earned.

*****

Helga reluctantly looked for work too. It was no longer a case of sending Hari to boarding school, it was the necessity of getting food on the table. In Weissbruegg people had started crossing to the other side of the street when they saw her. She was mortified.

To work in a factory didn't carry the same recognition as being a foreman at a large sawmill, but Helga desired to keep up at least a minimum of appearances for herself. No way could she possibly work in Weissbruegg, but the mayor in Reichenbach was looking for an additional clerk. She bit back her humiliation of looking for employment, put her best dress on and a hat, and walked to the town hall in Reichenbach.

She knocked at Ursula Huber's door.

"Wait!" a voice barked from within.

Helga waited. There was nowhere to sit, so she remained standing for over half an hour. She was wondering if she had been forgotten and whether she could knock again when the door was flung open from inside.

Mrs Huber looked at Helga, standing timidly outside her door.

"What do you want?" she demanded.

"I've come about the position for a clerk," Helga said quietly, hardly daring to speak out boldly in front of this dragon.

"We've no place here for the likes of you."

"What? What do you mean the l-likes of me? Why, I'm more respectable than—"

"You know perfectly well what I mean. Thieves and swindlers, your family. Away with you now, be off!" Mrs Huber slammed the door in Helga's face.

Helga couldn't believe it. She looked around but thankfully no one seemed to have witnessed the episode. She hastened home as fast as she could, took a half-full bottle of schnapps from the top shelf in the pantry and drank until it was empty.

When Hari returned from school he found his mother fast asleep at the kitchen table, snoring. He carried a wooden stool into the pantry and reached up to a ceramic pot. His mother thought it was a secret, but he had discovered it long ago. He took some of the coins out, and then left the house to go to the corner shop. Recently, Mr Brotz, the arrogant scumbag, demanded money on the spot whenever Hari wanted to buy sweets.

*****

In 1853 Reverend Moser from Weissbruegg, together with the reverends from Frutigen, Kandergrund and Reichenbach, wrote a letter to Mr Siebold, the district administrator and head of the General Council, complaining about the widespread child labour in matchstick factories. They criticised the fact that school children often worked, without a break, before and after school, sometimes well into the night, and unfortunately with the knowledge and permission of their parents. Even younger children, under the compulsory school age, often worked twelve hours or longer in the factories. The clergymen requested that the government take measures against this widespread grievance. Nothing happened.

To the contrary, since then, the district administrator had written several reports to the government in Bern, commending the benefaction of the factories. The report stated that through and because of them, a significant number of children and adults of few financial means had been given the opportunity to work, and thus considerably disburdened the poor relief fund in Weissbruegg.

The deaconry felt that something had to be done, at the least to help orphans and adults of unsound mind who had no relatives to take care of them. They decided to build a poor house, next to the Tellenburg, a ruined fortress between Frutigen and Kandergrund. To help counteract the substantial cost of care, accommodation and food, the deaconry established a box factory next to the poor house where the residents had to work. But at least they were clean, warm and received regular meals. The deaconry needed a number of charitable women, housewives, to look after the general running of their newly founded establishment and put an advertisement in the Parish Weekly.

Helga read the advertisement and pondered over it. She didn't really fancy working with, what she in her own mind, called imbeciles. On the other hand, matron of a charitable organisation sounded much more ostentatious than factory worker, and this above all, moved her to apply for the job. Reverend Moser, as her parish pastor, was given the duty to interview Helga. He talked about the establishment and duties she would be expected to perform. Helga asked about the hours of work and was happily surprised to hear how flexible the pastor sounded. The interview was going well, both parties knew that they couldn't be too fussy, until Helga asked about the actual earnings. Reverend Moser's complexion, already pale, turned white at the thought of the time he'd lost speaking to this pretentious woman.

"Pay? You expect to earn money? My dear lady, it was stated in the advertisement, quite clearly, that this is an honorary post!"

Helga felt sick. Honorary? She was sure she had read honourable. She stood up abruptly.

"Oh, I see. I'm afraid there's been a misunderstanding. You see ... well, I need to earn money ... for food." Helga felt her cheeks glowing hot. "I'm sorry," she said, stumbling out of the door as quickly as possible.

*****

It was summer again and the hill farmers prepared to move their livestock up to the alm. Jakob was excited, this would be his third year accompanying his uncle and looking after the goats. This year, his teacher Mr Stettler had entrusted his goat to Jakob too. He was very generous, offering Jakob the kid, should his goat have one, in return for the cheese. Jakob loved his time on the alm and felt very fortunate to be given the opportunity.

The only drawback was leaving Josef behind. Josef had started school the previous year and was old enough to accompany them, but Uncle Gustl couldn't occupy both boys throughout the summer. Their father, Anton, promised that Josef could visit several times at the weekends though. He said that he was old enough to walk all the way by himself when the weather was fine.

On the day of the procession, farmers and villagers, cattle, goats and pigs set off noisily along the grassy tracks, leaving the rest of the town behind them in an unusual calm.

*****

At the matchstick factory in Kandermatt, Chasper rubbed his hands together. Finally freedom, he thought. No Mr Schneider reacting like a hysterical woman whenever he tried to bring a little fun into the monotonous, boring work.

In the devil's kitchen the air was hot, stale and stank repulsively. Outside it was a beautiful summer's day. Chasper decided to move his stove outside under the leafy shade of a huge elm tree. He stirred the bubbling mass of phosphor mixture dreamily. The steam drifted lazily upwards into the branches. Suddenly, all sorts of beetles, gadflies and other insects began to rain down upon him, dead. They fell onto the ground, into the pot of phosphor mixture, onto Chasper's hair and clothing. He let out a scream that brought the factory workers all running outside.

Chasper had run a small way away and was shaking his head and body, desperately trying to rid himself of dead insects. The factory workers laughed at the spectacle. Mr Haeberlin watched sourly as the downpour of insects gradually receded, and then he grabbed Chasper by his ear and dragged him all the way to his office.

The workers returned reluctantly inside and went to their respective places. Berta shook her head at her brother's brainless escapade and was about to go back to the filling station when she passed Heinz at the chopping stool.

"Hello, Mr Stoll," she greeted him politely. "My mother asked me to bring a sack of wood shavings home, we've nearly run out. Do you have a stockpile in store?"

Heinz stopped his movements and looked at Berta.

"Yes, if you wait a couple of minutes until this pile is full, you can take it right with you."

Berta didn't really want to wait, she had her own work to get on with, but now she'd asked, she thought it would be impolite to say no. To hurry things up, every time Heinz brought the blade down, she grabbed the bundle of shavings and put them in the sack. They gained speed, Berta's fingers were still partially under the blade just before it came plunging down. Suddenly Heinz let the blade drop as Berta's left hand was still under it. It sliced through her middle two fingers. Blood gushed everywhere. Berta looked at her hand astonished, she felt no pain, and then she fainted.

*****

Helga wandered through the local market checking the prices of potatoes, wondering if she waited until just before closing time, she could get a bargain offer. She saw Mrs Buehler chatting to Mrs Siebold, and curious, sidled up to them, pretending to examine the cheeses but with her ear antennae ridden out to maximum hearing level.

"... yes, my friends in Bern are literally ripping Mrs Piller's lace out of my hands before I can unpack it," Mrs Buehler said.

"I would love a collar for my new velvet dress," Mrs Siebold answered. "I heard that she even masters Venetian point lace."

"Oh yes, it is so beautiful, but she has a long waiting list nowadays. She can't make lace fast enough for all the demand."

"Really – how long do you think I would have to wait for a collar?"

"I don't know exactly, but I expect three months at least."

"Oh."

"She's very accurate. She would never sell anything under perfect, just for the sake of being quick."

"No. Well, I see I must visit her soon. Tell me, is it true that her niece, the poor girl with the foot, can already make lace too?"

"Yes! Isn't it amazing? Mina's only six but an exceptional talent. You ought to see her little fingers flying as she makes lace trim for handkerchiefs! I tell you ..." Mrs Buehler leaned in closer to whisper to Mrs Siebold.

Mrs Siebold's eyes widened. "Really?"

"As true as I'm standing here," Mrs Buehler answered, noticing Helga.

Helga moved on quickly, annoyed that she hadn't heard the whole conversation. She hadn't wanted to belittle herself in front of Margot up till now, but they were relations after all, and if even a six-year-old could make lace ... well, it couldn't be that difficult! She would visit her tomorrow and offer her services. Margot would be grateful and could obviously afford to pay her well.

She waited until the market stands started packing up and then approached Barbara Urban's stall.

Barbara's sister, Bernadette, nudged her.

"She's coming, punctual to the dot."

"I told you she would," Barbara answered. The women continued packing their wares up, as if they hadn't noticed Helga.

"Good morning, Mrs Urban," Helga said. "I see you're packing up. I could take some potatoes off you if you wish, to save you carrying them home."

"Good day, Mrs Stoll. How many would you like? It's seven centimes for two pounds."

"Seven? But that was your price this morning! I'm doing you a favour by taking the potatoes off you."

"I wouldn't say that. We can sell them at the Reichenbach market on Saturday. But I tell you what, as you're a regular customer, I can throw an extra potato in for your loyalty."

Helga felt her cheeks going hot. "Yes please," she said, looking at her feet. She counted out the coins and walked home.

Barbara and Bernadette waited until she was gone.

"I'd feel sorry for her if she weren't such a stuck-up cow," Barbara said.

"I don't feel sorry for her at all," Bernadette answered. "Why doesn't she get a job like the rest of us instead of sitting on her backside all day?"

*****

The next morning, Helga walked to Margot's house and knocked at the door. She wore her everyday dress; there was no need to put on good clothes for Margot.

Margot sighed and put down her lacework. The rate people were knocking on her door that morning she'd get no work done. She hid her surprise at seeing Helga and invited her in.

"Would you like a cup of tea?" she asked.

Helga's complexion turned as green as fresh pea shoots pushing their way through fertile soil. Tea? How on earth could Margot afford tea? You could only buy it at Mr Brotz's shop for colonial wares. She swallowed and was about to accept when Margot misinterpreted her hesitation and asked, "or would you prefer coffee?"

Coffee? Helga felt suddenly very hot. A funny sensation went through her body. Surely she was yet too young for hot flushes? She sat down quickly at the table, although Helga hadn't invited her to, and stuttered, "Tea would be lovely, thank you."

Margot put cream and sugar on the table and a dish full of dainty cakes.

"I didn't make them myself," she told Helga apologetically. "I don't have any time lately, but Mr Brotz assured me that they were quite fresh."

Helga couldn't stop herself: "Ah, what a shame, homemade is always best, don't you think?"

Margot removed the cakes from the table and returned them to the pantry. Helga bit her lip, her mouth was drooling from the aroma of the cakes and her stomach rumbled.

"How can I help you?" Margot asked quite severely. She was annoyed at herself for allowing Helga to always get to her. "I'm afraid I've not much time, I have a schedule to fulfil."

"Ah yes, well, that's why I've come, to offer you my services. I heard that you'd be glad of some help and we are relations after all. Mind you, I couldn't do it for nothing, I mean, I would be giving up a well-paid job to help you."

Margot was silent a moment, trying to understand Helga's words.

"Helga, what exactly are you offering to do?"

"To make lace, of course."

"Make lace? I didn't know that you could make lace."

"Well no, not yet, you'd have to show me how. But it can't be that difficult if your disabled niece can do it."

"There is nothing wrong with my niece's hands. The girl you expected to die is an exceptionally talented needle worker. Even so, she has been learning and practising every day for the last three years. I can't just show you how to make lace in an hour or two." Margot caught her breath. She would have liked to say so much more. She would have liked to scream and shout at Helga. However, she was her husband's sister and it was no secret that they were struggling. She put all her self-control together and said, "I'm sorry I can't offer you work, Helga, but if you would like a loan, to tide you over bad times, then I'm sure we can work out something."

Helga pursed her lips, like she often did. Wrinkles had already started to etch themselves into her demeanour, giving her a perpetually sour expression, even when she did her best to smile.

"I'm not sure," she said, timidly now. "Maybe we could speak again on Sunday."

"Yes, bring the family round to lunch," Margot offered. "Gustl will be happy to see you."

*****

Gustl asked his brother-in-law how he could best help him.

"I don't like to ask for something for nothing," Heinz replied, "I have a portion of forest just behind Maeggisserenegg. If you could buy half of the section from me, that should tide us over this rough period until I get a better paid job."

"I think that should be manageable," Gustl replied. "I'll come and have a look at it with you next Sunday, if you like."

The following Sunday they went up to the forest together and agreed on an over-generous price for the small strip

The Matchstick Boy

of forest. Gustl didn't mind, he thought it honourable of Heinz to offer something for his money. If he sold the trees one day he wouldn't make a profit, but the loss would be bearable to help his sister.

163

16

1856–1859

The autumn sun illuminated the dying leaves hanging tenuously onto the maple branches, enhancing the yellows to glistening gold, the oranges to burnished copper and the reds to shimmering rubies. During the day the sunshine warmed the skin, but the nights were getting longer and a whiff of snow came drifting down the alpine heights.

The schoolchildren went outside for their lunch break. Ferdinand had left the village school to attend the same upper-class boarding school as Ramun in Bern. This had made Hari resentful and he cast his eyes around for a suitable target for his anger.

It was Mina's second year at school already. The cobbler had made her a special boot for her left foot and lined it with sheepskin to ease any pain. She couldn't run as fast as the other children and walked with a limp, but she had quickly made friends with Sylvia, Franziska Gehring's daughter.

Mina picked up her bottle of milk and apple from the table and was walking across the playground to Sylvia when Hari went up to her and knocked her arm viciously, so that the bottle fell to the ground and broke. She hadn't even had the chance to open her mouth to protest when he started taunting her.

"Oh dear, ha, ha, ha. Lame duck is so clumsy, she's spilt her milk. Well, it's no use crying over spilt milk, ha, ha, ha, that's a pun!" Hari's mates, Buolf in his last year at school and Utz from the Spissen, joined in his laughter and surrounded Mina, blocking her way. Josef, not far away, turned round and charged up to Hari.

"Leave my sister alone, you moron!" He pushed the flat of his hand against the older boy's chest.

"Or what?" Hari sneered. "Are you going to beat me up?" He raised his fists in a mock boxing pose and laughed. "You gutless sissy! Your father—"

The fist came quicker than Hari could finish insulting Josef. The right-handed punch landed directly on Hari's nose and blood spurted. Hari touched it, surprised, and then fell on Josef. Buolf and Utz joined in the fight and Jakob came rushing to help his brother, Urs right behind him. They all scrambled in the dust, fists flying.

"You scumbag!" Hari insulted Josef.

"At least my father's not **a thief!**" Josef retorted loudly. Silence fell, the children were shocked. This was a really bad defamation and none of them had heard the accusations before. Their parents had kept the subject taboo.

Hari withdrew a clasp knife from his pocket and all the children stopped in their tracks and watched, paralysed. Manfred Klopfenstein, the head boy, hurried indoors to fetch Mr Stettler as Hari took up a stance, ready to attack.

"Put the knife down!" Jakob yelled at Hari. "Don't you dare hurt my brother!"

"Like your little chick, Berta? Shame my father didn't cut

off more fingers." Hari started thrusting his arm forward with the knife and Josef dodged back and forth avoiding it.

"Stop! Stop immediately! Put that knife down, Hari, now!" Mr Stettler had run up to the circle of boys. Hari and Josef stared at each other, Hari determined to harm him and Josef equally intent on avoiding the knife.

"Hari, put that knife down!" Mr Stettler repeated. "We can talk this out sensibly with one another."

"He called my father a thief," Hari answered.

"He pushed Mina on purpose," Josef defended himself.

"Stop. It's of no consequence, put the knife down, Hari!"

Hari looked at the knife in his hand, looked defiantly at Mr Stettler, and then threw the knife half-heartedly away from himself, towards his teacher. He hadn't meant any harm but the knife landed unfortunately on Mr Stettler's hand, inflicting a gash. Blood ran down Mr Stettler's fingers and he hastily withdrew a handkerchief from his pocket and wrapped it tightly around the wound. He picked up the knife wordlessly and then said: "Inside, all of you, now!"

Inside the classroom Mr Stettler told the children to sit down at their places but held onto Hari as he was about to go to the back row.

"Not you. Wait here!"

Mr Stettler made Hari wait at the front of class until he had cleaned and dressed his wounded hand properly. He took his time purposefully. He folded his bloodied handkerchief together neatly and placed it in his briefcase. The whole time he didn't speak a word and the children sat silently, wide-eyed and holding their breath. Just Hari stood next to the blackboard sneering at the thought of writing lines. When Mr Stettler had finally finished, he told Hari to come to his front desk.

"Before you receive your punishment, Hari, have you anything you want to say?"

"No."

"Then pull your trousers down and bend over my desk."
The children gasped. This was something new. Hari undid his trousers and bent over. He bit his teeth together, determined to show no weakness.

Mr Stettler took his cane and thrashed Hari's backside five times.

"You can pull your trousers up," he told Hari, who had managed to suppress any cries or tears. "Now go to Wilhelmine and apologise."

Hari pulled a face but he walked up to Mina. "Sorry," he said curtly. He turned dispassionately to his teacher awaiting the next order. Mr Stettler shook his head sadly. He could read through Hari's demeanour as easily as a newspaper.

"You may sit down," he said.

The teacher returned to the front of class and held the knife up for all the children to see clearly.

"This knife is confiscated. I shall return it to your parents personally, Hari. It is forbidden to bring knives, or any other sort of weapon, to school." He spoke seriously. "If I catch any of you with a weapon, you will not only receive the same punishment as Hari but you will be suspended from school for a week. Now open your history books at page twenty-four."

School finished for the day and Hari began to walk towards Kandermatt with Buolf and Utz. He didn't work himself but he usually went with his friends at least part of the way. Buolf thumped his back and said, "Well done mate, you showed them."

"Did it hurt?" Utz wanted to know. "You were very brave."

"No, didn't feel a thing," Hari lied. "But just you wait, I'm going to pay them back for it."

"Yeah!" Buolf cried. "What are you going to do? Count me in to help!"

"Yeah, me too!" Utz joined in, more or less enthusiastically.

"Don't know yet, I need a good idea. Tell Chasper at work, together we'll work something out."

"Yeah, see you tomorrow then."

Hari walked back to his own home and now he was alone he could let the tears of pain and humiliation run. He hadn't spoken lightly to Buolf and Utz; he was determined to get revenge.

*****

Mr Stettler walked to Dr Koefeli's practice. He wanted him to give his wound a quick eye-over, and if he had time, have a small drink with him. It had been a hell of a day, the five strokes with the cane hadn't come lightly, but he was at his wit's end with Hari and Buolf. Buolf was just a plain idiot but he had had better hopes for Hari. Now Utz was falling under their influence too. As if the lad's chances in life weren't bad enough.

The door was open and Karl Stettler walked inside, presuming to see Helga Stoll at the reception. Since she had started working there, people were avoiding the doctor's practice, preferring to walk all the way to Reichenbach to see Dr Roessel, if necessary, so he wasn't surprised to find the waiting room empty. He could hear something though. He peered round the half-open door to the doctor's visitation room and backed away hastily. Lukas Koefeli with Helga Stoll? My God, the rumours were true then! No wonder Hari was so angry. Well that did it! He would go to the Goldenen Ochsen and grant himself a beer and a schnapps. He didn't believe in excessive alcohol consumption, but some days a drink was really necessary.

*****

Chasper had been waiting to pull a specific prank with someone for ages. Up until now the target and the motive had been absent. Hearing of Hari's misfortune and subsequent plan for revenge gave him the perfect excuse to try it out.

The four boys met on Sunday afternoon and Chasper explained his idea to them. He wanted to linger on after work and steal some phosphor. Buolf and Utz could meet him in the devil's kitchen as soon as Mr Schneider had gone home and Hari could wait outside until one of the boys came to help him sneak inside. They would then take the phosphor to the Schneider's house. The boys knew that the phosphor would glow green and white in the dark and intended to use this phenomenon to make a huge green boelima, a spooky ghost, to scare Mina out of her mind! The boys discussed a few minor details about how to get Mina to look out of the window, laughing with pleasant anticipation of the uproar they would cause and the screams she would holler.

On Monday evening Mr Schneider made sure that all safety precautions had been taken and then left the devil's kitchen.

"Sweep the floor before going home," he told Chasper.

The bars of yellow phosphor were kept under water in a sealed tin because they very easily caught fire when exposed to air, and burning phosphor caused the gravest type of burn, reaching deep into the dermal tissue and only healing very slowly.

Once Mr Schneider had left, Buolf entered the kitchen.

"Utz is getting Hari," he told his brother. Soon the four boys stood there, looking at the sealed tins and rubbing their hands in joyful expectancy of their adventure. Hari insisted that he be the one to carry the yellow bar of phosphor, but he let Chasper break the seal to open a tin and lift the lid. The boys' eyes sparkled at the sight of several bars of yellow phosphor.

Hari picked one bar out of the tin and stuffed it into his trouser pocket to make a fire later that night.

About thirty steps away from the factory, next to the well, the phosphor in Hari's pocket ignited and his trousers began to burn. He screamed out in pain and shock and beat his trousers trying to stop them burning. His three friends looked on, not knowing what to do. Mr Haeberlin, still in the factory, heard the screams. He ran outside, saw Hari, and threw him quick-wittedly into the well. The fire was extinguished and he helped Hari clamber out. Instead of undressing him immediately, there by the well, he made the mistake of carrying Hari indoors into the factory to undress him indoors. The phosphor began to burn again and continued to burn the flesh of Hari's right thigh deeper and deeper. Hari screeched and bellowed like a pig being slaughtered.

"Run to the director's home and tell him to send someone urgently on horseback to fetch the doctor," Mr Haeberlin ordered Chasper. He ran his fingers through his hair, out of his depth with the situation. "Fetch buckets of water," he told Buolf and Utz. Hari passed out. "More water," Mr Haeberlin told the boys, not knowing what else to do. The doctor came and treated the wound carefully before Hari was taken home.

Over the next days and weeks, it was uncertain whether he would live or die. After a high fever he seemed to be on the way to recovery but had one relapse after another. Several times he was near death. He stayed in bed and received appropriate medication and meticulous treatment, but he spent six months at home before he was fit enough to go back to school.

The burn still didn't heal completely. Helga was given a special ointment to apply to Hari's wound and told to bandage it with fresh bandages twice a day. Dr Roessel, the canton doctor who had been put in charge of Hari's case by the authorities, expressed hope that the wound would heal entirely.

Hari's young body grew but the scar tissue refused to stretch with the rest of the surrounding skin. The wound inflicted terrible pain and opened again and again repeatedly. One day when he was alone at home, he saw the bottle of plum schnapps that his father liked, on the table. He opened it and took a large gulp and then another. The alcohol deadened the pain a little.

After that first time, he reached for the bottle again and again, until his body craved for it daily. He worried his father might notice that his bottle of schnapps emptied quickly and give him a beating. He tried to stop drinking it but couldn't. The schnapps made his pain more bearable.

At first Heinz didn't notice anything. Then he started looking at his bottle, surprised that so little liquid was left inside it. He wondered whether Helga had started drinking secretly and began to watch her. He didn't notice any difference in her behaviour or demeanour at all. He forgot about it.

In November 1859, three years after the accident, the wound still hadn't closed permanently. Dr Roessel put the blame on Hari's family, claiming that the wound had been neglected.

Hari walked with a limp and bore the pain stoically. He had already made his mind up. As soon as he could, he would leave home and go to America. He never wanted anything to do with Weissbruegg or its inhabitants again, but first he would take revenge on Josef.

17

1859

Chasper, Buolf and Utz all lost their jobs at the matchstick factory. Their age alone saved them from being prosecuted by the court. Even Berta nearly lost her job, but everyone spoke highly of her and Mr Haeberlin, who knew her family relied desperately on her wages, left it with a severe warning not to follow in her brothers' footsteps.

Chasper left Weissbruegg and found work with the Swiss Central Railway, a private company that was extending the rail line from Bern to Thun. He slept in a container that belonged to the firm, together with most of his workmates, and he got a warm meal daily. The pay was low but a little better than at the matchstick factory and at least he could keep it himself.

The work on the construction site was hard and dangerous. Experienced men blasted dynamite through rock to build tunnels and Chasper's job was to clear the rubble away. Chasper worked hard, contending temperatures of over a hundred degrees inside the tunnel. Inadequate ventilation and dynamite fumes caused his eyes to water and made breathing difficult. The rock strata was unstable, and sometimes rock fell unexpectedly, burying workers underneath ton-weight stones. The company was always looking for replacement workers. In the summer of 1857, Buolf joined him.

Berta was glad that her two older brothers had left home. It saved conflicts with her mother and other siblings and made life more peaceful. She missed Anneli, but she came home once a month and had even found jobs for her other two older sisters, Trudi and Dorli, in service. This was a major improvement for them from working at Slaters, a rival matchstick factory. Her sisters already looked cleaner and healthier and much happier. Now Berta was alone with her mother and the twins, two years younger than herself.

The disadvantage was that her father, when he came home drunk from the pub, had fewer targets to victimise. Whenever he was at home, Berta tried to make herself invisible. His temper would roar up for no apparent reason, and if he even just saw her, she knew she was in for a beating. When she could, she tried to outrun her father, but there weren't many hiding places. He usually got her in the end and beat and kicked her until his temper subsided. She was covered in blue and green bruises, which she always put down to falls if anyone asked, but usually they didn't. Worse than the physical injuries was her mental state. She jumped at any unexpected sound, her schoolwork suffered, her answers when spoken to were monosyllabic and she became quiet and depressed.

An intelligent girl, she contemplated how she could change her situation, but she was only just thirteen. In summer she would finish school and her father had already said that she was to work full-time at the factory. She couldn't go into service until she was at least sixteen. She didn't know if she could survive that long at home.

The next day was Sunday. She waited until her father went to the pub at noon, grabbed a crust of bread, and ran off to meet the other three musketeers. Urs told her that his aunt was visiting that afternoon and that he had to stay at home. Now that he had left school and was apprenticed to his father as a saddler, she had the impression that he no longer wanted to play with them, they were younger than him after all. She shrugged it off and went to the Schneiders. Jakob was already putting his boots on. He told her that Josef had been punished for some misdeed and must stay at home gluing matchstick boxes together.

"So it's just the two of us," he said cheerfully. "What shall we get up to?"

Berta kicked the dirt with the tip of her shoe. "I dunno," she said listlessly. "You decide."

"Well the sun's shining," Jakob answered "and I can smell summer in the air. If we run like mad, we could just have time to go to the Aris Castle ruins. You can be my Lady of the Castle and I can be your jester." Jakob pulled a face and conjured up two pieces of cake, wrapped in a handkerchief, from his pocket.

Berta clasped her hands together in front of her heart and mimicked, "A true gentleman knows the way to his Lady's heart. First one there gets the biggest piece!"

She set off running and Jakob followed happily. They managed to run all the way to the affinage. Nobody was there, of course; it was Sunday and the entrance was locked. They drank some water from the River Chiene and then sat down to get their breath back. Berta reached out for the cake but Jakob shook his head.

"No, we're not there yet and the cake tastes much better with the view from the castle wall." He stretched his hand down to pull Berta up. "Quietly now," he whispered, 'we don't want to disturb the Grueenmatti innkeeper."

174

"What?"

"Tell you when we're there," he answered, racing on ahead.

Ivy and moss covered the crumbling stone ruins so that the castle blended in perfectly with its surroundings. Jakob and Berta sat on a wall, legs dangling over the side and looked down to the River Kander, a silver streak reflecting the sunlight in the valley far below them. Jakob removed the cake from his pocket and unwrapped it.

"We've got Mina to thank for this," he said. "Mrs Siebold was so pleased with some lace handkerchiefs she had made that she gave her a whole bag of sugar in addition to the agreed price."

"That's really good, she deserves it. My sister Anneli told me that she sometimes gets tips from clients too. My mother only ever showed me how to mend ripped clothing and darn socks."

"Well, that's useful—" Jakob stopped speaking as shrieks ripped through the peace. He leaned forward to see the direction the screeching came from, and losing his balance, began to topple forwards. Berta grabbed his jacket and pulled him back.

"Er, thank you. What was that?"

"Probably two herons, they always squawk like someone getting murdered."

"No, no. It was different. There, again!" Jakob and Berta heard desperate screams. They were coming from the direction of the affinage and they sounded human.

"Quick!" Jakob told Berta, stuffing the remains of his cake back into his pocket and racing down the mountain. As they approached the affinage they heard sobbing and crying. They hid behind a tree and saw Ramun brushing down his jacket and then striding off. Berta whispered to

Jakob that he should stay put and she went up to a woman curled up on the ground. Berta touched the woman's shoulder lightly so as not to scare her, but the woman jerked around shocked. It was Magdelena, Mr Brotz's eldest daughter, she was most distraught. Although she only knew Berta from sight, she clasped hold of her tightly and wept.

Berta waited until Magdelena's tears were spent and then signalled to Jakob.

"Shall I go and get help?" he asked, "the doctor, or your parents, or someone else?"

Panic-stricken, Magdelena registered Jakob's presence. "No, nobody, don't tell anyone, please!"

"If you're sure, Miss Magdelena, but you seem hurt. There's blood on your dress."

Magdelena wiped her tears away and looked at herself. She fastened some buttons on her bodice and gazed at Berta.

"Do you think I could come home with you and get tidied up?"

"My father is probably still at the alehouse, yes, of course you can come. Don't worry, my mother won't tell a soul if you don't want her to. We'll wash the stains from your dress and comb your hair."

"Thank you." Magdelena beheld Berta gratefully. "My parents will kill me if they ever find out."

"They won't hear a word from me, I promise," Berta said. Both girls stared at Jakob expectantly. He held his hands up.

"What? I already said I wouldn't tell."

"Promise!" The girls demanded in unison.

"Yes, of course, I promise."

Jakob thought he was missing something but didn't

know what. He wondered what Ramun and Magdelena had been arguing about. He sighed and followed them home, waving good bye as they turned off to Berta's home.

*****

Jakob already had eight goats of his own and another twenty from neighbouring hill farmers. Anton had four cows again, as before the fire. It was no problem for Jakob to persuade their father to allow Josef to accompany them on the annual procession to the alm, to help Jakob with the herd of goats. Jakob cut a long hazel rod for Josef and told him not to hit the goats properly with it, but just touch them lightly.

The march to the Griesalp was uneventful. Jakob made a fire and the men sat around it, eating, drinking and smoking. There was just one difference, Eddie was no longer with them. His grandson Emil, in spite of always insisting he wouldn't, had emigrated to America. Eddie was so heartbroken that he rarely left his home nowadays. This gave the men something to talk about for the first few minutes. They also spoke about the new rail line from Bern to Thun. They wondered how long the journey to Bern would take in a steam train. The conversation naturally led to Chasper and Buolf, who were working for the rail company, and onto the whole of the family Ebner. Fridolin had a persistent bad cough and was so weak that he could hardly walk to the alehouse anymore. Further conversation about the family was stopped as Karl Stettler pointedly reminded the men that Jakob and Josef were sitting amongst them, listening intently.

"Now then men, don't gossip. What will these two young lads think of us?" He laughed good-naturedly and changed the subject. "Tell me, Edwin," he asked Mr Brotz, "how is your daughter Magdelena? I spoke to your wife the other day and she told me that she's gone to take the waters at Baden-Baden. It's nothing serious, I hope?"

Mr Brotz coughed and went a little red in the face. Mr Stettler kicked himself for asking, Edwin obviously didn't want to talk about it.

"No, it's nothing serious," he replied, "but we thought a change of air would do her good and we have friends there whom she can stay with." Mr Stettler frowned, a little puzzled, but asked no further.

The men chattered on until it was time to milk the cows. The next morning, they returned to the valley, Josef with them. Jakob and Gustl remained back, alone on the alm.

The next two weeks passed quickly. Gustl and Jakob settled promptly into their now customary routine. Jakob, already twelve years old and a tall, strong lad used to hard work, could help Gustl more and more.

"I found a dead chamois not far from the Gamchibach on the slope of the Gspaltenhorn," Jakob greeted Gustl in the dairy. He'd brought the goats back to their enclosure as dusk was falling.

"Oh yes?' Gustl waited for more information.

"It looked as if a lynx had got it, but when I came with the goats, the area was deserted. There wasn't even any carrion in the sky. Anyway, see what I've got." Jakob held out a tuft of hair taken from the neck of the chamois. "I cut it off with my knife, it's going to be terrific on my hat."

"So it is," Gustl agreed. "It's got nice colouring too. I'll help you bind it properly later. Did you see many ibex up there?"

"A few more than usual, yes. The snow's hanging on and the ground is boggy. Nothing much growing this year, I'm not surprised they're moving down."

"I've heard a couple of small stone-falls the last couple of days. It doesn't take much when the ground is as wet as this. A full-grown ibex jumping from one rocky outcrop to the next can easily dislodge stones and rocks. And you know what they say: 'it just takes one stone to start the whole mountain rolling'."

"I can't believe it's already Saturday again tomorrow and Josef will be coming."

Gustl couldn't help smiling. "What?" he asked playfully, "just twelve years old and you already sound like one of us old men!"

Jakob blushed slightly and laughed back.

"It's true though! Just one day at the factory seems to last much longer than two weeks up here."

Gustl smiled, sadly now. He hadn't had to work in a factory as a child, there hadn't been any, thank goodness. Although he had often been hungry, he was still alive. Others had died though, there was no denying that. The world was changing, he just didn't know whether for better or for worse. He finished turning the cheeses.

"Come on then," he said. "Let's get your chamois hair bound up nicely. You can show it to Josef tomorrow."

*****

Jakob was up as soon as the first streak of light crept over the alpine peaks. He decided to take his goats into a side valley and check the area for stone-fall before Josef came. He followed a brook, walking slowly so that the goats had plenty of time to graze. He scanned the top of the valley ridges looking out for ibex or a tell-tale dark line of rocks. The alm was peaceful, the only sounds came from an occasional meh from his goats, the tinkle of their bells and the gurgle of the stream.

He continued his way, thinking excitedly that in a few hours his brother would be walking up the mountain just the other side of the ridge on his left. He decided to climb up the ridge a small way. He still had his goats in plain sight, guzzling their stomachs full below him. He sat on a rock and waited. A marmot emerged from its burrow and sensing no danger started to look for food. More marmots appeared. Three chamois began to descend from the ridge above him. He always marvelled at the way they seemed to just let themselves drop, but always landed sure-footed from one rock to the next. No living being could descend the heights as quickly as chamois, he thought.

But wait! What was that? Half a dozen more chamois started dropping down from the heights as if something had startled them. A marmot let out a high-pitched squeal and they all scuttled back into their burrows. Jakob squeezed his eyes together and searched the horizon for the cause of their panic. He thought he saw a person moving along the ridge. There! He hadn't imagined it. With a blue jacket! No, it couldn't possibly be! What on earth was Ramun doing up here?

Jakob's heart raced. He wasn't sure why, except that every time he saw Ramun something bad happened.

18

1859

Jakob followed the movements of the person until they disappeared completely from his view. Then, for no logical reason, he raced down the slope to his goats and started driving them back to Gustl's wooden chalet. The goats bleated in protest – it wasn't time to return yet! But Jakob was rigorous and herded them determinedly back and into their fenced-in enclosure. The sound of their bells and loud bleating brought Gustl running out of the dairy.

"What's up? What's happened?" Gustl asked, his voice full of worry. Not once, in all his years on the alm, had Jakob brought the goats back so early.

"Up there, on the ridge, there's someone moving about, I think it's Ramun."

Gustl stroked his chin thoughtfully.

"Someone up on the ridge, you're sure? That's unusual." He continued without waiting for an answer. "But maybe it's a tourist, hiking or something. Some people from the towns, I've heard they do that nowadays."

"Not here. I've never seen anyone, ever. Anyway it wasn't a tourist, it was Ramun."

"What makes you think that, lad?"

"He was wearing a blue jacket."

Gustl shook his head.

"I know you think that the blue jackets from that school are posh, lad. Truth is, in the cities, well, there are lots of people that wear blue jackets."

Jakob began to calm down. His uncle had strewn seeds of doubt in his mind. He was right, it could've been anyone, and even if it had been Ramun, so what? There wasn't much harm he could do up here.

"I'm sorry, Uncle, I don't know what got into me, I'm not usually like that."

Gustl patted Jakob's shoulder.

"That's all right lad, everyone has a small drop-out now and again. Now then, you're twelve years old, I think that's old enough to have a small sip of your auntie's special schnapps, then you can help me in the dairy."

Gustl went indoors to fetch the bottle and Jakob sat down on an old wooden bench in the porch. His heart still thumped, but slower now. Suddenly, he heard a deep low rumble, like thunder, but it didn't stop. He looked up to the sky as Gustl came dashing out of the house.

The sound boomed louder. It didn't pause. It thundered and growled and there was a strange grinding sound. Gustl crossed himself.

"Oh my God, help us please in your goodness!"

Jakob felt his chest compressing, he had difficulty breathing.

"Uncle?" he asked, terrified.

"A rock avalanche – a big one – serious."

Gustl continued to listen, concentrating. The sound reverberated, bouncing back and forth off the mountain walls that surrounded them. It roared and rolled and grumbled. Jakob had never heard anything so terrifying in his whole life. Even the ground beneath his feet trembled. Eventually, the sound slowed down and stopped. Just an occasional, smaller rumble revealed that the mountain was still moving.

Gustl let himself fall down on the bench. He crossed himself again and stared at the bottle in his other hand as if it were an alien body. With a shaking hand he poured two good measures into two beakers. He knocked his own back and refilled his beaker before Jakob had even tried his. His voice wavered as he spoke.

"I've never heard one that big," he told Jakob, "not in my entire life. We'll bring the cattle into safety and then make our way towards Lake Tschingel. Maybe we can see more on our way. Hopefully no one's hurt; one that size, it could easily bury a whole village beneath it."

The cattle had already added to the cacophony of noise by mooing agitatedly and running from their pasture back towards the hut. Gustl just had to open the gate and they all went into their stockade voluntarily. Gustl ran back and forth grabbing a coil of sturdy rope, a pickaxe, a shovel and a spade. He gave the latter to Jakob, urging, "Come on!"

They started running down the steep mountain trail that zigzagged unevenly in a north-westerly direction. It was just a narrow path covered in loose stones, dead pine needles and fallen cones, between a forest of firs and conifers. In his haste, Jakob stumbled over a stone and fell onto his hands and knees. Gustl stopped, turned around and gave him a hand to help him up.

"Are you all right?" he asked.

Jakob got to his feet and brushed a hand over his grazed knees to wipe the grit and dirt away.

"Yes, I'm fine, nothing broken," he answered, stamping his feet to check. "Uncle, will Josef be all right?"

"Yes lad, of course! There's no saying that the avalanche crossed the route up here, and anyway, it's not very likely that Josef was passing the exact spot just at the very second it occurred."

"I knew when I saw Ramun that something bad would happen, it always does!"

"I only know about the fire at Ramberts. Is there more you haven't told me?"

Jakob realised that nobody knew about Magdelena.

"Nothing like that," he avoided answering directly, "but little things, like throwing stones at me across a stream and such." He finished, realising how lame it sounded.

"Well, he's an arrogant young man, always was even as a lad, but we don't know for sure that it was him up on the ridge, and even if it was, you can't blame him for an avalanche – that's nature."

"If an ibex can upturn stones setting a rock fall in motion then so could a person."

Gustl stroked his chin, like he always did when considering something seriously.

"I suppose if a person upturned one or a couple of large boulders, setting them rolling in motion down the mountain, then they could maybe trigger off an avalanche, but," he added, "there is a lot of chance involved. No way could someone actually plan an avalanche. Come on now, instead of speculating, let's find the damned thing and see if anyone needs help."

The track hugged one side of the creviced mountain and fell steeply down on the other. Just a tottery rope, attached loosely to short wobbly stakes, separated them from a dizzying, sheer drop hundreds of feet to the valley below.

184

They progressed with respect from the Griesalp through the Gries ravine. Below them the Gornernbach thundered, as white as frost, between jagged rocks jutting out of the river bed; a whirling vortex of white-water raging in counter-currents. Above them, tall evergreens towered towards the light. Shade-loving plants and damp moss lapped at their feet.

Gustl and Jakob crossed a rickety wooden bridge arching over the brook. The path snaked upwards again, and turning right, circumnavigated an impassable wall of rock. They followed the course of the river towards the witch's cauldron, a deep whirlpool, and the tumultuous Pochten chute. The waterfall cascaded from the heights above them, crashing down into the river.

Further along, a tributary, the Duendebach, bordered by fresh lime-green larches, formed a multilevel waterfall before making its way resplendently into the Gornernbach. Following the trail around a rocky outcrop towards a field of scree, they suddenly saw it, sooner than they had expected – a black river of granite rocks and stones, newly arisen, stretching from the towering mountain ridge above them, down into the valley.

Gustl and Jakob stood frozen, their eyes tracing the flow of the avalanche, the dark anthracite-coloured, sharp, broken rocks contrasting starkly to the green meadows and forest trees fringing the edges. As Jakob tried to take in the harshness of the scene before him, his heart turned suddenly to ice.

"There!" he screamed, pointing to a bent wooden handle sticking out awkwardly between some rocks. "It's Josef's handcart!" He scrambled across the broken rock fragments on his hands and feet like a wolf who had espied his first meal in a fortnight.

"Wait!" Gustl screamed after him. "Stop, it's dangerous!"

Occasionally, stones were still in movement, rolling downwards. Jakob paid no heed to Gustl's warnings and continued to scramble his way clumsily towards the tell-tale wooden handle. Rocks gave way under the pressure of his feet and began to slide downhill.

Gustl grabbed the rope, there was nothing to fasten it to, and using the long handle of the spade as a support, picked his way carefully across the rocks, after him.

Jakob reached the handle and frantically started to lift up the stones burying it and throw them away. Tears and snot streamed down his face, he wept like a baby, but he channelled all his energy into dispersing the stones quickly in all directions, digging the hole deeper, intent on uncovering whatever might be beneath.

"Josef!" he cried, "Josef, where are you? We're here to help. Josef, hang on we're coming!" He continued heaving the rocks away until, unexpectedly, he had the whole handle, broken off from the cart, in his hands. He held it up and crying turned around to Gustl who had nearly reached him. He sat back on his buttocks.

Gustl took the rope and tied one end around Jakob's waist and the other end around his own for safety. He bit his lip to stop himself swearing at Jakob for his foolhardiness.

"There's nothing we can do alone," he told him instead. "Help is on its way; the whole valley has born witness to the avalanche. There is hope for Josef yet, that is just his cart. Now follow me carefully back to the path, out of danger. We don't want to send more stones rolling."

Jakob stared at the river of rocks and knew his uncle was right. Josef could be anywhere. The chance of uncovering him was nil. He turned round and followed Gustl obediently to the track.

There was just one path through the Chiene valley on the right side of the River Chiene, leading out of the valley into the Scharnach valley and then onwards to Reichenbach. The path was blocked. They must return to the alm and wait until the path was cleared and secured. He supposed that he could climb the ridge where he had seen Ramun, and descend the other side, along the left of the Chiene. It would lead him directly towards Aris, but it was at the most a foot trail, including rock climbing and definitely not accessible for cows.

They reached the track above them safely and Gustl undid the rope.

"Never do that again!" he told Josef. "No matter how urgent it is. You are no help to others by putting yourself in danger. You could have started a new avalanche and been killed yourself!"

Having let the steam out, Gustl retrieved his bottle of schnapps and took a slug. He offered it to Jakob, who sunk his head and shook it.

"Right!" Gustl said, wiping his mouth with his dusty sleeve, "here's a good place to let them know over there that we're alive but in need of help."

He took a few deep breaths and then began to yodel across the hills in the direction of a solitary farm, about half a league distant, nestled in the folds of the Mittelberg. He hoped that it was occupied now, in summer.

"Ho lo-di ri-di jo ho-la djo di-ri di-a-di ri-di jo." He repeated it three times. Eventually a faint answer drifted across the valley.

"Ho-la djo di-ri-di-o di-ri-di-djo." And again. "Hola ra-di-ri di-ro di-ri-di-o."

"They'll be coming. We must return to the livestock," Gustl told Jakob. "They can't milk themselves."

The yodelling continued repeatedly, ever fainter to hear, as the message was sent from one farm to the next down and across the valleys to Weissbruegg.

*****

Help came, provisions were brought and news that nobody had been injured, but that Josef was missing. Farmer Ruedi from Reichenbach offered to walk across the fallen rock with his Saint Bernard dog, Gundi. She was given a pullover of Josef's to sniff at. Both the farmer and the dog were secured with ropes held by men lining the course of the avalanche. The rescue operation failed. It was quietly presumed that Josef lay buried too deep for even the dog to trace a whiff of scent. The temperature had dropped too.

After a week, no one hoped to find Josef alive, and he was presumed dead.

Work began securing the rocks above the path. Sturdy iron posts were hammered into the granite mountain and metal nets fastened in between. When the danger had been minimised, twenty men cleared the path and stabilised it ready for further use.

Jakob returned home from the alm for two days while his father continued to work. The grief was unbearable. He went back and stayed with his uncle, looking after the goats, until autumn arrived and it was time to return to the valley.

There was no alpine procession that year. No festivities, nor dancing, nor music. It was a solemn return and the few people lining the path removed their hats and stood in silence out of respect.

Jakob went home. He could no longer imagine sleeping on the mattress in the living room with Mina alone, without Josef. He told Anton and Regina he would sleep in the hayloft with the cattle in future. Yes in winter too, despite the freezing temperatures.

He told his father and stepmother that he had seen Ramun, on the mountain ridge above where the avalanche had begun, shortly before it happened.

"He murdered Josef!" he maintained.

"Murder? Josef? Don't be ridiculous, you cannot murder someone with an avalanche!" Anton answered crossly. He had terrible toothache that refused to go away and he'd lost his son. He had failed Lena. The last thing he needed were wild accusations from Jakob.

"He must've had something to do with it. Maybe he didn't want to actually kill him, just scare or injure him. But then it's manslaughter, I know, I've read about it!"

"Enough, Jakob. I forbid you to speak such nonsense. Isn't it bad enough that we've lost Josef?"

Jakob went to the loft. He tossed back and forth, unable to sleep. He couldn't forget Ramun. If his family refused to listen to him then he would go to Constable Struenzli, he decided.

*****

The next morning, Jakob walked to the village and took a right turn into the street where Constable Struenzli's house stood. It was painted pale green and had red wooden shutters. It stood alone, a two-storey house with a steep gabled roof and surrounded by a white picket fence. The garden was abundant with bright flowering hollyhocks, sunflowers and dahlias. They encroached on the path leading to the front door, some of them taller than grown men.

Constable Struenzli was returning from his morning round. When he saw Jakob he hunched his shoulders up, and leaning forwards slightly, began to take a lot of short tripling steps. He gained speed and it looked as if he was about to topple over any second. Reaching Jakob, he grabbed hold of his fence to stop himself falling over. He pulled himself up and giving Jakob his hand said good morning as if everything was perfectly normal, as indeed it was.

Constable Struenzli always ran like this and nobody raised their eyebrows at the sight of it any longer. Even the children who used to giggle at Sausage had grown used to this characteristic. Only when he ran together with his son, August, who ran identically, and when they stopped nearly knocked the whole fence down, were the villagers' laughing muscles overstrained.

He led Jakob inside and asked him to wait in the front room, which served as the police station. He was wearing khaki trousers and jacket over a white starched shirt with a high collar that looked as if it pinched his throat. Jakob sat on a wooden chair and peeked behind himself. He saw the constable remove his green peaked police cap and looking in a small round mirror, comb his short brown hair neatly with a side parting, and then he twirled his moustache up into two tidy curls. Satisfied with his appearance he entered the room and sat behind his desk. He took a pad of paper from his drawer and removed a pencil from a holder before him, checking that the tip was sharp.

"Now then, how can I help you?" he finally asked.

Jakob retold his story, pausing at times so that Constable Struenzli could take notes. When he had finished, the constable chewed the end of his pencil thoughtfully.

"I can visit Ramun Lauber, should he be at home, and ask him where he was that day, but if you didn't actually see him push a boulder down the ridge, well, I'm afraid there's not much I can do." The constable sounded a little disappointed, as if he would've liked to have a crime to solve.

Jakob's face fell, but as he retold all that he had seen, he realised that the facts were needy. He himself was absolutely certain that Ramun was mixed up in it somehow, but he couldn't prove it.

"I suppose I could ask the mayor too," Constable Struenzli added. "Ferdinand goes to the same school."

"Ferdinand? No, no." Jakob assured him. "Ferdinand's not like that, it was definitely Ramun."

*****

At home the atmosphere was tense. Wilhelmine, ten now, spoke with Margot and then with her parents. It was decided that she could live with Margot and Gustl permanently. It was nearer to school and she could assist Margot, making lace after school; Anton was hardly at home anyway. They would see each other on Sundays.

Jakob went to visit Berta. She had lost weight and was pale. She told Jakob that her father was ill, something to do with his lungs because of working so many years in the slate mine. He was unable to work and was bedridden. She helped her mother to tend him and often got no sleep at night.

"At least he can't beat me anymore," she said and grimaced. "What about you? I'm so sad about Josef."

Jakob told Berta the whole story again. She listened carefully.

"But why would Ramun want to kill Josef? It doesn't make sense."

"Maybe Josef saw something. You know," he said lowering his glance and whispering, "like with Magdelena or so."

"Maybe," Berta answered, "but to kill him? What could Josef possibly have witnessed to justify that?"

"I don't know."

Berta took her time considering.

"That Sunday with Magdelena, do you remember, Josef had to stay at home all afternoon as a punishment? He had to glue matchstick boxes together or something."

"Yes I remember, why?"

"Well, I'm just wondering, do you know what he had done wrong? I mean, that was a fairly harsh punishment, all afternoon. Your parents aren't usually that strict. An hour or even two yes, but all afternoon?"

Jakob saw what she was getting at.

"No, I don't know. He didn't tell me, and well, my mind was full of Magdelena, I didn't think to ask. I didn't tell him about Magdelena either, I'd promised not to tell anyone. Hmmn, maybe Mina knows, I'll ask her."

*****

Jakob saw Mina at school the next day. At break time he went up to her in the school yard, where she was drinking her milk with her friend Sylvia.

"Uh sorry, Sylvia," he said, would you mind if I spoke to my sister privately? It's very important."

Mina looked at her brother crossly and was about to protest but Sylvia shrugged her shoulders. "No problem," she said, walking away.

"What?" Mina demanded.

"That Sunday afternoon when Josef was grounded, do you know what he had done?"

"Yes, of course. Why that's not so important as to send Sylvia away!"

"What did he do?"

"He told Mum and Dad that he'd seen Hari's mother kissing the doctor."

"What? Which doctor?"

"Koefeli of course. It's not a secret, everyone knows, even Auntie Margot knows. She asked me not to mention it in front of Uncle Gustl, it's his sister after all. She said that it was only gossip but that he would be upset if he knew."

"I didn't know!"

"Well yes, but you're a boy."

"Then why did Mum and Dad punish him so severely if it's so well known?"

"I don't know. Maybe Dad hadn't known and he had toothache again. He said that Josef shouldn't repeat gossip, and particularly not such slander, and that Helga was a relative and he didn't want to hear the word kiss again, it was a dirty word and so forth. There was a big row."

"And Josef?"

"Well he grumbled of course, especially as he'd seen them himself, but he didn't dare say any more."

Jakob returned to the classroom more confused than ever. Hari's mother with Dr Koefeli? What did that have to do with anything? He racked his brain until it felt like sawdust and Mr Stettler threw the blackboard rubber at him to wake him up.

"Pay attention, Jakob! Now tell us all when the Old Swiss Confederacy established its independence from the House of Habsburg and the Duchy of Burgundy."

19

1859–1860

Anton had a bitter taste in his mouth and even he himself noticed his own foul breath. His toothache was unbearable and now the pain reached to his head. He didn't want to go to Dr Koefeli. Not just because of the rumours of his affair with Helga, but since she worked there quite a few people had complained about their medical details becoming known, sometimes to the point of ridicule. Like poor old Bert Fechtig with his piles. Half the village knew all about them, in the finest detail. Toothache wasn't so embarrassing, but he still didn't want everyone asking him about it, especially not his employer.

Dr Roessel in Reichenbach sometimes worked for the local authorities and was expensive and so Anton walked the whole way to Muelenen to Dr Tobler. The doctor pulled his tooth out with some giant pliers and charged five francs. Anton was annoyed. He walked back to Weissbruegg muttering under his breath: "A swindler, a scoundrel!" He had a rag in his mouth to stop the blood and pus oozing out and it still hurt like hell. He grumbled aloud, if that was all, he could've pulled the tooth out himself and saved the money.

Six months later he was still in pain. He considered going back to the doctor to complain and demand his money back. But then Josef died and he had difficulty concentrating at work. The director's suggestion came as a Godsend.

Anton knocked at Director Lauber's office door, not knowing why he had been sent for and hoping that it wasn't bad news. Carl Lauber bade him in and offered him his condolences about Josef, and a seat.

"As you know, Mr Schneider, we sell our matchsticks directly to convenience stores and … well, I'll get straight to the point, I'm looking for a new sales representative and Mr Haeberlin and I thought you might be interested."

"Me? But I haven't got a horse and cart."

"No, but we are pleased with your work the last eight years here and we would be willing to grant you a loan to buy a horse and cart. In fact, we already have one that you could buy from us. You would be working for a commission and should easily be able to pay the loan back in a year, or maximum eighteen months."

"Oh, so I would travel around the general stores delivering the matches they have ordered and for each order I get a commission?"

"Yes, but if you show some initiative and sell matches to additional stores, then of course you could earn even more."

"Thank you very much, sir, I would like that very much."

*****

Constable Struenzli knocked on the front door of Director Lauber's villa. A maid answered and led him indoors and into a study. Two walls were lined with books and a small fire burned in the hearth. He didn't have to wait long for Mr Lauber, who entered and poured them both a small whisky without asking. He thrust a glass into Constable Struenzli's hand, bade him to sit down, and then seated himself on a dark red leather sofa. He leaned back, crossed his legs, took a sip from his tumbler and then asked the constable what he could do to help.

The constable took out his notebook and a pencil, turned to a blank page and said: "Mr Lauber, I'm here to ask about the whereabouts of your son, Ramun, on Friday, the second of July."

"Ramun? Why on earth do you want to know? Oh wait, wasn't that the day of the rock avalanche? Oh, I understand, but that's preposterous! Why would Ramun have anything to do with that? My son studies in Paris, as he did that day also." Mr Lauber stood up brusquely and snatched the half-full tumbler roughly from the constable's hand. "I must ask you to leave now. I shall make a complaint to your senior officer in Bern." He rang a little bell and a maid entered.

"Show the constable out," he ordered.

*****

Easter came and Jakob got a good price for his goats. With only a few months of school left, he counted his money together, deciding that it was time to concern himself about an apprenticeship. Whenever he had asked his father, his questions had been dismissed with the answer that there was plenty of time yet. But his father was often away for long periods now and Jakob had seen his school friends making arrangements. He wanted to do something with his hands, preferably mechanical. He had heard that the wainwright, Franz Egger in Kandergrund, was looking for a new apprentice in autumn and thought he would try his luck there before the position was snapped up.

Jakob had no idea what an apprenticeship cost. The few boys he knew that were lucky enough to have one, were the sons of craftsmen, tradesmen or merchants. The son of the notary and apothecary, as well as Ferdinand, went to higher schools and a few even studied. Most of the boys he knew though were the sons of farmers and ordinary unqualified workers. Their future would be similar to that of their parents; a life of hard work in order to scrape enough money together to live by. He didn't want to be like his parents, he had glimpsed a better alternative.

Jakob had often been tempted to spend some of his earnings. He would have liked a toboggan, or skis, or at least his own football, but apart from Millie's coffin and the lollies after the sale of his first goat, he had been very disciplined and saved every centime for an apprenticeship and better future. He took the money from his tin and started counting. At the bottom, the money from 8 years at the factory, he had 380 francs. So much, he felt rich! With excited fingers he counted his goat money – another 253 francs. He couldn't believe his luck. Together, 633 francs. Jakob had never even heard of so much money. He was exuberant. It had all been worth it, he thought.

He replaced his money in its tin and dressed in his clean Sunday clothes. Then, with the tin under his arm, he set off to Kandergrund.

Mr Egger was filing a wooden wheel, making it smooth. He looked up when Jakob entered his yard.

"Hello lad. Aren't you Jakob, the goat boy?"

"Yes, sir. I've come to ask about the apprenticeship."

Franz Egger stopped working and wiped his hands on his trousers.

"Have you now?" he said, playing for time. He didn't want to be unkind but he couldn't imagine the boy's father having money for an apprenticeship. "Well, you'd better come in and sit down. I'm surprised because normally the fathers of the applicants come to see me. It's a matter of finances, I'm afraid."

"Yes, sir. My father is a representative for the Lauber factory and often away. He gave me permission to speak to you myself," Jakob fibbed.

Jakob took all of his money from the tin and put it on the table in front of him.

"That's six hundred and thirty-three francs, sir," he said proudly. "I've saved it all myself."

Franz Egger was impressed.

"That is a great deal of money, Jakob, you can be proud of yourself."

"Can I start working for you then, is it enough?" Jakob looked at him eagerly.

"Jakob, do you know what an apprenticeship costs?" he asked kindly.

"No, sir." Jakob was uncertain whether he had enough. Or maybe it was too much?

"Let me explain. No matter what trade you learn it is customary to lodge and eat with your master during the whole duration of the apprenticeship. Your master has to take time to teach you. He must provide your clothing. And then there are insurances to pay and you must be registered with the guild and take examinations. This all needs to be paid for. An average apprenticeship costs around eighty francs a month."

"Eighty francs a month!" Jakob did some quick mental arithmetic and was horrified. "Nine hundred and sixty francs a year!"

"At least," The wainwright confirmed sorrowfully.

Jakob's face turned bright red. He stuffed his money back into its tin, mumbled "I'm sorry, sir" and ran out of the premises.

Once out of sight of the wainwright, Jakob took to his heels and fled. Nine hundred and sixty francs for just one year! His father must've known! Why hadn't anyone told him? He was embarrassed about his appearance at Mr Egger's place. What on earth had he thought of him? Some stupid country bumpkin! He ran past the Tellenburg ruins along the river towards Schwandi. He ran long after he had run out of breath. His tin of money bumped against his hip, rattling, tormenting him. Mocking his trust in his parents. He was so furious that he nearly threw it away. Finally, out of sight of any houses or people, he threw himself to the ground and began to cry.

He cried about all the years that he'd worked at the factory without complaining. He would never return there, that was for certain. Neither before nor after school, he decided stubbornly. All those years for nothing! Nothing except a tiny dairy that his stepmother had wanted. She wasn't even his proper mother, he thought with pure hatred. She had said that she would earn so much with her cheeses that both the boys could get apprenticeships and enjoy a better life than their forefathers. Wait – it had only been finished since Josef died. A horrible suspicion crept into his mind. Had she used Josef's money? The money that he had saved up. What had happened to that? Well, just let her wait, he would confront her.

He stopped sobbing and turned onto his back angrily. He didn't bother to take heed of his Sunday clothes. He looked at his white shirt and rubbed the sleeve on the grass. Hopefully it would get some stains, that would keep his stepmother busy. He was so enraged that his thoughts swapped back and forth rapidly between asking himself what he would do now and seeking revenge upon his parents. Why hadn't his father stood up for him when Pastor Moser had visited them? They weren't really poor, not like Utz's family. And Auntie Margot and Uncle Gustl would've helped them.

He would've given them half the goat money, gladly! He enjoyed going to the alm. He wondered if Uncle Gustl knew. Of course he did, he thought bitterly. He had already offered to train him as senn. But you couldn't live from being senn and farmer. Uncle Gustl worked on building sites most of the year.

Jakob stared at the blue sky above him. A red kite circled looking for prey. His tears dried.

What did he want?

He didn't want to go to America, he wanted to stay here. This was his home. He would not go back to the factory with its dark rooms and foul air. He would like to have a house and garden here, a barn for animals and land for potatoes. He could be senn and learn how to make cheese. Maybe he could save up and build a large dairy, make more cheese and sell it to grocery stores all around the Canton, or make specialities and sell them to the big hotels in Bern and Thun.

As he thought this, a plan formed in his mind. First, he would finish school, it was just another eight weeks. Then he would go to the alm with his uncle and take him up on his offer of training to become a senn. He didn't know how many years it took to qualify, probably a long time because the training was only three months a year, but that didn't matter, he was only thirteen and he needed to earn money for a house. He could try to get a job with a railway company, like Chasper and Buolf. Work nine months there and three months on the alm.

Jakob began to get excited as a prospective plan for his future formed. He would earn his own money and save it, but not all of it. In future he would indulge in a little enjoyment too. He didn't know exactly what yet, but he wanted to enjoy life all the year round and not just in summer and on Sundays. He picked a long stem of grass and chewed on it. Eventually he sat up, and then stood up, and returned home.

When he arrived home his stepmother was still at work at the factory. He went up into the loft, and taking eight francs from his tin of money first, he put it back with his other few belongings. He lay on the straw and waited for his stepmother. He had never had so much time in his life before. Feeling hungry, he went downstairs and took some bread and butter from the pantry. He sat down and began to eat.

It was already dusk when Regina returned home, weary from work. When she saw Jakob sitting at the table in his Sunday clothes, dirty and stuffing himself full of bread and butter, she exploded.

"What are you doing here? Why weren't you at work today? Look at you in your best clothes, filthy! What do you think you're doing helping yourself to food? No work, no food!" She snatched the rest of the bread loaf away from the table.

Jakob had had plenty of time to still his temper. He took the eight francs from his pocket and laid them on the table one after the other, counting them out loud.

"There you are, eight francs for eight weeks, paid in advance as I have no intention of returning to the factory. In eight weeks I shall go to the alm and I'll never return here, ever." He stood up, and taking the loaf of bread from her hands, replaced it on the table.

"Paid for," he said.

Regina crossed her arms in front of her chest.

"Well, if you've so much time on your hands the next few weeks, you can wash your own clothing. And while you're at it you can wash mine too." She removed her dirty apron and threw it to the floor.

"Tell me, stepmother, what happened to Josef's savings? Did you steal them to pay for your dairy?"

"How dare you stand here making accusations?" Regina screamed at him. "You have no idea what it costs to feed a family. Why, your one franc a week barely paid for that loaf!"

"If it is so little then why did you make me work?" Jakob screamed at her. "I went to the wainwright today and learnt what an apprenticeship costs. You and Papa lied to me all along! You knew that I could never save enough!"

Without waiting for an answer Jakob stormed out, slamming the door behind him.

The next day Jakob went to Gustl and Margot with his tin of money. He asked his uncle to look after his savings. He no longer trusted his parents.

20

1860–1868

Early one spring morning, Utz and his younger brother, Mathis, were walking through Weissbruegg when Mathis saw Constable Struenzli in the distance. He tugged at Utz's sleeve, said "Sausage" as explanation, and ran off quickly in the other direction.

"Stop!" Utz cried to his younger brother, sprinting after him. "We haven't done anything wrong!" But Mathis had been caught a few times stealing food from a market stall. An apple, or a bun, or anything to still his hunger. He didn't want another beating or telling-off and his experience told him that it didn't really matter whether he was guilty or not. Anything happened, Sausage would come looking for him first.

Utz realised that he couldn't catch his brother up, and he didn't want to arrive late for work, so he stopped pursuing him and turned back.

The constable might have had short legs but there was nothing wrong with his eyesight. If someone started to run away from him, then he was always suspicious and

Rowena Kinread

immediately gave chase. He hunched his shoulders up, took a deep breath and charged down the road, his eyes on the ground, watching out for loose stones.

He hadn't expected Utz to turn around and completely oversaw him until he smacked straight into him, knocking him over and landing with his belly on top of him.

"Oof!" Utz yelled, trying in vain to push him off.

Constable Struenzli was completely surprised. He had winded himself and wasn't quite sure where he was or what had happened. His vision blurred until his eyes adapted to short distance and focussed on a blue blazer.

"Oy you!" he accused Utz, "what are you doing with that jacket on? It doesn't belong to you."

"I found it. Get off me, you're heavy!"

Constable Struenzli pushed himself into a sitting position, realised that he really was on top of the boy and struggled to his feet.

"Sorry, I didn't mean to knock you over. Where did you find it? You'd better come with me to the station, I need to take a statement."

"I'll be late for work."

"Stop complaining and then we'll be quicker."

At the station, Constable Struenzli told Utz to remove the blue jacket, and examined it. It was faded and dirty. In two places it was torn and a brass button was missing. He looked at the lining and there, faint but clearly readable, was a tag with the name Ferdinand Buehler.

"There!" He showed Utz the name tag. "Now where did you say you found it?"

"In Lake Tschingel, under water covered with stones. I saw a brass button glistening in the sun and took it out and dried it. I didn't steal it, I thought someone had thrown it away."

"And buried it under stones? That doesn't sound very likely. What were you doing up there anyway? It's the other side of the valley, a long way from your place."

"Fishing. We were hungry and my uncle said he'd made a good catch there. It's allowed, it's not forbidden!"

"All right, you can go to work now. I'll speak to the mayor though and see what he has to say about this."

*****

Karl Stettler was in his mid-thirties. He enjoyed living in Weissbruegg, he got on well with the inhabitants and he enjoyed his job as teacher. At first, he had wanted to change the fate of every one of his pupils for the better, but after all these years he knew that it was impossible. He helped in small ways wherever he could, but he realised that there was a limit as to what he was capable of achieving alone.

He decided that it was time to take care of his own future. He had a house and a garden, both small but comfortable, a goat and a few hens. What he needed was a wife, and be it God's will, one or two children of his own.

Karl had long ago set his eyes upon Regula Brotz. She was the youngest, and in his opinion, the prettiest of the three Brotz sisters. He had waited until now because of her age. Last week she had turned eighteen and had left school five years ago, long enough to dismiss any malicious rumours of scandal. He had spoken to her often in the street, or in her father's shop, and believed that she wouldn't be averse to his proposal, but he had never spoken to her privately and was anxious about her reaction. First, however, he must speak to her father.

On Saturday evening, like most of the inhabitants of Weissbruegg, Karl took a bath before Church the next day. On Sunday morning he dressed and groomed himself with more attention than usual and then set off to St Martin's. Mr Brotz sat before him and Mrs Brotz and her daughters were on the other side of the congregation. He was so nervous that he couldn't concentrate on the sermon and the service seemed twice as long as usual.

Afterwards, he waited outside for family Brotz, and when they had emerged from the church, shaken hands and exchanged a few pleasantries with Reverend Moser, he stepped forwards to greet them. He shook hands with Mr and Mrs Brotz and then with each of the daughters. His palm was damp with sweat. That had never happened before. He should have left his gloves on, he thought, horrified.

"I wonder if I could have a word with you?" he asked Mr Brotz.

"Yes, of course. Come back to the house with us and have a beer with me before lunch."

Mr Brotz hoped that the teacher was going to ask for Magdelena's hand in marriage. It was time she married but the number of suitable bachelors in Weissbruegg was wanting, and neither were there many social occasions to meet somebody from outwards.

Back at the house he showed Mr Stettler into his study and exchanged a few words about the weather until Mrs Brotz brought the beer and left them alone.

"So, Mr Stettler, what did you want to speak to me about?"

"Well Sir, I've settled down nicely in Weissbruegg now and find that I like it. In fact, I like it so much that I would like to settle down here permanently. I have saved some money and have a house and occupation, and well ... er ... I'd like to get married, and may I have your permission to speak to Regula please?" Karl finished in a rush.

"Regula? But she's only eighteen. No, no. First our eldest daughter, Magdelena, must get married, then Gertrud and only then can I let Regula marry!"

Karl's heart sank. "But that could take years!"

"Yes, but you may speak to Magdelena if you wish, she is available."

Karl had never even given thought to Magdelena. She looked well enough he reflected now, considering, but Regula had such sweet little dimples. But two sisters to be married first! Magdelena should find someone easily enough, but Gertrud? Well, that could take longer. She already had a distinct moustache over her lips, which he found quite disconcerting. On the other hand, Regula might not like him. She had always been sweet and polite, but well, he was a lot older than her and not very good-looking either, he admitted to himself.

"All right, I'll take Magdelena!" he told Mr Brotz. "If she'll have me."

*****

Constable Struenzli knocked at the mayor's door. He spoke briefly to Mr Buehler who referred him to his wife.

"My wife deals with all household matters; she will help you if she can."

Mr Buehler showed the constable into the front room, asked the maid to bring refreshments and said he would fetch his wife. Constable Struenzli sat down, inwardly groaning about the heat from the tiled oven. He removed his peaked cap and placed it on the low coffee table before him, along with Ferdinand's jacket.

The maid entered with a tray of cups and saucers. Quickly, he tried to stand up, as he thought a gentleman should when a female enters the room, but the chair was so low that he fell back into it, knocking the table with his knees and sending the tray with cups and saucers clattering to the floor. Mortified, the constable tried to stand up again, this time with more momentum. He succeeded, and bending over, began to help the maid pick up the china. At this moment, Mrs Buehler entered the room.

"Good morning," she said.

Shocked, the constable straightened himself up rapidly into an upright position, knocking his head on the underside of the table and sending the china flying again. Mrs Buehler rushed over to him.

"You poor man!" She said pushing him down into a chair. "Have you hurt yourself? Luzia, fetch a cold cloth for the constable's forehead, he looks quite heated."

Constable Struenzli felt his cheeks burning. He tried to calm himself by getting his pencil and notebook out while Mrs Buehler collected her broken china together.

"No, it's really not necessary, I'm fine. I'm sorry about the cups and saucers. Please let me know what they cost so I can refund the damage. I'm here about the jacket."

"Nonsense, it was an accident and probably just as much Luzia's fault as yours." Mrs Buehler was glad that she had told Luzia to bring the ordinary cups and saucers and not the good ones they usually used for visitors. But after all, it wasn't the constable's first visit here.

"No, I insist, now about the jacket."

Luzia returned with a cool damp cloth. Mrs Buehler stood up, and telling the Constable to lean back, placed it on his forehead.

"I'm fine, really." The constable struggled to sit up straight but Mrs Buehler pressed him back.

"Just a minute, it will do you good," she spoke soothingly.

"But about the jacket."

"Immediately."

"Please, let me sit up."

"There now." Mrs Buehler gave the cloth to Luzia. "As you wish."

Constable Struenzli felt completely disorientated.

"About the jacket, I found it, well not me, Utz Schmidt, I saw him wearing it."

Mrs Buehler took the jacket in her hands and saw the label.

"Yes, this belongs to Ferdinand. Thank you for bringing it, Constable, but well, quite frankly, Ferdinand has a new jacket now and this one is quite beyond repair. Utz would have been welcome to keep it."

"That is very charitable of you, Mrs Buehler, but tell me, didn't you notice it missing?"

"Yes of course, but we didn't want to bother you about such a bagatelle. It was the day after the rock avalanche you see, and you had much more important things on your mind."

"You are sure it was after the avalanche?"

"When we noticed it, yes. Why? Is this important?"

"I'm afraid the information is confidential. So, although you didn't notice it missing until after the avalanche, it could have disappeared beforehand?"

Mrs Buehler sighed. She had had her suspicions about the jacket but she hadn't wanted to accuse anyone without proof. She still didn't want to name anyone. It was only a jacket after all.

"On the day of the avalanche Ferdinand went with his school class on a field trip to Lake Oeschinen. They wore suitable outdoor clothing and boots and he left his jacket here. The next day we couldn't find it."

"Right, thank you very much." Constable Struenzli

closed his notebook and took his leave. He felt that he was getting closer to solving the mystery but was missing something. Even if he found out who took the jacket, that didn't prove anything, sadly. He would so like to solve an important crime.

*****

Karl and Magdelena went on a picnic to get to know each other better. Gertrud went with them, not so much as a chaperone – Mr and Mrs Brotz trusted the teacher to be a gentleman – but to prevent any gossip amongst the old women in Weissbruegg. They walked along a path following the Heiti Brook and then across meadows until they found a suitable place to spread out their picnic rug. Gertrud and Magdelena busied themselves unpacking the picnic basket while Karl poured them all a glass of lemonade.

They sat down and ate. Karl pointed out various mountain peaks, naming them and explaining where the mountain passes led to. It was companionable. Soon, Gertrud made an excuse to leave them alone and said she'd be back later. Magdelena had dreaded this moment, although she had pre-arranged it with her sister. Her conscience could not allow her to marry Karl without telling him the truth first.

Karl took hold of Magdelena's hand and stroked it.

"Thank you for agreeing to come on this picnic, I'm enjoying it very much. What about you, can you bear my company?"

Magdelena looked into Karl's eyes.

"Yes, very much so. But before this goes any further ..." she said, gently withdrawing her hand from his, "... I have a confession to make. I don't believe you will want to marry me when I have told you."

"What!" Karl looked startled. "I cannot believe that you

could possibly tell me anything so terrible as to make me want to change my mind."

"It was six years ago." Magdelena removed a handkerchief from her pocket and dabbed a tear from her eyes. "Do you remember me travelling to Baden-Baden?"

"Yes, your parents said you had been unwell."

"Hmmn. Well, before that, I'm afraid I acted very foolishly."

Karl took her hands in his.

"But you were so young, it can't be anything bad."

"Please, let me finish before my courage fails me. One Sunday, Ramun asked me to go on a picnic with him. He said lots of young people would be there. I really wanted to go but I was afraid my parents might forbid it, so I didn't tell them. When I arrived at the meeting point, Ramun was alone. He said that the others were waiting at the affinage. I wanted to return home but he had a large picnic basket with him and begged me to go with him. He said he couldn't eat everything alone." Magdelena wiped the tears from her eyes. "I should've known; I was so stupid! We walked up the Chiene valley to the affinage and there was nobody else there. It was deserted." Magdelena broke down, crying.

"Tell me no more!" Karl took her in his arms. "What a despicable, vile man! But it wasn't your fault Magdelena, there is no need to reproach yourself. You were young and believed in the good of people."

Magdelena sobbed. Her body heaved while Karl held her.

"I-I'm so sorry. I understand that you no longer want me now."

"My darling! What you have told me makes no difference to my feelings for you." Karl got on his knees and removed a small box from his pocket. He opened it, showing Magdelena a ring.

"Magdelena Brotz, I love you. Will you do me the great honour of becoming my wife?"

Magdelena looked at him unbelievably, and then she smiled and leaned forward to kiss him.

*****

Ramun finished his studies in Paris and returned home. His father was glad on the one hand; Ramun's escapades with women were not only getting expensive but also his reputation was becoming compromised. It was time he settled down, got married and raised a family. The only question was how to occupy him. Carl Lauber wasn't ready to retire yet and give his son the factory, but maybe he could let him take over a part of the business. He decided to speak to him first and see if he'd actually learnt anything in Paris, apart from having the makings of a Casanova.

Carl need not have worried. Ramun was eager to lay out the new ideas he had learnt before his father. He suggested opening a factory shop. The workers could buy their groceries and other necessities there, right next to their work place, instead of walking all the way to town and then all the way home again.

His idea was to let their factory workers shop there, offsetting the account against their wages. It was easy to convince the workers of the advantages of buying on credit. Should they miss a day from work, for example because of illness, then there was no need to go short, they could buy all they needed and then pay the sum back the next week.

Ramun proposed not to actually buy the products they would sell retail; he suggested exchanging the matchsticks for groceries. Convenience stores short of cash were enthusiastic. They could get rid of shelf holders, or nearly past the date wares, in exchange for matchsticks, which they could sell for cash. The factory directors passed the wares on to their workers, thus saving their wages.

Carl was pleased with Ramun. He built a shop next to the factory and appointed Ramun manager.

Ramun brought more good news home. He had met a young lady, Beatrix, the fourth of six children of Niklaus Lehmann, a private banker in Geneva.

Niklaus Lehmann was a highly respected citizen, director of several firms and town councillor in Geneva. Ramun asked his father if he might invite Beatrix and her parents to Kandermatt for a weekend.

Mr and Mrs Lauber were delighted. They organised a ball and a hunt. They hired two dozen additional maids, cooks and footmen, all to make Kandermatt shine in the best possible light.

Ramun Lauber married Beatrix Lehmann in 1867. In 1868 their son Friedrich was born. Ramun's parents sighed with relief. Ramun would settle down now, they thought.

*****

Anton backed his horse and cart up to the packing station at Lauber's factory. He loaded the cart full with crates filled with matchboxes. Then, waving goodbye to his workmates, he moved the reins to set his horse off. At first he stayed in the canton of Bern and bordering areas. Later he began to deliver the matches all over Switzerland and was often journeying for weeks on end. He visited his purchasers, mainly owners of convenience stores, and to improve his turnover, sometimes exchanged matches for wares rather than cash.

The competition was crippling. Just in the area of Weissbruegg alone there were fourteen matchstick factories, and soon cheap competition started to arrive from Scandinavian countries, which had even more forests than Switzerland.

He slept overnight in barns of friendly farmers to save money, but it was proving harder and harder to make enough profit to pay back his debts. Director Lauber didn't put him under pressure, he was only too happy to have workers dependent upon him. But then Anton got sick.

It was the winter of 1868. The temperatures had dropped to sub-zero and no matter how many layers of jackets Anton wore on top of each other, he was permanently cold. He sat on the driver's seat of his carriage, a rug over his legs, scarf around his neck and hat pulled low over his ears. The wind attacked him from all directions, howling around his ears, and depending on how high or low above sea level he was travelling, either rain drenched him, penetrating through all his layers of clothing, or snow fell upon him, not budging and turning him into some kind of abominable snowman. There weren't many people outside on the roads, and those who were didn't stop to chat and maybe buy something like they did in summer; they just gave him a quick nod and hurried on their way.

He continued to spend his nights with his horse in a cow shed, but the warmth radiating from his horse wasn't enough to warm his bones. His clothes were still damp the next morning when he reluctantly put them on again to brave the next day. He developed a cough and had terrible headaches but he continued to work, travelling and desperately trying to sell the matches.

One day, dusk had fallen as he approached a farm where he had stayed overnight several times before. He felt lightheaded and inwardly he was unusually glowing with heat. As he got down from his driver's seat his knees gave way beneath him and he fainted into the foot of snow on the ground. Luckily for him the farmer's wife happened to be looking out of the window and had seen him coming. When he keeled over into the snow, she got her husband and together they carried him indoors. They laid him down on the floor by the fire and covered him with rugs. He had a raging fever with delirium and they weren't sure if he'd survive.

Anton drifted in and out of consciousness for a whole week. Blood and pus from his mouth stained the rug below his head. Eventually, his temperature subsided and gradually he could sit up and drink some warm broth; just an excruciatingly painful toothache remained. After another week he felt strong enough to continue his travels. He thanked his Samaritans and set off back towards Bern. His toothache didn't go away and his jaw was swollen, so he tied a piece of string around his tooth and pulled it out. Part of his jaw bone broke off with the tooth. Anton held it in his hand, his breath stopped, he was terrified.

He asked people on the street where the next doctor was and they recommended Dr Weber's surgery. Dr Weber was away on house visits but his son, fresh from medical school, said he'd look at him.

Anton sat on a chair and waited. When Dr Weber junior entered, Anton's jaw fell open in surprise. The doctor looked about fifteen.

"I think there's been a mistake," he said, "I need to see a doctor. No offence, but I mean a proper one."

"Well I'm qualified, I studied at the Inselspital in Bern, but you can wait for my father if you prefer. I don't know how long he'll be though."

Anton gazed at the youthful face before him, he didn't even need to shave.

"Oh," he replied, "I'm sorry, you look so young." He

handed the doctor his tooth, still attached to a small piece of the jaw bone. "I've been having some terrible toothache and when I tried to pull my tooth out this morning, well, this came out with it."

Dr Weber stretched his hand out and looked at the tooth and bone interestedly. He pulled a large petroleum lamp nearer to Anton and asked him to open his mouth wide. Anton did so and the doctor reeled back two steps. He put the back of his hand to his mouth and turned around to a drawer. There he opened a jar of strong smelling eucalyptus cream and rubbed it under his nose. and then he covered his nose and mouth with a white linen mask. Returning to Anton with a long wooden spatula he prised his mouth open and looked again.

"Your gums are red and inflamed. Does this hurt?" He pressed the spatula against the gums on the lower jaw.

"Mmmm," Anton mumbled, unable to speak.

"And this?" The doctor pressed against the upper gums. "Nuh."

The doctor removed the spatula, turned the oil lamp lower and washed his hands. Then he sat down at his desk and began to write notes. Finally, he turned his attention to Anton.

"Mr Schneider, your gums are swollen, particularly around your lower jaw. They are red and inflamed and several of your teeth are loose. You have putrefying ulcers on your jaw and some of them have discharged into your mouth, which is why you have probably noticed a bitter taste and bad breath. Some have discharged internally into your jawbone and I'm afraid that these have caused your jaw to decay. I strongly advise you to go to the Inselspital for an operation."

"What? No! An operation for toothache? I can't afford that."

"Mr Schneider, I'm afraid I've not made myself clear. Your condition is serious. It is called phosphorus necrosis. If you leave it untreated, then it will spread to your upper jaw and eventually affect your brain. It is a life-threatening disease."

Anton slumped in his chair.

"Are you sure? How come the first doctor I went to didn't say anything?"

"I cannot judge that. Maybe the symptoms weren't so bad when he saw you, but when you go to hospital, I can assure you that they will only operate if my diagnosis is correct."

"And when do I have to go?"

"If you wish to live, as soon as possible."

"But how long would I be there, not working? I have a family to feed and debts to pay, if I'm not earning ..."

"If you die you will not be earning either."

*****

Anton rode back to Weissbruegg. It took him three days. He went straight to the matchstick factory, and finding Carl Lauber in his office, explained the situation to him.

"Can you buy the horse and carriage back from me?" he asked, hoping he would receive enough to pay the hospital bill and tide him over the time he wouldn't be able to work.

Carl took time, scribbled some figures on a scrap of paper and considered. He twirled his moustache between his thumb and finger irritatingly. He didn't have his gloves on and Anton noticed that his finger nails were missing.

"We don't usually do this, you know. It is specifically stated in the contract of purchase that a return sale is ruled out. But I'm not unsympathetic to your circumstances. If you return the horse and cart, and pay one hundred Swiss francs, then I'm prepared to consider your debt to us as balanced."

"Me pay you! But Mr Lauber, where am I supposed to find such a large sum of money?"

"You can accept my offer or leave it, but I assure you that I'm being very generous here. You will not get a better offer elsewhere."

"But I'm returning the horse and cart!"

"Now, now Mr Schneider, you have had the use of the horse and cart for many years now. You cannot expect to get that for free."

"I paid you money every month towards my debt!"

"And two hundred Swiss francs remain. I've cut that debt in half."

Anton was exasperated, but he had no choice. He left the horse and cart at the factory, and splitting phlegm on the ground outside in disgust, went to see his sister.

*****

Margot's initial delight at seeing her younger brother after so many months soon turned to concern when he told her about his illness. They had always known that working with phosphorous entailed a risk of getting necrosis but they never really thought that he would actually be affected. When Anton told her about Mr Lauber she was outraged.

"What a cheating, fraudulent, contemptible piece of shit. The arrogance! No wonder they're so rich! How dare they go to church on Sundays pretending to be good Christian people. Why it's absolutely preposterous! And to think that poor mite Utz got arrested for wearing a jacket he found. The police should spend more time arresting the real criminals. That son of his is no good either. I could tell you ..." Margot stopped before she revealed something that she'd promised not to tell. Still inwardly boiling, she went into the pantry and fetched a bottle of homemade schnapps and two glasses. She sat down at the table and patted the seat next to her. "Sit down, Anton. I'm sorry but people like that, well, they make me so angry!"

"I'm sorry, Margot, I'm so sorry but I need help, again! I'll have to pay the hospital too."

"Don't worry, Anton. The main thing is that you get better. I'll speak to Gustl when he gets home. We'll find a solution, I'm sure."

Anton left to go back to his own home and to tell Regina his news.

Margot remained brooding at the table. She didn't know what the hospital would cost, she hoped not too much, but she worried about the time afterwards. When Hans Hofstetter got necrosis he couldn't work for a whole six months.

Luckily, Jakob was self-reliant now and Mina earned enough for her keep with lace-making. Regina, however, earned merely a pittance at the factory, it wouldn't be enough to see them through. Even worse, she no longer got paid with actual money. Like all the workers there, they were given their pay in the form of vouchers that they could redeem at the factory shop. Everyone knew that the goods in the shop were overpriced, and some things simply weren't available, but it was no use complaining – they would lose their job and be replaced with somebody else the very next day.

Margot stood up to count their savings. She did well with her lace but you couldn't get rich as a craftswoman, no matter how accomplished you were. There was plenty of cheap industrial-made lace available and only a limited number of women were prepared to, or in a position to, pay for the superior handmade lace. Making her exquisite lace was also very time consuming, so she didn't have all that much to sell. Mainly she stuck to commissions.

She was still sitting at the table brooding over their tin of savings when Gustl returned home.

"What's up, no dinner? I'm starving," he said, sitting down opposite Margot and quickly helping himself to a glass of schnapps before she tidied the bottle away.

Margot told him about Anton.

"That is bad news," Gustl said, stroking his chin and feeling justified to pour himself a second glass of schnapps. "How much have we saved?" He nodded at the tin. "You've obviously counted it."

"Not as much as I'd hoped. We shouldn't have built the extra room onto the house."

"Ah, but Mina has something of her own now. Jakob will take over Anton's house eventually. Anyway, we couldn't know that something like this would happen."

"That's the trouble isn't it? Something always happens. Just when we thought we weren't doing badly. Why, I even indulged in luxuries: sugar, coffee and cocoa powder. Even perfumed soap! Really I don't know what I was thinking. What do the likes of me need with perfumed soap?"

"Now, now, don't be too harsh with yourself. We all enjoy small luxuries," Gustl said, pouring himself a third glass of schnapps. "It's not a sin, we work hard and have paid for them. What about that strip of forest I bought from Heinz to help him out? We could always sell some trees to tide Anton over."

"Oh yes! I'd forgotten all about that. That's an excellent idea! Thank you Gustl, you're the best husband ever!" Margot plonked a kiss roughly on his cheek, prickly with stubble because he'd had no time to shave that morning, and poured him another glass of schnapps.

*****

The very next Sunday, straight after church, Gustl walked up to Maeggisserenegg to inspect the bespoken section of forest. The wood from a few of the trees would be worth quite a bit now and Peter Zaehler might be interested in buying. He remembered seeing a stately oak, was a walnut tree there too? The higher he climbed, and the nearer he got to his piece of forest hidden behind the ridge, the more excited and hopeful he became. He reached the top of the ridge and looked down to the forest in the deep cleft below him.

He sank to his knees and his chest squeezed together as if in a vice.

"No, surely not!" He had difficulty in breathing and plumped down on the ground, his hand to his chest. "We're family! I helped him out!" A strange tingling sensation passed through him, he couldn't breathe. All that remained from his section of forest was an ugly scar, eaten out of the surrounding forest and completely bare of trees. "He can't do that!" he mumbled.

Gustl's brain sent him warning signals. He tried counting calmly to a hundred and then to a thousand. Gradually the pain in his chest subsided and his breathing became less ragged. He wouldn't give Heinz the pleasure of a heart attack, he thought. What a thieving devil, a rotten piece of dirt!

This betrayal from a family member hurt much more than the injustice they suffered at the hands of the rich. Gustl considered what to do. Although the notary had written his name down in the land register, he and his brother-in-law hadn't exchanged a detailed contract. They hadn't considered it necessary amongst family. Gustl had never heard of such an act before. If you sell forest, that includes the trees in it. That goes without saying. Without trees it's worthless. You don't just chop them down and sell them all afterwards. They take hundreds of years to grow.

He wondered whether to file a complaint with the magistrate. But even if the magistrate ruled in his favour, Heinz wouldn't have any money to make amends, the money from the trees would have been spent years ago. And in that case, Gustl would have to pay for the magistrate too.

He went home thinking about what to tell Margot. The truth, he supposed. But one thing was certain: as long as he lived, he would never utter one single word to either Heinz or any member of his family, ever again. They could rot in hell!

21

1860–1868

Jakob returned from the alm and celebrated with the villagers of Weissbruegg. It had been a summer without any lethal losses and the festivities were merry and carefree. He was thirteen, he had finished school and he would look for work somewhere outside of the valley. He took some of his savings from his tin that was still with Gustl, said goodbye to his aunt and uncle, his sister Mina and Berta, and then lifting his rucksack onto his back, he walked towards Thun. It was already dark, the festivities had lasted until midnight, but he only needed to follow the road beside the River Kander, and the moon shone brightly to mark his way.

Two hours later he arrived at Spiez, a small town imbedded on the shores of Lake Thun. Seeing an open barn, he decided to rest until the baker's opened, then he would have some breakfast and visit the castle. He was in no rush and had long ago decided to have the occasional day free from work, to enjoy life. He walked around the castle walls and gardens, admiring the solid square keep towering into the sky. He'd like to show this to Berta, he thought.

Jakob continued walking towards Thun. He could already see Castle Thun, far in the distance, from where he stood. It sat high, atop a hill, presiding over the city. First he had to cross the River Kander, and as he looked over the stone bridge to the water thundering down the valley from the Kander Neve glacier into the lake, he felt his stomach flutter. The sound of the water was deafening, the force of the mass of water fearsome. He was glad he was passing now, in late September, when the mass of water was considerably less than in Spring.

Scarcely a league away from Thun, he asked passers-by if they knew where the Swiss Central Railway company was based. The people enjoyed interrupting their work to stop and chat. They asked Jakob where he came from and wanted to hear news. It soon became clear, however, that since the railway had reached Thun, nobody knew for certain where the company was working now. One man suggested he go to the railway station in Thun and ask. It belonged to the company, so someone must know how to contact them.

Jakob walked to the station and found the station master who told him that the Swiss Central Railway company had their headquarters in Olten.

Jakob stared at him blankly.

"Olten? Where's that?"

"Look, here it is." The station master pointed to a town on a large map of the railway lines.

"So far away?" Jakob was dismayed. "It's way up north, I'll need at least three days to get there."

The station master grinned at him, revealing a mouth with at least half the teeth missing. "A few years back yes, not now we've got the railway though. You can be there in three hours."

"Three hours! What does a ticket cost?"

"Fourth class? Just five francs, forty-five."

"Really?" Jakob started to do some sums in his head. Why not? he decided, already excited about the thought of a new adventure.

"When does the next train go?" he asked.

He had to wait two hours, so he bought some bread and a bottle of beer. He ate, trying to remember everything anyone had ever told him about steam locomotives.

Jakob had known it would be loud but nothing had prepared him for just how loud. He stood on the platform, waiting for the train to arrive, searching down the line. The station master told him to step back. He heard a blaring horn and looked again, exuberant. Quicker than he could ever have dreamt, the huge black engine raced into the station, steam hissing and blowing in all directions. He jumped back a few steps, surprised and momentarily scared, then there was an ear-splitting screeching of metal upon metal as the brakes squealed and the locomotive stopped. When it was finally still, the last puffs of steam emerging gently from the engine, passengers began to step down from the carriages, he let his breath out and relaxed. He walked to the end of the platform and climbed up the steps to the fourth-class carriage. He sat down on a plain wooden bench screwed to the floor next to the window. He would've liked to open the window and stick his head out to see better, but the windows didn't open in this carriage, they just had a small slit at the top for airing.

His heart raced as the train got louder again and set off, chugging along through fields and meadows, past cows and buildings, at an incredible speed. Hardly had he glimpsed a building than they had already shot past. It was the most exciting thing he'd ever done in his whole life. Such a pity Berta wasn't there.

They arrived at Olten and he found the personnel manager. A badge on his dark blue blazer said he was Wilhelm Koch. He had thick black eyebrows, like two hairy caterpillars, and mutton-chop whiskers going a little grey.

"I'm sorry lad, we don't employ workers here in Olten, just the constructors and development planners. If you want to find work you must ask the foreman at one of the sites. Where do you want to work?"

"I don't mind, anywhere really. I know someone, Chasper Ebner and his brother Buolf. I don't have to work at the same place though."

"Wait a minute, I can look in our records to see if I can find their names, Ebner you say, hmmn, yes here we have one, Chasper, I can't see the brother's name though."

"He would've started a year later."

"Ah, I see. Well, sometimes the workers move on quickly from one company to the next, wherever they get a better offer. Here it says that one Ebner, Chasper, is employed in Thoerishaus at the moment."

"Thoerishaus?"

"Just south of Bern, look here." Mr Koch showed Jakob Thoerishaus on a wall map.

"Oh no! I've just come all the way from Thun, now I'll have to go back again."

Mr Koch smiled.

"Sorry about that. Before you go there and get your hopes raised, I should tell you, we get people looking for work all the time. Even if the foreman in Thoerisberg needs someone, it doesn't mean the choice will fall on you. They need good strong men, older than yourself."

Jakob looked glum.

"I don't really know what else I can do; I haven't got any qualifications. I might as well return though, I'll be nearer home. I'll say hello to Chasper first, it won't harm. His sister and mother will be glad to know he's all right."

"As you wish. The next train isn't until tomorrow. I'll speak to the station master and he'll let you stay in the station tonight, if you want, it'll be warmer than outdoors."

"Thank you."

Wilhelm Koch felt a little sorry for the boy, but there was nothing else he could do.

The next day Jakob rode the train to Bern, and then following new, unused railway tracks, walked until he came upon a work base camp. Several metal and wooden containers, like disused carriages, living quarters for the men, stood in a semi-circle around a space with a fire in the centre and logs for sitting down upon. A couple of people were about and Jakob asked his way to the foreman to whom he introduced himself.

"Sorry lad, we're not hiring at the moment," the foreman answered immediately.

After the pre-warning from Mr Koch the day before, Jakob wasn't surprised.

"Is it all right if I wait around for Chasper Ebner?" he asked, "or Buolf, to say hello? I know them from home."

The foreman looked up from his papers.

"Yes, that's no problem at all. Just sit down by the fire and they'll be back towards evening."

Jakob sat down on a log by the fire. He took his only book, the Bible, out of his rucksack and read to pass the time. As dusk fell more and more workers returned to camp. Dirty, dusty and weary, they sat down to drink and wait until the cook finished preparing a meal. Nobody paid him much attention. Suddenly, Chasper appeared. He looked taller, broader and more muscled than in Jakob's memory. Chasper recognised Jakob immediately and stopped short.

"Jakob, what are you doing here? Has something happened?"

"No, no, don't worry. I was looking for work actually, and I thought I might as well say hello now I'm here."

Chasper put a hand on his heart.

"Oh, thank goodness for that, it gave me quite a shock seeing you sitting there! And did you get a job?"

"No, the foreman said he's not looking for anyone at the moment."

"Did you tell him you can climb? We need a good climber."

"No, I had no idea."

"Come on then, I'll come with you."

*****

"Are you scared of heights?" The foreman asked.

"No, of course not!" Jakob grinned, amused at the thought that this could be a qualification.

"And you can climb well?"

"I'm on the alm every summer looking after the goats. They often get stuck on rocky outcrops and I have to rescue them. So yes, I suppose I can climb quite well."

"Ah, he's too modest, always was," Chasper interrupted. "He can scamper up and down and across all manner of rock wall faces as quick as a chamois."

"All right, we need a climber, I'll give you a trial," the foreman answered. "Get some food in you. Chasper will show you where you can sleep tonight and anything else you need, and tomorrow we'll begin."

The railway company needed to blast its way through rock to get level lines and ledges, and to build galleries along the base of hills beside lakes, to build tunnels. Experts had long ago planned where the dynamite must be placed to achieve the desired result. These places were often remote and difficult to access. They needed mountaineers to place the dynamite.

Jakob wore a leather belt, with a chisel and hammer, and sticks of dynamite. He was secured with a rope and two men watched out for him as he scurried as nimbly as a squirrel from one rocky outcrop to the next. Instinctively, he found the right irregularity in the rock for his hands and feet. He knocked holes into the rock, and hanging on the end of the rope like a spider on its thread, stuck the dynamite into the appropriate spaces. He soon earned respect from his comrades. He worked fast in all kinds of weather, never complaining that somewhere was too difficult or too dangerous to reach.

Jakob was content too. He worked outdoors, got food and accommodation, and the wages were all right too. He didn't need much and began to save for a house. He got on all right with his comrades, knowing Chasper and Buolf made it easier for him, and surprisingly they both seemed to have grown up and become sensible. The work was dangerous for everyone, but particularly for those like Chasper and Buolf who worked in the tunnels. Accidents were frequent and sometimes lethal. Considering that, it wasn't strange that Chasper and Buolf had changed, Jakob thought. Their family would be glad.

Most of the workers went to church on Sundays and Jakob joined them. Afterwards, he wrote letters and occasionally arranged to meet Berta, or his aunt, uncle and Mina. Sometimes he just explored the area.

The foreman wasn't pleased about letting him go in summer but Jakob insisted.

"If your job's gone then that's your bad luck," the foreman threatened, but when Jakob returned in September after a summer on the alm, he was eagerly awaited with a long list of jobs. Eventually, it was accepted that he was absent in the summer months.

For many years Jakob had never seen his father nor Regina. His father was hardly ever in Weissbruegg and he didn't feel connected to Regina. They didn't starve but she never really loved them. His initial anger about the apprenticeship had subsided a little over time, the church taught forgiveness, but he couldn't bring himself to take the first step towards a reunion.

*****

Hari finished school the same year as Jakob. Similarly he had no qualifications for a job, nor could his parents afford to pay for an apprenticeship for him. In addition to these negative factors he still walked with a limp due to the burns on his leg. He couldn't take on any hard manual labour; he couldn't even stand on his legs all day.

He could've glued matchstick boxes together but he told his parents that he refused to work fourteen hours a day, six days a week, for a mere two francs. His parents let him be. They felt a little guilty that they hadn't been able to give him better schooling. Something will turn up, they thought, and continued to work themselves to bring food to the table.

On Sundays, they went to church and insisted that Hari accompany them. He gave in, having already won the bigger battle. However, he stood now on the right-hand side of the congregation, next to his father, with the men. After the sermon a long hymn with many verses was announced while the offertory basket was passed along each row, and Hari put in the five centime coin that his mother gave him every week before the service. As the basket was passed along, instead of looking discreetly away while the men put their donations into the basket, he stared at their hands, mesmerised by the amount of paper notes disappearing into the basket. An idea formed in his mind.

Hari told his parents he wanted to go to confirmation classes. They were delighted. Six months later he received his confirmation. Every Sunday he dressed and groomed himself as smartly as possible and went to church ten minutes early. His zeal was noticed and occasionally he was asked to do a reading. Sometimes the pastor needed help and asked a few boys to attend a wedding or funeral service. Hari was always willing and eager, and more importantly, he had time.

In a matter of a few months Hari gained respect and trust from Pastor Moser. Along with Manfred Klopfenstein and Paul Zaehler, he was given the job of standing in the aisle at the end of the back row, taking the collection basket from the last parishioner and bringing it to the vestry. This was the opportunity he had been waiting for. Exaggerating his limp a little, he dragged behind and by the time he entered the vestry, the other boys had left and taken their places again. It was easy to remove a handful of notes and coins and push them deep into his trouser pocket, before tipping the collection into the offertory box and returning innocently to his place.

At home he put his booty into a sock and then into an old tin. He went to the outside shed and hid the tin at the back of a shelf. Hari was pleased with himself. He had taken more than twenty Swiss francs. He continued to take money at every service, never too much, he didn't want the pastor to become suspicious. In addition, at weddings and funerals the boys were often given a coin or two for helping, and the collection on these occasions was bountiful. His sock stretched, the tin became full. He buried it under an apple tree in the meadow behind their house and began to fill a new sock. His parents told everyone how pious he was and even the villagers were impressed that he went to every single service.

One day an old lady at church pressed a hundred franc note into his hand.

"This is for you," she said. "I admire your piety in spite of your disability. I expect that life was not kind to you, I on the other hand, have been blessed with a good life. Take it and treat yourself to something."

"Oh no, I couldn't possibly accept so much." Hari pushed the note back into her hand. "Not without working for it." The lady studied his face attentively but said no more.

The following week there was a knock at the Stoll's house door. Hari was alone at home, his parents were working and his sister was at school. It was the old lady. She introduced herself as Mrs Clara Vogel. He invited her indoors and made her a cup of herbal tea while she took in her surroundings.

"Mrs Vogel, I'm honoured by your visit. As you see I'm alone. Did you want to speak to my parents?"

"Not necessarily, I came to see you. I'm a widow, I live alone with my maid and cook in my house on the road to Adelboden. I'm often lonely and my eyes are no longer as good as they once were. I have made some enquiries and hear that you have difficulty finding work because of your leg injury. I wonder if you would like to visit me occasionally and read to me? I would pay you of course."

"Mrs Vogel, how can I thank you? I would be delighted to spend some time in your company."

They agreed that Hari would visit the next afternoon

and Mrs Vogel left. Hari thrust his fist in the air. He too had made enquiries and he felt as if he'd struck gold. Mrs Vogel was the widow of a rich industrialist from Geneva. She had two children, a son and a daughter, who both lived in Bern and hadn't visited her in over six years. If he played his cards right, he'd soon have enough money to travel to America.

Within a couple of months Hari was visiting Mrs Vogel nearly every day. He read to her and she taught him card games. He often stayed to dinner, and learnt which spoons and forks to use, and when. She taught him manners and which wines suited which type of meat or fish. He ate food that he hadn't even known existed and began to grow tall. One day they took the post carriage to Spiez and she bought him a suit and shirts. He was ashamed of his own family and spent as little time as possible with them.

Occasionally, Hari let a silver teaspoon disappear, or a brooch, or a ring that Mrs Vogel never wore and wouldn't miss, small sums of money, or a silver saltcellar. He took the things home and buried them with the rest of his booty in a tin under the apple tree. He didn't think the items would be missed, nor that any suspicion would fall upon himself, but he wasn't taking any chances, just in case the police came looking and searched the house.

And then suddenly, and quite unexpectedly, Mrs Vogel died.

Her children came from Bern and she was buried. Hari received a note from Mrs Vogel's notary asking him to attend the reading of the will. He was so excited he couldn't sleep. He congratulated himself on his cleverness. Other people worked hard for their living; he would inherit enough to live comfortably wherever he wished.

He dressed smartly and arrived punctually at the notary's

office. Mrs Vogel's daughter and son sat at the top of a table with the notary. The cook, the maid and Hari stood at the end of the room. The notary read the last will and testament, which left everything to Mrs Vogel's children. Then he informed everyone present that Mrs Vogel had also made some bequests. Her children smiled benevolently as the cook was bequeathed a small brooch and the maid a woollen cape. Hari held his breath, the suspense was unbearable "... and to Hari Stoll, my dear companion, I leave my bible." Hari choked. Those present presumed that he was overcome with gratefulness.

Mrs Vogel's daughter handed him a leather-bound bible with gilded pages.

"Thank you so much for being a friend to my mother," she said. "She spoke very highly of you in her letters. She said she had never met somebody so pious as yourself." Hari took the Bible and rushed from the room.

"The poor boy," the daughter spoke. "He's obviously quite upset by her passing."

Hari went home and threw the Bible onto the kitchen table. Then he went behind the curtain that separated his bed from the rest of the room and lay down, seething with anger. His mother picked up the Bible.

"Why, it's beautiful," she said. "How kind of her, she must've thought a lot of you." Hari didn't answer and his mother let him be, she thought he was grieving.

A week later at dinner, Helga spoke to Hari again: "You know son, I'm proud of you, you have done well for yourself. I have heard that some rich people in the big cities, widows and spinsters, they quite often have companions or secretaries. Maybe if Mrs Vogel's daughter or son would give you a reference, well, you could try ..."

Hari perked up. "Really? I didn't know that!"

"Yes, yes, I believe so."

"How can I find out if someone is looking for a ... secretary?"

"I don't know. Maybe Mr Stettler will let you read the paper when he's finished with it. There will be advertisements."

"Thank you, Mother, that's a good idea, I'll visit him straight after dinner."

Helga put her spoon down and smiled. Now that was a pleasant surprise, she thought.

Two months later, Hari began to work for Ernst Pfister in Bern. Mr Pfister had inherited a large city house and a fortune from his forefathers. This enabled him to indulge in his hobby, botany. He travelled the world looking for, and finding, new, unknown plants. He spent his time sketching them, pressing samples of their leaves and blooms and collecting their seeds. He was single, he didn't feel comfortable in the company of the opposite sex, and now he had returned from possibly his last journey.

Sixty years old Mr Pfister was tired. He decided to advertise for someone to help him organise his vast collection of plants and make a written memoir of his findings. He hoped that once all his sketches and scribbled notes were sorted out, that he might be able to find a publisher willing to print it all as a book. That would be his legacy.

He placed an advertisement in the Bernese Weekly Paper. Hari applied along with nearly twenty other young men. Hari showed Mr Pfister his reference from Mrs Vogel's daughter. Mr Pfister had known Mrs Vogel's late husband and so the decision was easy.

Hari was happy. After several interviews where he hadn't got the job, he had been losing hope. He was given his own room in the house and a whole day off work every week. He dined with Mr Pfister who desired company, and as Mr Pfister liked meat and had a partiality for wine, Hari soon became accustomed to these luxuries in life too. He realised that he would no longer be satisfied with a small house, or farm, with a wife and children somewhere. No! He wanted to live like Mrs Vogel or Mr Pfister, to have so many valuables that he didn't even notice when something went missing.

Hari used his days off to sell the objects that he had stolen from Mrs Vogel. He changed all his small coins into notes. When he went to America, he wouldn't want too much bulk. He gradually eased himself into Mr Pfister's trust and soon he was taking twice as many ill-gotten gains than his weekly wages. He was clever. He didn't open a bank account. He didn't want anything traceable should he be accused of stealing. Not having a good place to hide his growing fortune, he began to sew it into his clothing. He bought two new suits and a wooden travelling chest. His target was approaching rapidly, but yet he had to be patient. To travel to America alone he must be sixteen years old, and he needed a new identity.

On his next day off Hari went to the railway station. He sat down in a restaurant and watched. He studied the people passing, he looked at shady characters standing in corners and he observed silently. Towards evening he approached a man in an old torn coat, who had been standing by the kiosk smoking for over an hour.

Hari handed him a twenty-franc note folded together and said: "Laudanum." The man pocketed the note and said: "Follow me."

He stopped at a stand selling hot roasted chestnuts and digging into his coat pocket gave Hari a small phial.

"I'll give you twice that amount of money," Hari said, "if you can tell me where I can get identity papers."

Hari's preparations were complete. He had new identity papers, which made him eighteen years old and gave him the name of Ferdinand Buehler from Weissbruegg. He had thought of this when trying to come up with a name and birthplace. It was better to keep the lies to a minimum. One last big coup, he thought, and then I'm gone.

He knew the combination to Mr Pfister's safe. He had been asked to open it on several occasions and his eyes had nearly left their sockets at the sight of so many bank notes and gold coins. Of course, an empty safe wouldn't go unnoticed and the suspicion would fall on him, but by then he'd be gone and it wouldn't matter. It was unbelievable how trustworthy Mr Pfister was; he deserved to be robbed!

All the same, Hari didn't want any surprises. On the fourth Monday in November, Bern always celebrated the Zibelemärit, a traditional folks-festival. Mr Pfister gave all his household staff the day off, so that they could enjoy the colourful market stalls and the fairground. He said he would spend the day at his club.

Hari waited until everyone had left the house, saying he would join them later, and then he went downstairs to the safe. His travel chest was packed; he would take the train to Amsterdam at 10.15 a.m.

He opened the safe and started emptying the contents into a carpet bag.

"Hey! What are you doing there?"

Hari swivelled around on his feet horrified to see Mr Pfister staring at him.

"Mr Pfister! Why are you here?"

"I forgot my eye-glasses, luckily so it seems! Why you thieving—"

He started walking towards Hari but didn't get far. Hari had picked up a long, sharp letter opener from the top of the desk and plunged it forcefully straight through Mr Pfister's heart. Blood sprayed out in all directions. Mr Pfister's eyes opened wide in surprise and then he fell to the floor.

"Damn, damn, damn!" Hari cursed, quickly filling his carpet bag and running up the stairs three at a time. He washed his hands and face and threw his blood stained clothes to the floor. He put a new suit on, grabbed his carpet bag in one hand and dragging the wooden chest with the other, went out of doors quickly. Please let me find a carriage, he begged to nobody, please! But they were all busily engaged bringing people to the festival. Hari began to drag his chest down the road. It was hopeless. He looked around. The street was empty.

"Shit, shit, shit!" he cursed, stamping his healthy foot. He was wondering whether he should carry the chest and leave his bag behind when he saw a lad with an empty barrow returning from the market.

"I'll give you twenty francs if you take my chest to the railway station," Hari offered.

The lad's eyes opened wide. He tipped his cap. "Yes guv, thanks!"

They made good progress until they reached the inner city. The whole city was congested with hundreds of stalls selling everything from plaited strings of onions and garlic to ceramic pots and tasty foods giving off spicy aromas. Young visitors were scattering confetti in the streets. There was so much bustle that they had to fight their way forwards.

Hari cursed again. He hadn't thought this through properly. He promised to himself that if he ever managed to get the train, he'd never make such a stupid mistake again. The minutes ticked by quickly. Hari glanced around in all directions dreading to see policemen pursuing him.

"I'll give you an extra ten francs if you get to the station by ten," he told the boy. The lad pushed and jostled, threaded and weaved his way through the throngs of people. Hari stuck close to him, pushing from behind. The Bernese housewives in their best dresses swore at them heftily but they bored their way through the masses like worms eating their way through wood. They arrived at the station at ten past ten. Hari snipped his fingers for a porter, thrust two bank notes into the lad's hand and then raced to the platform. He climbed into a first class cabin and sat down on a red velvet cushioned bench. The train left almost immediately.

Slowly, he let his breath out and began to calm down. That was close, he thought, ordering un café americano from the waiter. But he was safe now. In fourteen hours the train would arrive in Amsterdam where a sailing ship would set sail for America tomorrow, and nobody would be looking for Ferdinand Buehler.

The next morning, Hari boarded a proud three-master, ready to set sail to New York. A steam-run tugboat hauled them out of the harbour into the open sea. A light wind came forth and the captain gave orders to hoist the sails. The sailing ship gathered speed and the tugboat returned to harbour. Hari went on deck and took deep breaths of salty air. Free, he thought, I've done it!

The passengers were sleeping. Towards midnight, a steam ship coming from the English coast collided with the left side of the three-master tearing away the upper part of the rigging and about thirty feet of the ship's panelling. The impact caused an almighty jolt whereby the crew and passengers awoke. The crew ran back and forth, one commando followed the next, the male passengers were ordered on deck to help fix the mast, however possible.

Women and children, and even men, screamed and shouted. With huge effort they finally managed to fix the mast and to seal the leak on the waterline. The noise quietened, especially now the return to harbour was initiated. The distress flag was pulled up but was of no use until at one o'clock the next day, the tugboat that had pulled them out to sea, came hastening towards the ship to bring it safely back to harbour.

Hari feared the worst and truly the dock was teeming with policemen. Swiss authorities had asked for the help of French, Belgian and Dutch police to watch the European harbours for the murderer of Mr Pfister. As the passengers began to disembark, young men travelling alone were sorted out and their papers scrutinised. Hari's heart plummeted, he saw no other way but to try to bluff his way out of the situation, but this time nothing helped him. His papers said he was Ferdinand Buehler and that he came from Weissbruegg. That alone with his age was enough for him to be led away and imprisoned in Amsterdam for further investigation.

*****

Berta's father, a former slate miner, had fallen ill with silicosis, a lung disease caused by breathing in the dust at the quarry. He was sick for many years, the illness progressing until he became bedridden. Berta had finished school a year before Jakob, but as long as her mother needed help to care for her father, she knew she couldn't leave the valley. Eventually, her father died and Berta and her mother became used to sleeping through the night again without interruption.

They didn't need to work at the matchstick factory because not only did Chasper and Buolf send money home every month, but also her eldest sister Anneli, now head of housekeeping at the hotel where she worked in Thun, and her two other sisters Trudi and Dorli, who worked at the same hotel, contributed to their living costs every time they visited. Berta's mother, Elsa, felt very blessed to have such loving children. In 1862 her youngest children, the twins, finished school too. With a heavy heart Elsa decided it was time to let Berta go. The young girl needed to see something of the world before she settled down to get married. When Anneli next visited, she agreed to let Berta go with her. At least Thun wasn't too far away and she knew Berta would visit.

Berta was happy. She loved the valley but she needed to get away for a while. She brushed her long brown hair neatly, fixing a low roll at her neck, and she put on her best brown dress with a lace collar. She didn't have many belongings but she packed a bag with her second dress, a brush and comb and some underwear. Tying a bonnet under her chin, she kissed her mother goodbye and set off along the road to Spiez with Anneli.

22

1868–1875

The brutal murder and theft in Bern made the headlines. Detectives came to Weissbruegg searching for Hari and questioning his family as to where he might be hiding. His parents insisted upon there being some misunderstanding, their son was a good boy and pious, he wouldn't hurt a fly. Nobody had any information.

"He'll be in America." Jakob gave Berta his opinion when they next met.

The Swiss police also suspected that Hari would try to flee Europe. Had the three-master not been involved in the havarie, they would have been too late. As soon as they received a telegram from the Dutch police informing them about the arrest of a suspect named Ferdinand Buehler, they spoke to Ferdinand's father and satisfied themselves that Ferdinand was at boarding school. Three detectives were sent to Amsterdam to bring Hari Stoll back to Bern where he was thrust into prison to await trial.

Clara Vogel's daughter felt awful about having recommended Hari to Mr Pfister, whom he had then murdered. She even wondered if Hari had had anything to do with her mother's death. She remembered his reaction at being left her mother's bible. Maybe she had misinterpreted his grief and he had in truth been hoping for more. She asked to speak to the detective in charge of the case.

Hari had been robbed of his fine clothes in Amsterdam. His prison mates had torn them apart and argued over the gold. Sewing money in clothes was an old trick and his fellow prisoners were hardened criminals. The duration in prison had been hell. His body had screamed in pain at the loss of addictive laudanum. He had no money to pay bribes and his hardened outer shell crumbled away, leaving an insecure, shaky young man.

The three detectives that brought him back to Bern were rough and harsh. He was put in a cell together with twenty other callous convicts and he spent his time cowering in a corner, hoping not to get beaten.

It was a relief when he was brought to a detective for questioning. He admitted killing Mr Pfister. He said he hadn't wanted to, but that he'd been caught stealing red handed and had automatically reached for the knife and used it..

"That is no excuse!" the detective retorted angrily.

"Yes, I know, I regret my action and would like nothing better than to make it undone."

"What about Mrs Vogel? Did you act in affect too? What did she do to you?"

"What? No, no, you've got it wrong. I didn't murder Mrs Vogel, nor Josef! I liked Mrs Vogel, I wasn't even there when she died, and with Josef, well, it was a mistake. I just wanted to frighten him, I didn't know that moving a few rocks would start an avalanche!"

The detective knew nothing about a Josef but did not reveal the fact. He sent Hari back to his cell and determined to speak to Constable Struenzli before he presented the case against Hari to the judge.

Back in his cell, Hari made himself small in his corner and thought about Josef.

He hadn't thought about him in years, but he remembered every minute of that fateful day perfectly.

He had been bored. School had broken up for the summer as it was usual for farmers' children to help bring in the hay and the rest of the harvest. Chasper and Buolf had been unavailable, and even Utz had been kept well occupied by his parents in the Spissen. He had brooded, indecisive about what to do.

He had gone to Ferdinand's house, hoping he was bored too, bored enough to communicate with Hari again. He had walked to the mayor's house and lifted the shiny brass knocker. A maid had answered and let him step indoors.

"I'd like to speak to Ferdinand," he'd said.

"I don't think he's in but I'll ask the mistress," she'd replied and had hastened down the corridor. She'd knocked at a door and entered, closing the door behind her. Hari had heard voices but he hadn't understood what they were saying.

Looking around, he had seen Ferdinand's blue jacket hanging in the cloakroom. He'd hesitated, then grabbed it quickly and stuffed it into his rucksack.

The maid had returned.

"I'm sorry but Master Ferdinand isn't here. He's on a school trip."

"Thank you. Goodbye," Hari had said before leaving, furious. School trip? What was his blue jacket doing there then? Typical high and mighty folk, thinking they could just lie to him, as if he was some goof straight from the gutter.

He'd kicked his feet angrily on the ground and marched off towards Reichenbach. He hadn't really been thinking, nor had he had a plan in his head, but he'd crossed the River Kander and had started walking up the Chiene valley. When he'd thought nobody would see him, he'd stopped, taken the jacket out of his rucksack and put it on. He'd carried on walking all the way to Lake Tschingel, but even the strenuous exertion had failed to dispense his anger. He had felt as if the whole world was against him.

He'd continued to walk up the Chiene valley, still dissatisfied and disgruntled. It'd annoyed him that Ferdinand wouldn't have anything to do with him. It was all Josef's fault for calling his father a thief. The scar on his leg had begun to ache. That was Josef's fault too! If he hadn't called his father a liar, then Hari wouldn't have wanted to scare Wilhelmine with a boelima.

He'd started climbing up the creviced mountain away from the path. He'd hoped that the different kind of movement would hurt his leg less. It didn't, but he had been halfway up the mountain, and had decided that he might as well go the whole way up. He might discover an eagle's nest and could steal some eggs. He could sell them for a huge amount of money. He had cheered up at the thought of it.

When he'd reached the top of the ridge, he'd looked down. Far away in the distance he'd seen a figure pulling a handcart up the Chiene valley path. He'd squeezed his eyes together but still hadn't recognised who it was. He had begun to walk along the ridge in search of an eagle's nest when he'd heard goats bleating below him. He'd looked down and seen a goatherd. That must be Jakob, he'd thought, the alm his uncle used was up there. Then the boy coming along the path, the one with the handcart, that must be Josef! An idea had formed in his head.

He'd gone back along the ridge, hunting for a suitable place. At one point, a rocky outcrop jutted over the mountain, directly above the path Josef had to take. Ideal, he'd rejoiced. He'd found some heavy boulders, several about the size of footballs, and had rolled them to the edge of the outcrop. Perfect, he'd thought. He'd waited until he'd seen Josef coming around the corner and had pushed the first boulder over the edge. He'd heard it crashing on the path below. Then he'd pushed the other boulders off in rapid succession, one after the other.

Suddenly the mountain below him had growled, grumbled, and then it had started to slide. He had been terrified and had run backwards as fast as he could, just before the whole rocky outcrop upon which he'd been standing, gave way and crumbled downwards. Hari had darted further away, the mountain ridge roaring and disintegrating before his eyes. He had raced without stopping, as quickly as his legs would carry him, stumbling in his fright, scrambling to get away.

He had sprinted all the way back to Lake Tschingel, then he had sat down, shocked and trembling. He'd stayed there, petrified, realising what he had done. Eventually, his mind turned to self-preservation. He'd bent down to drink and seen his reflexion in the surface of the lake, but he'd found no pleasure in it. It wasn't the jacket that was desirable, but rather the position it represented. A scholar at the Berchtold Haller Gymnasium in Bern. He'd torn the jacket off, and wading a little into the lake, pushed it under water and covered it with stones. Nobody would find it there. He could never have worn the jacket publicly anyway. Everyone would have known he had stolen it and put him together in one pot with his father.

Had Josef died? He must have, no way could he have

survived such a gigantic rock fall. He had known that he had to get home undetected. If anyone saw him, they would immediately suspect that he had had something to do with the avalanche, but it hadn't been his fault! How could he have known that moving a few rocks would cause an avalanche? Maybe Josef hadn't died. Maybe he'd got out of the way in time, but it would be best not to take any risks. Soon people would be coming to help. They would come up the Chiene valley path on the right side of the river. He had taken the other way, along the rough tracks on the left. If he'd have seen anyone, he would've hidden.

The detective spoke to Constable Struenzli and learnt about Josef's death in an avalanche. No judge would call that murder; at the most manslaughter. He told the constable what Hari had admitted, leaving it up to him whether to inform Josef's parents or not. The detective completed his case against Hari for the murder of Mr Pfister. A trial took place and Hari pleaded guilty. Due to his age and remorse, the judge ruled that he should be imprisoned for life instead of the death penalty. Hari would have preferred the latter.

*****

Anton had his operation on the 23rd of May 1868 at the Inselspital in Bern. Half of his lower jaw was removed. He spent two weeks in hospital and then returned home. His head was bandaged from under his chin, over his head, and from one ear to the other with a narrow slit for his mouth and under his nose. Regina mashed his food and he ate with a spoon. He tried to speak but nobody could understand his mumbles.

Jakob returned to Weisbruegg the first week in June. He had heard that his father was ill and knew that the time had come to let bygones be bygones. He walked home and found his father half-asleep in a chair. He picked up their only book, the Bible, and began to read aloud to him.

"Is it all right if I stay here for a few days before I go up to the alm?" he asked Regina.

"Of course, it'll be nice to have your company."

Regina hadn't hugged or kissed him upon his return, but she had baked his favourite cake and put a candle on the table. Jakob appreciated that.

When night fell he climbed up to the animals' quarters and made himself comfortable in the loft. He fell into a deep sleep immediately but was awoken a few hours later by voices, cries of pain, and Regina moving about downstairs.

The next morning he took over some chores, fetching water from the well, lighting the fire and milking the cows.

"Thank you," Regina said when she came to breakfast.

"I heard Father in the night. Does he wake often?"

"Yes, every night. He's in pain."

"Did the doctor prescribe something?"

"Yes, laudanum," she said, showing him the bottle on the table, "but the doctor said I shouldn't give him more than five drops, three times daily."

"Is it expensive? Do you need money? I mean ..." he added, a little embarrassed " ... you can't work if you're looking after Papa."

"If you can spare anything, then yes please. We have debts too. The hospital fees and Mr Lauber wanted a hundred francs for taking the horse and cart back, but that's paid. Gustl is helping us and Mina, as much as she can, too."

"I have some savings, enough to tide you over. Let's hope he recovers soon."

"If I ask for poor relief I must mortgage the farm."

"No, don't worry, I have enough."

"If-if your father dies, he promised that I could always live here."

"Yes of course, the farm belongs to you as much as Mina and me."

"Can I keep my room?"

"I don't see why not." Jakob felt slightly irritated now. "But Papa is still alive and will hopefully get better soon."

The summer passed and Jakob returned from the alm. His father was no better. His jaw was disfigured, he couldn't chew and his speech was unintelligible. He was suffering unbearable pain. Jakob took him to Dr Tobler in Muelenen.

"The necrosis has spread," Dr Tobler told them, "the other half of his jaw must be removed."

Jakob didn't return to the railway company in autumn. He stayed in Weissbruegg and helped look after his father. He took over the farm work and with his savings he made some repairs. When a field came up for sale he bought it. He bought a horse, a cart and a plough.

Anton's condition worsened. In 1869 he died and was buried in St Martin's graveyard. After the funeral, Jakob wondered whether to stay in Weissbruegg or to return to the railway company. It depended on one person.

Jakob wrote to Berta and arranged to meet her in Weissbruegg on her next day off. He bathed and dressed in his black, traditional leather suede jacket. He packed a picnic basket with roasted chicken, freshly baked bread and strawberries, cream and a bottle of bubbly wine. He covered everything with a soft rug and reflected whether he had forgotten anything. He tapped his pocket to make sure the small box he'd gone especially to Thun for was still there. His other pockets were full of candles and a box of matches.

On the way to Berta's mother's house, Jakob picked a bunch of wildflowers, then with a heart thumping with nerves, he knocked at the door. Berta opened it. The sight of her took his breath away and he nearly ruined all his plans by proposing to her there and then. Her brown hair shone like horse chestnuts, her eyes sparkled and she smelt like a summer meadow. She too wore her traditional dress and she carried a shawl across her arm.

Jakob and Berta strode out into the sunshine, the fresh alpine air engulfing them. "Where are we going?" Berta asked.

"It's a secret, but no doubt you'll work it out soon enough."

"The Tellerburg?"

"No."

"Am I dressed suitably?"

"Yes. You are beautiful," he added, turning to look into her eyes.

"Maybe the waterfalls?"

"If I tell you then it won't be a surprise."

Berta pouted playfully. "Can you at least tell me how far we're going?"

"Not much further now. Shall I carry you?"

Berta squealed and ran on ahead. "You'd like that wouldn't you?"

"Yes."

Berta continued running on ahead, just out of his reach.

"No chance!" she said and laughed.

They wandered uphill for miles until they came to a forest that Berta had not previously explored. A path entered the woods. It wove its way on soft earth, over tree roots and loose rocks, around proud fir and deciduous trees and mighty boulders. They held hands and walked along the trail silently, listening to the songs of the birds, animals and insects. The sun's rays filtered through the branches overhead and warmed their limbs.

The path led abruptly downhill. It was narrow, trodden down by an animal, or several animals walking in single file. It twisted and turned around huge boulders, some covered or partly covered in moss, resembling grotesque monsters. Berta stepped over a fallen tree, startling a red squirrel. It raced up the trunk of a tall pine, running vertically, and then sat motionless on a branch, watching them. The path wound its way steadily downhill, sometimes so steep that Jakob stretched out his hand to help Berta. Then suddenly she saw it. Somewhat to the right, hidden in the fir forest, lay a small lake.

Enchanted, she went down to the lake's edge and gazed into the shimmering water. It was crystal clear, every fish and every single stone at the bottom of the lake, easy to recognise. She gasped in delight.

"How did you find this?" she whispered to Jakob, so as not to disturb the peace.

"That is my secret, we should keep it as our special place together." He laid his rug on the ground and set the picnic basket upon it. Berta removed her socks and shoes to go to the lake.

"Wait here!" he said, "I won't be a minute."

Berta dipped her feet into the tiny ripples at the water's edge. Sand and tiny morsels of grit danced between her toes and tickled the soles of her feet. She swept water up between her hands and drank the pure, icy water. Berta had never had any doubts about her future. She had enjoyed experiencing something different than the valley and also taken pleasure in meeting different people, but she loved Jakob, at first as a brother but when puberty kicked in, she had dreamt of him quite differently. He always treated her with respect and listened to her thoughts and ideas. She hoped today would be the day he asked her to marry him. She wouldn't be sorry to turn her back on Thun. The town was picturesque, but so was Weissbruegg, and farm work was definitely preferable to emptying chamber pots. Jakob ran back quickly the same way they had come, to a small clearing. The firs surrounding the space were dense, so that only a little hazy sunlight penetrated through their needles to the floor. He pushed the candles into the soft earth, lit them, and ran back to Berta.

"Close your eyes," he said, taking her hand, "and follow me. No peeping!" He led her to the clearing. "All right, you can open them now." Berta opened her eyes and gasped. The burning candles read 'I LOVE YOU'.

Jakob fell on one knee, removed the ring from his pocket and holding it out to Berta asked: "Will you marry me?"

Berta clasped her hands together before her chest.

"Yes!" she replied and leaned forward to kiss him.

Jakob beamed. They had been together for a few years now, a proper pair not just friends, but he had still been uncertain of her answer. She had tasted life in a city with all its attractions, and met plenty of well-dressed, well-groomed young men, many with much better prospects than himself.

They agreed to wait until a year after Anton's death before they married, it would be respectful and anyway, they had so many plans. Jakob wanted to extend the farm with an extra bedroom for himself and Berta. He didn't want to begin his married life on the floor in the sitting room or in the loft, and that way Regina could keep her room for herself. They also wanted to enlarge and improve Regina's dairy. He was an excellent cheesemaker himself now and was full of ideas about making gourmet cheeses for expensive restaurants in Bern and Geneva.

Jakob and Berta married in spring 1870. The wedding took place at St Martin's church, followed by a vibrant party on the village square. It had been decorated with flowers and long tables set out. Roast sucklings turned on three spits, beer was drawn from three large barrels and musicians played. In the centre was a wooden platform for dancing. It was a celebration to be remembered for years to come.

A year later, Berta gave birth to a baby girl. They called her Lena after Jakob's mother. Eighteen months later, a second little girl arrived. She had blue eyes and blonde hair. They called her Gretl.

Two years after Gretl's birth Regina started feeling unwell. Sometimes she would go about her work for weeks without complaining, but these periods grew shorter. She refused to go to a doctor.

"Don't you think it would be better?" Berta asked tentatively. "The pain is recurring more often, maybe a doctor can help."

"Steal my money more like! Look at all the money we paid them for Anton and he still died didn't he?" Regina retorted. It was difficult to argue.

"It's her own decision," Jakob told Berta. "When she is convinced of something, no arguments will change her mind. She distrusts all doctors; maybe something happened when she was younger."

Eventually, in 1875 the pain was so bad and so frequent that Regina allowed Jakob to take her to Dr Koefeli. He examined her and detected a tumour in her abdomen.

"I'm afraid that it is quite large," he told Regina frankly. "There is nothing that can be done. It is too late to operate, but I can at least prescribe you laudanum for the pain."

"I told you doctors were useless," Regina complained to Jakob as they walked to the apothecary.

Jakob had almost been expecting such a diagnose but he was still stricken with sorrow and concern.

"I hope the laudanum will reduce your pain," he said.

Regina answered with a grunt.

23

1875

Lena, now four, was playing with Gretl, two and a half. They had a small rag doll that Berta had made for them and were sitting on the floor playing families quite contentedly. A baby boy, Albert, aged six months was asleep in his cot. It was Saturday evening and their parents were preparing the weekly bath. They had carried a large metal tub indoors and placed it in front of the fire. It was half full with scalding hot water.

"Can you look after the children while I draw some more water from the well?" Berta asked.

Jakob looked up from his newspaper at the peaceful scene in front of him.

"Of course," he answered, "or shall I get the water?"

"No, it's fine," Berta said, "I need to use the outhouse anyway." She went out of the house.

At that moment Regina called from her room. "Jakob! Jakob come quickly!"

"Can you wait? I'm watching the children," Jakob shouted back.

"No! Come quickly, I've got the runs, aagh, quick, it's urgent – I can't hold it!"

Jakob got up sighing. The children were still playing peacefully. He went into Regina's room. She was sitting up in bed distraught.

"I couldn't hold it," she said miserably.

"It doesn't matter."

Jakob comforted her and helped her onto a wooden commode next to her bed. He took her nightshirt off and helped her put a clean one on. The whole time her bowels were blubbering and spluttering into the bowl beneath the commode. Jakob tried not to wrinkle his nose, the smell was worse than the outhouse on a hot summer's day. He grabbed one towel after the next, trying to wipe the worst away.

Suddenly, an ear-splitting shriek came from the sitting room. He heard an iron pail clattering to the floor and rushed next door, terrified that something terrible had happened to Berta. She had thrown herself to the floor and he saw her pull Gretl out of the tub of scalding water. His beautiful little girl lay lifeless on the floor. He got to her in two strides and pumped her heart, again ... again ... come on now! Gretl spluttered, he turned her head sideways so she could be sick and then carried her gently to the sofa.

"My poor little treasure," he spoke. "Does it hurt anywhere?"

Gretl looked at him and Berta bewildered. She started to cry. Berta undressed her and put some calendula cream on her red skin.

"This will soothe your burns," she told Gretl. "Would you like some warm milk?" Gretl didn't react.

"Me too," Lena wailed.

"Yes, you too," Berta murmured comfortingly. She brought two mugs of warm milk to the sofa and the girls sat next to each other and drank.

Jakob and Berta watched Gretl carefully over the next few days. She didn't get a temperature and the burns were luckily only mild, but she seemed to be daydreaming all the time and didn't always react when they spoke to her. Berta was worried; something didn't seem right.

"Did you see Gretl fall into the water?" she asked Lena. "Was her head under water long?"

Lena knew they had been naughty and began to cry.

"We wanted to bathe Baby," she explained. Baby was the name they called the ragdoll. "But the water was hot and I dropped her. Gretl bent over the edge of the bath to get her out and fell in. I called Papa but he didn't come, so I tried to pull her out myself but she was too heavy."

Jakob put his hands over his eyes.

"Oh my god, I didn't hear her! Regina was full of diarrhoea. I shouldn't have left the room but they were playing peacefully and Regina was shouting!"

"I think we should take her to the doctor," Berta said. "Something's not right."

They went to Dr Roessel in Reichenbach, not wanting to be interrogated by Helga Stoll who still helped out at Dr Koefelis. They didn't know what was wrong with Gretl, but whatever it was, they would need to come to terms with it themselves before the whole of Weissbruegg was informed by that evil woman. Dr Roessel examined Gretl carefully, asking questions. He looked inside her ears.

"I can't find any physical problem," he told the worried parents, "but watch this." He put his hands near to Gretl's right ear and clapped them loudly together. Gretl showed no reaction, she didn't even flinch slightly. The doctor repeated the experiment on the left side with the same result.

"I'm afraid that Gretl is profoundly deaf. It may have been caused by the shock of the accident. Maybe she will get her hearing back in a month, or a year, maybe not at all."

Berta and Jakob looked at each other.

"What can we do?" Berta asked Dr Roessel.

"Well, so long as she cannot hear you, you should always look into her face when you speak to her. Try to pronounce words slowly so that she can read your lips and make signs for certain things that recur often. For example, point to her bed when it's time to go to bed, or to a bowl of water to wash her hands. You will think things out for yourself with time."

Berta and Jakob left the doctor's surgery with Gretl and began to walk home to Weissbruegg. At first they were both very quiet, lost in their sorrow.

"It was my fault!" The words burst from Jakob's mouth. The guilt had been weighing heavily on him since the accident, although Berta hadn't accused him.

"I would have gone to Regina too, had you been getting the water." Berta told him sincerely. "We must think of Gretl now. It's happened, and putting the blame on somebody won't help."

"Why does everything always have to happen at once?" Jakob moaned.

Berta began to pick some dandelions and Gretl copied her. "Dan-de-li-ons," Berta spoke, looking at Gretl.

"Dan-de-lons." Gretl made an effort to repeat the word.

"It will be all right." Berta smiled at Jakob. "You saved her life. She is alive and we'll manage the rest."

Jakob took hold of Berta's hand and gazed into her eyes, deep pools of love. He thought his heart would tear apart. Gretl saw them holding hands and squashed herself between them, taking one hand from each, beginning to swing and laugh. Her parents laughed too.

"Yes, we'll manage," Jakob agreed.

24

1875–1877

Regina died and was buried, life for the Schneiders continued.

Gretl's hearing didn't return. She learnt to read lips and understood most things when people spoke to her carefully and slowly, mouthing syllables in an exaggerated fashion. When she spoke herself, the words came out unclearly, sometimes too loud and sometimes nearly silent, always with a small break between the syllables. Berta and Jakob treated her the same as their other children. After Albert, they had two more boys, Martin and Oswald. All their children had their share of farmhouse chores but none of them went to work at a factory. Jakob and Berta were proud of that.

When Constable Struenzli had heard about Hari's role in the deathly avalanche, Anton Schneider had been ill and he had decided to wait six months after the funeral before informing Regina and Jakob, but then he had heard about the forthcoming marriage and didn't want to spoil it. Gretl's accident and Regina's death had postponed his report further. Eventually, he saw no reason to delay any longer. One Sunday afternoon, he visited Jakob and Berta and repeated Hari's admission and remorse.

"So I was right!" Jakob said, "though it never occurred to me that Hari might've stolen the blazer. And Ferdinand?"

"He really was on a school trip; he was wearing outdoor gear. They noticed that the blazer was missing the next morning, and even suspected that Hari had stolen it, but they didn't want to make a fuss after Josef died, and neither did they have any proof."

"It wouldn't have changed anything," Jakob surmised. "Josef was already dead, because of calling Hari's father a thief, which we all know to be true!"

Berta took hold of Jakob's hand.

"At least you know what happened now, my treasure. Thank you, Constable, for letting us know."

The appalling situation in the matchstick factories had finally caught the government's attention. At the end of 1865, it had been forbidden to employ children under the age of seven. An order was issued stipulating that a curtain was drawn around the bucket that was used for a toilet, so that particularly the women had some privacy. The government also ruled that there be washing facilities and better airing. In fact, nothing much changed. The younger children worked at home gluing matchstick boxes together, which was better than sitting in the factory all day, but in spite of once-yearly inspections, there was still a lack of washing facilities and nothing changed to improve the polluted air.

When she was six, Gretl went to the village school like all the other children. She even learnt to read and write. She did her best, she couldn't keep up with the other children who had perfect hearing. There was a boy in her class who

260

had had meningitis as a toddler. He had suffered a high temperature over many weeks and lost his hearing too. Mr Stettler sat Gretl and the boy together and gave them different exercises from his other pupils.

Gretl worked as hard as everyone else and was capable of doing simple jobs. She was pretty with blue eyes and long blonde hair, which she tied in two plaits with a large bow at the end, but she had difficulty making friends with other girls her age.

*****

In 1875 Carl Lauber died unexpectedly. He had been walking home from the factory one evening when he just suddenly collapsed and died. The doctor said it was his heart. He was buried and Ramun, now thirty-five, took over his father's position as director of the matchstick factory.

Ramun built a separate wing onto his father's villa for his mother. He moved with his wife, Beatrix, and son, Friedrich, into the main house. Friedrich was already seven years old but after his birth no further offspring had come. Friedrich's birth had been difficult and the doctor had said that Beatrix's health was fragile and that they should wait a year before trying for more children. Beatrix went on long vacations to her parents' home in Geneva and visited expert doctors who specialised in women's troubles. She went to spas and took the waters, but she remained pale and of delicate health.

Ramun wasn't a patient person. He looked for other opportunities to satisfy his sexual drive and had no patience to be discreet. He always took what he wanted, with no consideration for other people's feelings. Nor did he care about gossip. He was so arrogant that he thought nobody would believe the word of a working-class girl against his own. The villa had staff: his wife's personal maid, a cook, a scullery maid and another girl for cleaning. The scullery maid was a bit unkempt but she was young and had a good figure. What was her name? Alice? Yes, that was it.

One day he cornered her in the stables and began to pay her compliments. He complained about his wife and offered her five francs if she would satisfy him.

Five francs was more than a month's wages for the girl and she agreed.

"Not orally, just with the hand," she determined, and he agreed.

After the first time, it became a regular occurrence two or three times a week. He offered her more money if she allowed him to see her breasts. Soon they started an intimate affair.

The cook complained.

"Where have you been so long, Alice Hofstetter? I hope you've not been flirting with the carriage boy. You're paid to work here and not to frolic about in the stables. The hay in the girl's hair was a giveaway.

"No, the master needed me. If you don't like it then you can complain to him."

The cook tutted. "You watch yourself, girl. The last thing you want is bacon in your drawer from him. He won't help, he's got a reputation, just like his old man, he is."

"He'll look after me," the maid retorted, and flounced off. She had already been thoroughly corrupted by his money and other generous gifts. The affair lasted until she told him she was expecting his child. He gave her a hundred francs and the address of a woman in Bern.

"She'll solve your problem for you," he said.

"It's not my problem," Alice answered, crying.

But no amount of tears or pleading moved Ramun in the slightest. The girl left the villa and the cook went about looking for a new scullery maid. Plenty of young girls wanted the job. She chose a girl from the Spissen. She had a plain face and long teeth. If the master attempted to bother her, then at least he'd get scabies, the cook thought with pleasure.

If they hadn't already guessed, then the other household members soon found out why Alice had left so suddenly.

"I wouldn't let my daughter work here," the butler said. "How old was the girl, eighteen or twenty? She could've almost been his daughter."

Everything was quiet for a month or two. Beatrix returned from her travels and peace was restored in the villa.

One day, Beatrix took a shopping trip in the carriage to Thun. Agatha, her personal maid, sat in Beatrix's boudoir sewing some lace onto one of her dresses.

"Ah, here you are!"

Agatha looked up, startled, as Ramun entered the room. He took off his jacket and began to remove his shirt. Agatha stood up quickly to leave the room. He held her back and said: "No, no. I just need a button sewn back on my shirt."

"Oh." Agatha's heartbeat subsided. "Of course." She held her hand out for his shirt. He grabbed hold of her hand, and falling to his knees, pressed it against his crotch. Agatha uttered a small scream and stabbed him with her needle. She jumped up and tried to brush past him and out of the room.

"Please," he said, hanging onto her skirt to hold her back. "I'll pay you."

"Let go of me immediately or I'll scream the whole household down and tell your wife," Agatha threatened. "I'm not that kind of woman!"

Ramun let go of her skirt and she rushed from the room. In future, she'd sew in the kitchen when the Mistress was away. It was a good job; she didn't want to lose it. She went there now, her heart still racing from the shock. Cook raised her eyebrows at the sight of Agatha. Usually calm and demure, she was red-faced, her hair in disarray and she swished her skirt back and forth like a torero preparing to attack.

"What's bitten you? You look as if you've just met the Stollenwurm."

Agatha humphed. "The bloody cheek of that man!" she blurted out. "He offered me money to shag him! Me! Like a whore!"

"What! Just like that?"

"Yes. I gave him a piece of my mind, I did. Said I'd scream the whole household down and tell his wife."

"That's unbelievable! Wait, I'll get you a schnapps."

Cook carried a stepladder into the pantry so that she could reach to the back of the top shelf where she hid the good schnapps. She poured them both a glass, and then a second, till Agatha calmed down again.

"It's a good job, I don't want to lose it," she complained miserably. "I pity that poor wife of his, no wonder she's always so pale."

"Do you think she knows about his affairs?"

"I don't see how not, he's not exactly discreet."

A few weeks later, Agatha was with Beatrix in her boudoir. Beatrix asked Agatha to sit down for a moment.

"Forgive me for asking, dear, but certain rumours have reached my ears and I really don't know who else to ask. My so-called friends titter behind my back, but won't speak straight to me. It's about my husband, you see. Have you heard gossip about him being unfaithful to me?"

264

Agatha couldn't bring herself to tell her the truth.

"The master? No, mistress, I haven't heard anything."

Beatrix sighed with relief.

"Thank you, dear. You won't tell anyone about our little conversation, will you?"

"No, mistress, of course not."

25

1877–1887

In 1877 Swiss factory law forbade the employment of children under fourteen years of age. The law was very unpopular, not just amongst the factory owners who were forced to forego the cheap labour, but also amongst the poorest of the poverty-stricken region. How could they survive without this income? Making matchstick boxes at home was one possibility, but sending their children illegally to the factories was more lucrative. Many a ten-year-old was indoctrinated to profess he was fourteen and the factory directors did not check.

The local authorities soon worked this out and instructed the village constable to carry out surprise inspections.

In May 1878, Constable Struenzli entered the matchstick factory Lauber in Kandermatt with no forewarning. He saw two young boys at the packing station. He approached them thinking he had caught them red-handed; they wouldn't be able to talk themselves out of it this time. The two boys sensed a presence, looked up from their work and saw Sausage. They dropped their work and fled like the clappers through the factory. They turned left past the director's office and ran out of a back door. Constable Struenzli hunched his shoulders up, put his head down, and scuttled after them like a blackbird espying a worm. He hurled down the corridor, tripped over something lying on the floor and took off. He stretched his arms out mid-flight and landed spread-eagled on the hard floor with a horrible crunch.

The factory turned silent in shock; then everyone became active all at once. The constable was well-liked. Six men carried him home on a stretcher and another two fetched Dr Koefeli. The constable had broken his leg in two places. The doctor secured the leg in splints and ordered strict bed rest for two months. Constable Struenzli did not recover entirely, although he could walk a short distance using crutches, his leg remained stiff and refused to bend at the knee. The local authorities who employed him saw that he would not be able to carry out his duties. He was given an invalidity pension, and his son August was appointed constable in his place.

August was sorry for his father but delighted for himself. He was given a small house and garden with the job and would earn enough to support a wife and family. He had been engaged to Sylvia for four years and he was becoming desperate, thinking that he would never earn enough income to get married. Now all the obstacles were cleared.

Sylvia had been Mina's best friend at school and remained so afterwards too. She was the daughter of Franziska and Linus Gehring, the next-door neighbours to Anton Schneider and his family. Sylvia and Mina shared all their secrets. Mina had confided that she had a crush on Sylvia's older brother, Franz, who unfortunately didn't reciprocate her feelings. Sylvia had told Mina how much she loved August.

She had already been engaged to him when one day Ramun had come across her, walking alone in the middle-high meadows, up until then a harmless pastime without danger. He had attacked her, pushed her down onto the grass, torn her skirt and ripped her blouse, exposing her breasts. Then he had raped her. It was over in ten minutes. He had stood up, fastened his trousers and told her not to tell anyone because no one would believe her word against his.

Sylvia had remained in the meadow crying, grief-stricken, until darkness fell. Then she had crept back to Piller's house where Mina lived. There she wept her heart out. She scrubbed herself clean while Mina repaired her clothes. She extracted Mina's promise not to tell anyone and then went home to her parents who were already wondering where she was.

"I'm sorry," she apologised. "I was chatting with Mina and forgot the hour."

From that day on, Sylvia never took more than two steps away from home by herself. She tried to convince herself that the rape had never happened. When her monthly bleeding came, she went to Mina and they celebrated with a glass of schnapps.

Sylvia had been quite content in her long engagement, but now, suddenly, August had a house and they could get married. August was exuberant. Sylvia went to Mina.

"What am I going to do?" she wailed. "He'll-he'll know he's not the first! Anyway it was horrible, I don't want to do it again!" She threw herself to the floor and burst out crying.

"You should tell August," Mina suggested. "He is so kind and good-natured, it wasn't your fault."

"No!" Sylvia screeched. "He will kill Ramun, I know he

will. Then his life will be ruined too, not just mine. He'll be hanged. Oh life just isn't fair!"

"You can't let him stand at the altar or call the wedding off, you will break his heart."

Sylvia continued to sob her heart out. Mina knelt down beside her and stroked her hair.

"Aunt Margot and Uncle Gustl make love all the time, I can hear them. It can't be that bad, I think they enjoy it."

Sylvia perked up.

"Really?"

"Yes, really," Mina reassured her. "Are you sure August will notice he's not the first? How can he tell?"

"I don't know," Sylvia answered, unsure now, "but I heard someone say so, I think."

"Well, if he says something or asks you, just deny it."

"Lie?"

"No, say that you have never loved anyone before him, that's the truth."

Sylvia dried her tears.

"I suppose that's really the only way." She sniffed. "And you're sure that your aunt and uncle like it?"

26

1887–1888

Gretl, now fifteen, blossomed into a pretty young girl. She always took time to braid part of her long, honey-blonde hair over the top of her head and drew the rest of her hair back from her face into a chignon. She made sure that her face was clean and brushed her teeth with her fingers. She had a straight nose and dimples when she smiled. Her lips were full and she knew how to bite on them to make them red and attractive. Her sister Lena had shown her that.

She washed her work dress weekly and her apron every day. She had two aprons, having sewn one herself with some material her Aunt Mina had given her for Christmas. She had one good dress; it was a traditional Bernese costume with a blue skirt and bodice and white blouse. It had been passed down a few times, but it still looked good because it hadn't been worn often, as there weren't many opportunities to wear it.

On Saturdays she and Lena were allowed to bathe in the tub before her brothers had their turn, and since becoming older with feminine figures, their mother stretched a sheet across the ceiling in front of the bath so that their brothers, who were banished outside of the house for the duration of the bath, could not peek in and make rude comments. They both shared the room of their deceased grandmother, and straight after their bath they would rush into their room to warm themselves up in their shared bed.

Gretl had left school a year earlier and stayed at home helping her parents with the farm work. Since she was ten, she had always spent her summers on the alm with Uncle Gustl and Lena. She loved looking after and caring for the goats, she even milked them, but she wasn't interested in the cheese-making process. Lena, on the other hand, loved making cheese. She was the first female goatherd on the alm and soaked up all the information she could from her uncle. He was actually their great uncle but he had asked the girls to leave off the 'great'.

"It makes me feel old," he had said and laughed. He showed Lena the edible herbs, told her when it was the best time to pick them, and showed her how to prepare them. They were often joined by Jakob too. He had gained the rights to graze cows on some meadows on an alm near Spiggegrund, only half a league distant. When the day's work was finished, he would sometimes visit them.

The summer drew to a close. The cows were decorated with garlands of wild flowers and Uncle Gustl, Lena and Gretl made ready to return to the valley. They passed the chattering mountain streams and took a final gaze at the breath-taking panoramic views. Gretl thought of the long winter ahead of them and felt a little sad.

Back at home Lena threw herself into working in the dairy. Her father's business was doing well and she enjoyed working for him. Gretl on the other hand, felt increasingly restless. It was all right doing farmhold chores but it was also getting boring. Her three younger brothers were still at school, her father and Lena spent all day in the dairy, and she had the feeling that her mother sometimes made up work for her to do. She certainly never let her out of her sight.

One day at dinner she told her parents, "I – want – to – work – some – where – else."

Jakob looked at Berta surprised.

"What? Did you know about this?"

Berta shook her head.

"No. Where do you want to work?" she asked Gretl.

"I – don't – know. Some – where – else," she replied a little sullenly.

"What do you want to do?" Berta tried again.

Gretl shrugged her shoulders.

"You're too young to leave home. You must find work in Weisbruegg or near here."

Gretl perked up. "You – a – llow – it?"

"Yes." Berta ignored Jakob's frowns.

"Tank – you!" Gretl jumped up and gave Berta a kiss. "Did – you – hear – Le –na? I – can – get – a – job."

That night in their room Jakob asked Berta: "Don't you think she's too young to work elsewhere? She's still vulnerable and you don't know how strangers will react to her speech impediment and ... er ... I mean ... oh you know what I mean!" he finished, a little frustrated. Neither of them acknowledged openly what they both knew. Gretl was disabled. Not severely, but she worked in slow motion and wasn't quick to grasp new chores.

"Maybe it will do her good to get away and meet new people. Adults are not so unkind as children. It could build up her self-confidence. It could turn out badly too, but then at least we're here to support her. We can't protect her forever. At some point we'll no longer be here."

"But what could she do?" Jakob persisted.

"That is probably the bigger problem. She can only really work in a factory, as an unqualified worker."

"Oh no, please don't suggest the matchstick factory."

"There are other factories too, and the new law has put a stop to the exorbitant working hours, it's a maximum of eleven hours a day now, ten on Saturdays."

"I almost hope that she doesn't find work, not yet anyway."

*****

The watch factory was looking for a worker to connect micro parts, but Gretl's fine coordination wasn't sufficient for the job. Neither did she have the sleight of hand to work at the lace factory. The box company, Edelweiss, said that Gretl was too slow and suggested that she work at the Church box factory near the Tellerburg. There were often accidents that occurred there, serious accidents. Her parents felt it was too dangerous.

Ramun Lauber offered her a job at the packing station of his matchstick factory, willingly. Her family members had always been good reliable workers and the employees were paid according to performance, so it didn't matter if Gretl worked a little slowly at first. Her parents weren't happy but they had already vetoed the job in Tellerburg.

"I think we must allow her to work there. She won't see Ramun much in the packing station and we can't keep on refusing to let her accept a position. She won't have a lot of choice." Berta tried to convince herself.

"I don't like it," Jakob answered. "I don't trust that man. He's getting on for fifty mind you, Gretl certainly won't be tempted. Can we allow it on condition that she returns home straight after work?"

"Yes, that might work. There's nothing he can do at the factory. I doubt he'll notice her anyway, and even if he does, well, maybe her disability is an advantage in this case."

"I hope she gets fed up after a month and stays at home with us, that would be the best solution."

In spite of a slight uneasiness, Jakob and Berta allowed Gretl to accept the position of packer at the Lauber matchstick factory. There were many other young girls and boys of her age there. Maybe she would find a friend.

*****

Gretl cleaned the dirt streaked across her face and twisted her hair into a neat chignon.

"You're too early," Berta told her, "you've got half an hour yet."

"No, be – tter," Gretl answered.

Berta sighed. It was true enough that if you had some sort of disability, no matter how serious, people were always watching out for mistakes, so you ended up working harder than everyone else. She let Gretl go; she must learn to deal with it herself.

On payday, Gretl took vouchers rather than money. This practice had been forbidden by law, but the workers didn't complain, and so the authorities were helpless to prevent it. Gretl bought a loaf of bread at the factory shop that Mr Lauber had bought from the baker at a special price, and then she carried it home past the very same baker where she could have got it cheaper.

It was noted which workers bought wares in the factory shop and what they bought. If a worker didn't spend enough money in the factory shop, then they got a mark next to their name in the pay-book. When work was slack, these workers had to stay at home, while those who spent more, could continue to work.

*****

Every morning when Ramun came to the factory to unlock the doors, he saw Gretl waiting there alone. At first, he congratulated himself for taking on what was obviously a hard-working girl, keen to work. He nodded good morning and then went to his office while Gretl went to the packing station. Gretl was flattered that Director Lauber spoke to her. After a week he even started tipping his hat. She began to study him.

He was probably as old as her father, maybe even a bit older, but he smelt better. He slicked his hair back with macassar oil that smelt strongly of coconut and ylang-ylang flower. His hair was still mostly black with just a little grey and he had sideburns and a moustache, which he kept neatly trimmed. He had dark eyes and was always dressed impeccably in a three-piece suit. He looked quite handsome, she thought.

When Gretl continued to arrive early, Ramun began to look at her more thoroughly too. She was actually very pretty. A pity about her speech defect, but ... well, it didn't really matter. He couldn't make up his mind whether to attempt to seduce her or not, but he started smiling at her whenever he saw her and sometimes visited the packing station specifically for this purpose.

His wife didn't take pleasure in his attempts to fulfil his nuptial duties and his rights as a husband, and eventually, over the years, he had stopped trying. In Bern and Geneva, in their social circles, he played the loving husband and never let his eyes stray. Back in Weissbruegg, however, he was constantly on the lookout for women.

In June 1888, Gretl told her parents that she didn't want to go to the alm this year, she wished to stay in the valley and continue working at the factory. Jakob let Albert take her place. It wasn't a problem; Berta would stay in the valley with their two youngest boys anyway.

It was one mild morning at the beginning of June when Ramun arrived at the factory, and as always, saw Gretl waiting. The grass was still wet from dew and birds were chirping joyfully. He made his mind up quickly.

"Good morning Gretl, first again I see. Come to my office."

"Goo – d – mor – ning – Di – rec – tor. Yes – sir."

Gretl hurried after Ramun and entered his office. Ramun let down the blinds over the glass screens and locked the door. Gretl looked a little worried.

"Take off your bonnet, Gretl," Ramun said. "Here, shall I help you?" He undid the ribbons and placed her bonnet on his desk. "There, that is better now. There is no need for you to hide your pretty face."

Gretl blushed and smiled uncertainly at him.

"You are so beautiful, Gretl." Ramun stroked her cheek. "May I kiss you?"

Gretl was agitated. She didn't know what to say. She thought of the goodnight or farewell kisses her father sometimes brushed against her cheek. She supposed there was no harm in that. She nodded.

Ramun gripped her arms tightly and thrust his tongue into her mouth. She didn't like it. She was frightened. She tried to push him away.

"No!" she managed to cry out.

Ramun grasped her even tighter. He swivelled her round and pushed her violently over his desk. He pulled her skirt up, her drawers down and opened his trousers.

"No!" Gretl cried out again. "Stop!"

Ramun forced his penis into her vagina.

"Ow! It hurts! Stop!" Gretl was sobbing.

Ramun didn't stop. Gretl struggled but he held her in a vice, pinned to the table. When he felt his orgasm coming, he withdrew his penis quickly. He didn't want any accidents to happen. He let go of Gretl and fastened his trousers. Using a comb, he looked into a small mirror and groomed his hair. Gretl was still lying stretched across the table, crying.

Ramun reached into his pocket for a five-franc silver coin. When Gretl still didn't move he tutted. He pulled her drawers up and her dress down distastefully.

"Come on now, it's over," he said.

"It – hurt!" Gretl wailed.

Ramun gave her the shiny coin.

"It only hurts the first time," he told her. "Next time will be better. This is for you. Thank you, you pleased me." He screwed his nose up at the off-putting snot running down hers. He gave her his handkerchief. "Come on now, dry your tears." He almost regretted having taken her, but something about the way she had protested had aroused him and given him the best satisfaction he'd had in a long time. Yes, he felt good.

Gretl blew her nose a few times and dried her eyes. She looked at the coin incomprehensively. It was more than double her weekly wage. She put it in her pocket and brushed her dress down, and then she left his office to go to her workplace. She felt as if hours had passed but still no other workers had arrived.

That evening, Gretl went home and gave her mother the coin.

Berta looked at it. "Where did you get this from?" she asked.

"Di – rec – tor Lau – ber. Good – work."

Berta was astonished. The director wasn't known for his generosity. He must be getting kind in his old age, she thought.

*****

Ramun assaulted Gretl several times throughout the summer. She didn't like it and began to go to work later, trying to avoid him, but he often found an excuse to get her into his office. She didn't know how to refuse. Sometimes he gave her one franc, sometimes two for her cooperation. Gretl gave the money to her mother. It wasn't much so Berta thought nothing of it.

Gretl didn't fully understand what was happening; she presumed it was usual. Her eyes lost their lustre and she dragged her feet to work. Berta thought that Gretl was bored with work and would soon ask if she could stay at home.

At the end of August, Gretl got up one morning, felt dreadfully sick and threw up into her chamber pot. Berta thought that Gretl was ill and told her to stay at home. When the sickness recurred daily, always clearing up by lunchtime, a horrific suspicion crept into Berta's mind. She thought back and realised that Gretl hadn't had her monthly bleed for weeks. She plumped down on a chair, shocked.

How could Gretl be with child? She hadn't been seeing anyone. She didn't have time to see anyone, and she always came home punctually after work.

She sat down next to Gretl.

"Gretl, are you with child? Who did this to you?" she asked kindly.

"Di – rec – tor – Lau – ber."

"What! No! Are you sure?" Berta couldn't believe it.

"Yes – Lau – ber – mess – a – round – with – me – don't – like – hurt." Gretl started crying.

Her mother put her arms around her and rocked her back and forth.

"Ssh, it's over now, it will be all right, don't worry."

27

1888

Berta couldn't sleep all night. She wondered what to do. She was torn between marching to the Lauber villa and sticking a kitchen knife straight through that monster, as she now thought of him, and climbing the pulpit in church on Sunday and denouncing him in front of the whole congregation. The sheer hate running through her blood was terrifying.

Much as she'd like to, and she had no doubts of her capability to do so – she had often slaughtered a pig – Berta dismissed the first idea. She would end up in prison or hanged and who would help Gretl then? She also dismissed the second idea. Pastor Moser wouldn't approve of her using God's house for revenge. Ramun would no doubt deny it and say that she, Berta, should be admitted to a mad house.

Summer was nearly over. In five days Jakob would return from the alm. She had to do something before he came home and killed Ramun himself.

Berta racked her brain, bringing up all sorts of solutions, only to dismiss them again, one after the other. Then she thought of Vreni. Vreni Stein, Willi's wife, their kind neighbour, had worked at the matchstick factory, on and off, ever since it opened. There wouldn't be much of the goings-on there that she didn't know about. Yes, she'd talk to Vreni – she was discreet, not a scandalmonger like most of the folk round here – and ask her what she knew. Berta believed Gretl but a second opinion wouldn't harm.

Berta got up, did the early morning chores, put a shawl around her shoulders and rushed around to the Stein's house, hoping to see Vreni before she went to work. She caught her about to set off and asked if she could accompany her part of the way.

"It's about Gretl," she explained. "Do you know if she's seeing anyone at the factory? Maybe one of the young lads?"

"Gretl? No, she's no time for that," Vreni answered. "She has her head buried in work, concentrating on keeping up with the others. Why? I mean, she's sixteen, if she found someone it would be nice, wouldn't it? It's no one at the factory though; I always notice the small smiles the young ones give each other. There's not much that stays a secret there for long, what with us all perched on top of each other."

Berta felt dismayed.

"Thank you Vreni. I know you won't tell anyone about this conversation, but you see it's Gretl, she's with child and she says it was the director!"

Vreni, up till now striding out quickly, stopped abruptly in her tracks.

"What? What did you say? Did I hear you correctly? Why that does it! Come with me," she said, putting her arm through Berta's and turning on her heels. "This is just too much. I've put up with his crimes all these years, never saying anything so as not to bring his victims into disrepute. Ha! Just listen to me! Of course, he is the one who should be scorned, but the women begged me not to say anything. But Gretl? How could anyone take advantage of the poor mite. Did she even realise what was happening?"

"I'm not sure. She said it hurt," Berta answered with a sob.

"There are no words to describe that swine! Oh Holy Maria and Josef, Jakob will beat Lauber's guts out when he returns from the alm. Come home with me now, we must work out a plan of action to stop Jakob from slaughtering the pig. We don't want the wrong man hanged. My God, he makes me sick!"

Berta felt enlightened to have trusted Vreni. She didn't have to explain much; Vreni understood the importance of preventing Jakob from committing a crime, instead of bringing the director to justice.

"The only way to stop Jakob from doing something stupid, is either to hold him back with brute force or have a very convincing alternative plan that would preferably cause Lauber more pain and more harm than mere death," Vreni said.

"But we'll need Willi to hold him down when we tell him," Berta answered quite seriously.

"You can't prove that he raped Gretl; it will be her word against his, but if we could persuade enough women to speak up in court against Lauber, then maybe the judge will believe her word against his."

"Oh, Vreni, even with an overwhelming number of women, do you think we can in truth ask them to break their silence? You know the people here in town, the women's reputations would be ruined, but indeed if they did speak up, Ramun Lauber is a powerful man with important friends in Bern and Geneva. Men in high positions. I feel daunted just at the thought of going to court or demanding Gretl testify there. They'll make mincemeat out of both of us."

Vreni considered Berta's words. Both women sat in silence, following their own thoughts.

"Forgetting Jakob for the minute," Vreni said, "what do you want to achieve?"

"I want the best for Gretl. Ideally, Lauber would admit the rape and pay alimony for the child."

"Would you be prepared to hush things up? Despite what the muckrakers will whisper behind Gretl's and your back?"

"The gossips will wag their tongues no matter what we do, or don't do. I'm not bothered about them."

"Well, in that case, all we need to do is persuade Jakob to confront Lauber peacefully. A dead man can pay no alimony."

*****

Every Monday evening, gentlemen from the Kander valley met at eight o'clock in a private room at the Wilder Mann in Frutigen. They called themselves The Liberal Centre Club and met for a drink, a smoke, political discussions or just for a round of dominoes. It was Karl Stettler's idea to stage a confrontation between Jakob and Ramun Lauber here, outside the public house, after the club meeting. There would be plenty of witnesses, and a member himself, he would make sure that Ramun Lauber neither left early, nor got into his waiting horse carriage, before Jakob had a chance to address him.

Berta had spoken to Karl Stettler's wife, Magdelena. Her marriage with the teacher had remained childless.

After detailed examinations in Bern Inselspital, specialists had found severe scarring in her uterus that prevented a pregnancy. The scarring was a consequence of the forced rape by Lauber in her teens. The inability to have children had caused them both incessant pain and grief.

It was too late to file a suit against Mr Lauber themselves. When Magdelena told her husband about Gretl, a child he had taught for eight years at school and to whom he felt in some way protective, he was so incensed that he went upstairs and shaved all his hair and beard off. He re-entered the living room and Magdelena raised her eyebrows.

"I had to do something," he explained. "Let anyone ask me why. I shall tell them of my utter disgust of that man."

Magdelena took hold of his hips and drew him closer to her. She stood on her tiptoes and kissed him tenderly. Afterwards they discussed the matter with each other, fully aware of the consequences for themselves if they spoke up, which was what Berta wanted.

"It's your decision, my love," Karl told his wife. "Whatever you decide, I will support you."

Magdelena sat down on a chair and thought things over.

"I can't let him get away with it," she said, "not again, not this time. That poor girl! And who will be next? I'm sorry Schatz, he must be stopped."

"I'm proud of you, darling. We won't listen to the gossips and we'll stop reading the newspapers, but we'll sleep well at night."

Karl Stettler wasn't the only outsider present. Wilhelmine had spoken to Sylvia. Sylvia had hesitated at first but then confessed the whole episode of her rape to August. She felt much lighter of heart after she had spoken. August had shown understanding of why she hadn't told him before.

"I was so ashamed but I loved you so much; I couldn't just go away and leave you standing at the altar."

"Thank the Lord for that," August answered. "And for our two wonderful daughters who wouldn't be here if you'd left me standing there. But now Lauber has abused the young Schneider girl, you say? And her aunt wants you to testify if necessary? Well, you know my opinion about that, justice must be done."

"But then the whole town will find out and oh, I'd never live it down, it's so embarrassing!"

"How would you feel if he got away with it and in a few years' time from now assaulted one of our girls?"

Sylvia went pale and caught her breath.

"Oh Jesus, Maria and Josef. I never thought of it like that. Yes, of course I will testify if needs be. But before you tell anyone, I must speak to my parents first. They don't know about it either."

Sylvia's parents were Franziska and Linus Gehring, next-door neighbours to Jakob and Berta. They had already been pulled into the plan by the Steins – Willi had thought he might need help holding Jakob back if the peaceful discussion got out of hand – and they knew about Magdelena. When Sylvia heard that she hadn't been the only one to be raped, she felt happier about agreeing to testify if necessary. She visited Magdelena and both women found comfort in talking to each other.

"If I'd known before that Lauber had attacked more women, I might have been brave enough to speak up," Sylvia said.

Both women were still hoping that the matter wouldn't go to court, but having experienced Lauber personally, neither thought that he would just admit the rape and pay alimony. His social status would be ruined.

On Monday evening, 29 September 1888, towards ten o'clock, Jakob, Linus Gehring and Willi Stein waited outside the Wilder Mann for Ramun Lauber to leave the premises. Constable August Struenzli leaned casually against the trunk of a horse chestnut tree, taking a smoke. Jakob hadn't asked him to be present but was warmed by the constable's support.

Jakob stamped his feet against the cold. The occasional gust of a bitter wind blew leaves from the trees and they fluttered to the ground. He looked towards the Alps.

"I can smell snow in the air," he told his companions, to break the silence. Willi nodded in agreement and pulled his woolly cap further down over his ears. Horses' hooves rang out clearly in the silence as Marty Fuchs, Lauber's servant, drove the carriage round the corner and pulled the horses up in front of the inn. He lit up a smoke as the church bell chimed ten.

"Won't be long now," Linus said, and then, "Ouch!" as a horse chestnut fell from the tree above him onto his hatless head. "Bugger an' all!" he swore rubbing his scalp. "Tha's thanks to 'im too!" He stopped as Willi nudged him and said under his breath: "There he is, he's coming."

Ramun Lauber trotted lively down the few steps from the Wilder Mann and headed towards his carriage, as Jakob stepped in front of him, blocking his passage.

"If I could have a word?" Jakob asked politely, removing his cap and holding it in his hands in front of him.

"What's all this about?" Lauber asked, looking around. Karl Stettler stood on the steps of the inn behind him. Constable Struenzli held the reins of the horse carriage and Willi Stein and Linus Gehring were close behind Jakob.

"It's about my daughter, Gretl," Jakob started, and then paused, waiting for the director to speak.

"Yes?" Lauber snapped impatiently.

"You know her; she works at your matchstick factory."

"I can't know everyone who works for me, there are a hundred workers there."

"She is with child; she says you are the father!"

"What? That is preposterous, what would I want from an imbecile young child?"

"So you do know her," Jakob replied calmly.

"If you mean the ungainly child who always arrives at work too early, then yes, I admit noticing her." Ramun Lauber didn't flare up angrily as one might expect of an innocent man. He continued speaking calmly and factually, no doubt convinced that no one could prove anything against him. "But I haven't ever touched her, nor any other of my female workers. Why, I'm a town councillor in Reichenbach and I lead an exemplary family life!"

Jakob clenched his fists at the arrogance of the man. Was he chiselled from stone?

"I have personally witnessed the contrary and have written testimonies from other citizens to the same account," Jakob retorted, equally composed. "Is it not true that you have assaulted several women against their will and indeed committed other crimes? I saw you set fire to Rambert's factory."

"Look, I confess that as a young child I was playing with matches one day and may have accidently caused a small fire. But I was a child, I didn't do it intentionally and the crime, under the statute of limitations, has long since lapsed. You claim to have seen me with a woman, but if so, then it was before my marriage and consensual."

Jakob didn't intend to argue about Ramun's many crimes. Here and now he was present to get justice for his daughter who was not strong enough to fight for herself.

"I am here for Gretl. I know my daughter; she would not lie about something so important."

"It is absolutely ridiculous. I would rather shoot myself than confess to getting your daughter with child. My wife would go mad!"

"Gretl insists that you assaulted her and hurt her."

"I may have got a little close to her, and she may have misinterpreted something, but I was not intimate with her."

"We have asked Gretl again and again. She is steadfast. She is constant in her account about how you pinned her to the desk in your office and forced yourself upon her."

Ramun put his hands in front of his face.

"If this gets spread around I shall be ruined. How much do you want to make this matter go away?"

"I only wish for alimony for the child and a small compensation for Gretl. The usual sum for this would be eighteen thousand francs."

Ramun gasped loudly.

"That is ludicrous! Are you insane? Go to court, no one will believe the word of your imbecile daughter against mine! But let me warn you – neither you nor any members of your family will find work at my factory, nor any other matchstick factory, ever again. I shall make sure of that!" Ramun got into his carriage and drove away.

Jakob's friends surrounded him.

"Phew, well done for keeping calm," Karl Stettler congratulated him. "I nearly fell over him myself when he spoke of consensual acts."

"Berta made me drink valerian tea before I came. That's it then. I promised Berta that I would try to solve the matter in peace in order to save Gretl from having to testify in court. It will be horrific for the poor girl, but I did my best. If it wasn't for Gretl, I would much prefer the only option left to me now anyway. We cannot let Lauber get away with his crimes again and again. The whole world can hear about this vile despot. He shall be compelled to take responsibility for his actions and his reputation shall be ruined, just as he's ruined the lives of so many others."

"He will no longer be welcome in The Liberal Centre Club," Stettler stated.

"Nor in the Wilder Mann," the innkeeper, who had joined them, added.

28

1888

Criminal Court in Frutigen, Schneider v. Lauber (1888).

The next morning, the whole valley was filled with gossip, bubbling back and forth along the rivers, a vapour penetrating the houses, echoing off the mountains, bouncing to and fro. Everyone knew someone involved, everyone had an opinion and many an old witch stirred her pot of evil lies. Some poor souls trembled, worried their own secrets might become uncovered. And one person started working on a line of defence should the matter go further.

Ramun Lauber made an appointment to visit his advocate, Mr Heinrich Studer, in Thun. As Marty Fuchs drove the carriage to the lawyer's office, Ramun looked at him and had an idea. Marty, a sixty-plus-year-old with a gammy leg, had taken the place of a young lad, Lutz Bieri. Lutz had been a charmer with the ladies. The housemaids flirted quite openly with him. He had given in his notice and emigrated to America about a month ago. Nobody could prove his own relationship with Gretl, so maybe he could say that he had seen Lutz with her. The boy wasn't here to deny the fact. Yes, he liked the idea.

He entered his advocate's office and an apprentice took his top hat and walking stick to the cloakroom. He sat down in a comfortable chair, flicking his tails behind him, and Mr Studer poured them both a small sherry.

"Now then, tell me what's worrying you, Ramun," the advocate asked.

Both men moved in the same social circles and knew each other well. Mr Studer's father had also been Gustav Lauber's lawyer. Ramun told Heinrich Studer about the confrontation the week before. Naturally he claimed his innocence.

Mr Studer couldn't care less whether Ramun was guilty or not.

"And he demanded eighteen thousand francs in front of witnesses?"

"Yes, a ridiculous sum! I might have paid five hundred, but that was way too much. These people think we have money to shit!"

"We have a clear act of criminal blackmail here. Don't ever repeat what you have just told me about being willing to pay a lesser sum. People would ask why, if you're not guilty. I know one of the magistrates in Frutigen, Ulrich Reinhard. Leave it to me, I'll get in touch with him and he'll see that Mr Jakob Schneider is arrested. That will quieten him. Now then, tell me, how is your charming wife?"

*****

Ramun left his lawyer's office in a mood to celebrate. Extortion, he chuckled to himself. Why hadn't he thought of that? Brilliant! This would be easier than he thought. He took his silver pocket watch from his waistcoat and checked the time. Not too early for lunch.

"Take me to Hotel Krone," he told Marty.

The carriage wheels clattered over the cobbled stones in the town centre; he couldn't have known that Anneli, Berta's elder sister, former victim of attempted rape by his father, had made an excellent marriage with an up-and-coming gastronome, Philippe Leconte, twenty years earlier. They had both worked hard, and five years ago had taken over the hotel and restaurant Krone. It was difficult to book a table less than a month in advance in the renowned restaurant that was currently en vogue.

Anneli heard a commotion at the entrance to the dining room. Her maître d' was politely trying to convince a gentleman that the tables were all fully booked. The conversation became heated and other guests began to look. She hurried to assist her maître d'.

"Mr Lauber," she said, recognising him immediately, "can I help you?"

Ramun looked Anneli up and down.

"Do I know you?"

"I doubt it, but I know you. I come from Weissbruegg originally."

"Ah," Ramun answered, flattered by this handsome woman. "Yes, you can. I would like a table."

Anneli was used to dealing with difficult situations. Prominent guests kicking up a fuss were never good for business. The thought of refusing Lauber a table, however, was so deliciously tempting that she had difficulty resisting. She hesitated, battling with her conscience and loyalty towards her husband's good name and reputation. With regret, she decided to be professional.

"I'm sure our maître d' will have told you, I'm afraid we are fully booked this lunchtime, but if you would consider being our guest at my own personal table ...?"

Ramun accepted. Had Anneli known at the time about Gretl, she would have thrown him out immediately, she said later. But she hadn't.

Ramun sat down at the table and ordered a bottle of the most expensive champagne on the wine menu. The wine waiter brought a silver ice bucket with the bottle of champagne. Anneli stood up.

"I'll deal with this," she told her employee. She deftly let the cork pop, and taking Ramun's glass, leaned over slightly to fill it up. Ramun locked his eyes on her cleavage. Removing his white gloves, he took hold of his glass in one hand to propose a toast, and with the other pinched Anneli's backside. Anneli screamed. No other client in such a respectable restaurant touched any of the waitresses, let alone the proprietress, in such an inappropriate manner like a cheap whore! She suddenly noticed Ramun's missing fingernails, his father's attempted rape flashed back and her vision turned red. Still holding the bottle in one hand, she poured the contents over Ramun's crotch.

Ramun leapt from his seat with a cry.

"Oh, I'm so sorry," Anneli mocked, snatching a serviette and slamming it on his balls. "What a waste of good champagne."

Ramun bent over double, in pain. His face turned beetroot. The guests at the restaurant stopped eating to watch the spectacle; it would be a topic of conversation in the noblest boudoirs for at least a week. Pointing his finger at Anneli, Ramun threatened her loudly: "You haven't heard the last of this, you bitch! Just you wait, you'll be hearing from my lawyer!"

He left the building quickly and ordered Marty to return to Weissbruegg. Anneli composed herself and went round each table apologising for the disturbance and offering drinks on the house. She hadn't been in the business for twenty years for nothing.

*****

Ulrich Reinhard, magistrate at the criminal county court in Frutigen, agreed with his friend, advocate Heinrich Studer, that there were enough grounds to charge Jakob Schneider for extortion and he let him be arrested. Mr Reinhard spoke to his two colleagues, Mr O. Abraham and Mr H. Braunbarth. Mr Abraham had said he wanted to question Gretl Schneider personally at the hearing.

"Miss Schneider, please can you tell us who the father of your child is?"

Gretl stood before the three men and trembled. Their formidable presence in front of her, earnest and severe, frightened her. Nonetheless, she summoned up her courage.

"Mr – Lau – ber." She spoke much too loudly.

The three men were shocked. Miss Schneider had looked and seemed perfectly normal to them, but these two words alone were sufficient to tell them otherwise.

They whispered to each other and then Mr Reinhard crooked his finger to beckon Gretl's father to their table.

"Is your daughter disabled?" he asked.

"Gretl had an accident when she was two and since then she is profoundly deaf," Jakob answered, matter-of-factly.

The three magistrates drew in their breath, slightly distastefully. Nobody had told them that; it gave the case a different turning. No wonder the father had tried to get support for his daughter. Mr Abraham spoke, kindly now, to Gretl.

"My dear girl, do you remember when the cohabitation took place?"

"Yes. Mon – day – June – sixth – in – his – off – ice," she replied determinedly.

The magistrates looked at each other surprised.

"The girl remembers the date exactly, that is clear evidence that she's telling the truth," Mr Abraham said.

"Unless her father instructed her," Mr Reinhard answered.

"We should listen to the father now," Mr Braunbarth intervened. "He is the person accused here."

"Mr Jakob Schneider, is it true that on Monday evening, the 29th of September 1888, you confronted Mr Lauber and demanded the sum of eighteen thousand francs from him?"

"Yes, sir, but not as he maintains at the beginning of our conversation, rather at the end and only after he asked me how much it would cost not to take the matter to court."

A murmur rumbled through the court room. Lauber's advocate sprang up.

"Were those his exact words? I remind you, you are under oath!"

Jakob considered.

"I think his exact words were: 'To make this matter go away,' but there were witnesses to the conversation, present here in court today, whom you can ask."

The magistrates spent all day listening to witnesses and hearing Mr Lauber. At 7.00 p.m. Mr Schneider was acquitted, and Mr Lauber ordered to pay the court costs, and for Mr Schneider's legal representation.

29

1889

High Court in Bern, Schneider v. Lauber (1889).

On the 5th of March 1889, Gretl gave birth to a healthy young boy. She named him Walter. All was well except that his thumbs and big toes had no nails, a minor issue.

During spring and summer, Jakob prepared intensively for the paternity suit against Ramun Lauber. It was due to take place at the Civil High Court in Bern in the autumn. He found overwhelming support from most of the inhabitants of Weissbruegg. Together with his advocate, Mr Simon Steffen in Thun, and assisted by Mr Albrecht Bertelsmann, an appointee for the poor, he built up his case to prove that Mr Lauber was the father of Walter, and to convince the judge to decree that Mr Lauber pay alimony for the child.

Jakob was aware that it would be a process based on circumstantial evidence. He knew that Ramun Lauber was highly respected in Bern and had many influential friends. It would be his word against Lauber's, and he didn't doubt which way the credibility would tend to sway. He spoke first to his neighbour, Linus, and asked him to write a character reference.

At the next town council meeting he asked formally for a certificate of good character for himself, Berta and Gretl. He could not ask Gretl's workplace for a reference, but Karl Stettler was happy to write a character reference for her.

The court in Bern itself, now fully aware of the circumstances, commissioned a psychiatrist, Dr Gutmann, to fully examine Gretl and to evaluate her state of mind. They also asked the District Court in Frutigen, who was familiar with local circumstances, for a character reference for Mr and Mrs Schneider themselves.

Not just the local newspapers and scandal rags, but even the national newspapers followed the case and every tiny development minutely, before the suit even appeared in court. The case of the profoundly deaf girl aroused feelings in the whole population of Switzerland.

Ramun Lauber had but one meeting with advocate Mr Studer in Thun.

"Nobody was witness to this accused assault," Studer told Lauber, "it's a matter of circumstantial evidence; in fact, I'm surprised that the case has got this far. But don't worry, we'll pull these coarse yokels back into the cesspit where they've come from. Nobody will believe them."

The day of the court case in Bern arrived. Jakob was nervous. He went over in his mind again and again, if he had thought of everything. Gretl could not defend herself, it was up to him to get justice for her.

The defendant, Ramun Lauber, represented by his advocate, Mr Studer, was asked to declare his affirmative defences. Mr Studer stood up and did his best to discredit Gretl and her family.

"Gretl is an unattractive, malicious and dishonest creature. Out of pure avarice, she has made false accusations. She no doubt had an illicit affair with some poverty-stricken lad, and seeing Mr Lauber at work, decided, out of greed, to accuse him, thoroughly unsubstantiated, of this ridiculous crime. I ask you," he looked at the judges, "what would a respectable, happily married gentleman, like my client Mr Lauber, want with a feeble-minded, dirty child like Gretl?"

Jakob had difficulty keeping calm. Berta, sitting next to him, squeezed his hand, and from behind, Karl Stettler laid one hand on his shoulder.

Jakob was asked to take the stand. He removed his cap, placed his hand on the Bible and vowed to tell the truth the whole truth and nothing but the truth. His heart thumping, he told the court how he found out about Gretl being with child. He repeated how that, despite asking his daughter on several occasions, she always said the father was Mr Lauber. He remained outwardly calm, even when Mr Studer cross-questioned him, suggesting that Gretl was a liar.

"No!" Jakob contradicted him, his heartbeat racing like a steam engine. "Gretl might fib about little things, if she wanted more cake or something like that, but she never, and would never, lie about something so serious. She even knew the date when it happened."

Berta was next to take the stand. Her voice caught when she reported that Gretl had told her it hurt. Although outwardly calm, tears ran silently down her cheeks. The court was subdued and several women dabbed at their eyes with a handkerchief.

Alice Hofstetter was called to take the stand. Although Ramun had paid for her services, Mr Steffen wanted her to testify to prove that Ramun Lauber was not so honourable as that he even paid for sex in his own home, where his wife and son lived. Mr Studer hadn't known about this and waived his right to question her.

Magdelena Stettler took the stand and told the court that Ramun Lauber had raped her and left her unable to bear children. The court was shocked at this, until now, well closeted information. When Mr Studer cross-examined her, she held her head high and stuck to her story.

"Is it not true that the cohabitation took place before Mr Lauber's marriage and that it was consensual?"

"It was before his marriage," Magdelena conceded, "otherwise he could not have tricked me into joining him on a picnic, but the act was not consensual, and there are witnesses who heard me screaming no!"

"Who are the witnesses?"

Magdelena realised her mistake.

"Jakob and Berta Schneider" she mumbled.

"Sorry, I didn't hear you properly, can you repeat their names louder please?"

"Jakob and Berta Schneider, but they weren't married then."

Mr Studer asked the judges to disregard Magdelena's statement as the witnesses to this alleged rape were obviously biased. Without a witness it could be possible, even probable, that Mrs Stettler agreed to the cohabitation and only made this ridiculous accusation afterwards to explain to her husband why she was barren.

"No, that's not true!" Magdelena said and wept. The judge asked her to keep silent when not spoken to and she was dismissed from the stand. Distressed, she left the courtroom and Karl hurried after her.

Sylvia was next on the stand. She told her story quietly, her head hanging in shame.

Mr Studer questioned her.

"Were there any witnesses to this purported rape?"

"No."

"Louder please!"

"No."

"So, if this act took place at all, then it could have been consensual. It is the word of Sylvia Künzli against that of Mr Ramun Lauber. Tell me, is it true that you are good friends with Miss Wilhelmine Schneider, Gretl's aunt?"

"Yes."

Mr Studer hadn't finished.

"The plaintiff's witnesses are all, without exception, untrustworthy and non-credible. Whether as near, or distant, relations to the Schneider family, or for some other selfish reason or resentment, they do not have the volition to tell the truth."

Mr Steffen, Jakob's advocate, stood up and calmly refuted the defendant's accusations.

"The District Court describes the Schneider family as highly respectable. The certificate of good character issued by the town council goes over and above the habitual formula to beneficially certify both Mr and Mrs Schneider's good character. The witness, Mr Linus Gehring, who makes a credible and favourable impression, testifies that Mr Schneider is industrious and thrifty and always endeavours to meet his obligations. The defendant's advocate has not one single piece of evidence that Gretl was, or had been, in a relationship with anybody else. A state that was certain to be noticed in a small village. The witnesses, Mrs Magdelena Stettler and Mrs Sylvia Künzli, were very brave to come forward and expose their secrets. They were both highly respected women in the community, wives of the teacher and police officer. They had no reason to lie and certainly would not have put their reputation at risk if the matter was not true."

The court ascertained that Mr Schneider's statements were calm and precise and by no means filled with hate. Even Mrs Schneider made the impression, from her tone and the content of her statements, that she was not trying to wilfully bend the facts.

A major point of circumstantial evidence was that Gretl Schneider had, on the 5th of November 1888, already stated that the assault had taken place on the 6th of June 1888. That was four months before the birth and it was absolutely impossible that Miss Schneider, at that time, could foresee the date of birth, and make her statement accordingly, as would have been possible after the birth. The natural explanation was that this date had engraved itself deeply and indelibly on the girl's, not quite fully fledged, mind.

The judge ruled that concerning the motion:

a. The defendant is determined as the extramarital father of Walter Schneider, born on 5 March 1889.

b. The defendant is ordered to pay the mother, Gretl Schneider, a sum of money, determined by the court, for the cost of childbirth, for the loss of wages for at least four weeks before until four weeks after the birth, and an appropriate compensation for damages according to Art. 318 Z.G.B.[3]

c. The defendant is ordered to pay the child, Walter Schneider, alimony as determined by the court until the end of his eighteenth year of life.

---

3. *Unlawful sexual intercourse with a woman against her will.*

The defendant's petition was rejected and the defendant ordered to pay the court fees and the legal fees for the plaintiff."

The finding had taken all accounts into consideration. As always in similar cases, that the mother knew the date of assault, and that this date lay exactly nine months before the birth, was a very significant circumstance for the truth of the whole of the claimant's account.

Jakob and Berta hugged each other. They stood up and shook hands with Mr Steffen and then went home with a huge weight lifted from their shoulders.

"I would have preferred Gretl to find a nice young man one day and live a life of happiness," Jakob confided to Berta, "like you and me."

"At least justice has now been done and they will not starve. And hopefully Ramun will stop violating women now. Vreni said that many female workers had been defiled by him over the years."

"Yes, hopefully he will stop now. His reputation is ruined at least."

*****

The verdict released a deluge of gossip in the Kander valley. Snow had fallen many feet deep, even in the lowlands, which made travel nearly impossible. But the newspapers, arriving several days late, were scoured for information, and where there was no written account, scandalmongering and opinions spread from house to house and from village to village, flowing unstoppable, like lava from a volcano.

The Schneider family, the Stettlers and Künzli family stayed at home claiming infectious colds, excusing them from leaving the house or receiving visitors. They didn't want to chatter with gossipmongers from the village. They spoke only to close family members and friends whom they could trust.

They hoped that the matter was settled, but Mr Steffen warned them that Mr Lauber might demand a revision. Jakob lived in a state between hope and despair waiting to hear what happened.

*****

Ramun Lauber suffered a severe blow to his arrogance. His wife and son, who at the time had been sojourning with her parents in Geneva, fled to Rome to escape the shame and whispers behind their backs. They were no longer welcome in the boudoirs of Bern, and at the theatre people had looked away and turned their backs on them. The whole family was shunned. Beatrix's father advised her to rent a villa in Rome and stay there until his grandson's education was complete. He promised to support her financially so that she could live there in comfort, but only on the condition that she divorced her husband. Beatrix complied willingly and her father assured her that he would make certain that Ramun would cause no more problems for her or their son, Friedrich.

Ramun spoke once again with his lawyer, seething at his previous ill advice and determined to win his reputation back.

"I don't care how you do it," Ramun fumed, "the verdict is inacceptable. I want to appeal and this time I shall win!"

30

1891

Bern, Nov.12th, 1890

Concerning the case Schneider v. Lauber,
paternity suit.

Mr President,
Your Honour,

During the proceedings of the High Court,
the defendant purposefully avoided following the
example of the plaintiff by consulting with all sorts
of unreliable witnesses.

An, up to this date, well respected family has
been morally ruined by the findings of the High
Court. The defendant, now determined to prove
his innocence, has made investigations on his own
account, and discovered facts that are crucial factors
for the clarification of this case.

The defendant, convinced of his innocence, has,
up until now, not brought it over himself to let his

ailing wife testify before court. Since the High Court convicted her husband, Mrs Lauber refuses any consideration of her own person. Therefore, we request that the court summon Mrs Lauber and ask her personally if she has ever, in her long marriage, had the slightest reason to doubt her husband's fidelity.

Further, we would like to include references of the defendant's good character from Mr Niklaus Lehmann, the defendant's father-in-law, banker in Geneva and Mr Simon Lehmann, the defendant's brother-in-law, banker in Geneva, who both explicitly state that the defendant's character is exemplary and as long as he has been known to them, has never given them any reason to doubt his moral righteousness.

The defendant has been made aware of a new blood test method tested in similar cases in the question of paternity in America. Similarly, a fingerprint method. He requests the court to consider these methods.

Finally, it has come to the defendant's attention, that the witness Hans Hofstetter is an incorrigible forger and scammer. He falsified the results of the Marksmen's Festival in the Canton Lucerne in 1884 by changing the stamp on individual scores. We petition, therefore, that his statement is removed from the case.

Yours truly,
H. Studer.

The court read the letter and wrote a letter themselves to Prof. Dr Stampfli in Bern, the renowned and respected chief physician at the Inselspital, asking a series of questions.

Prof Stampfli replied.

Honourable sirs,

After receiving your letter from 19th Dec. 1890, I have studied all the literature available to this day, in order to state my opinion to your extraordinary questions lying before me.

I have come to the conviction today that neither a special kind of blood test, nor the fingerprint method, nor the identification of a particular type of shared thumbnail defect between the child and the in-question-coming father, according to the present stand of science, can be utilised to come to a reliable result to either determine or to rule out paternity. None of the three methods suffice either singularly nor combined to reach a satisfactory result.

I wrote to Prof. Dr Zuckermann in Zürich, Director of the Forensic Institute, for his competent judgement. He replied that in his opinion 1. The blood test method was not as yet sufficiently researched to give a reliable result. 2. The assessment of fingerprints could not convey any critical factors. 3. Hereditary malformations: in the case under consideration the missing thumbnails of the father-in-question and child do not lead to any safe conclusions. Even if the malformation were indeed hereditary, this could only lead to a peaceful solution of the matter in hand.

I regret that I cannot help you further.

Yours truly,
Prof. Dr Stampfli

The court set the date for the Court of Appeal for 22 March 1891. Walter was two years old. Gretl had only been able to find odd jobs, cleaning people's houses or helping with the harvest. For a family, poor from the outset, the long court process was taking its toll. All reserves had been used up. Legal costs had been paid but not yet refunded by Mr Lauber, still fighting for a final judgement in his favour.

Ramun Lauber and his lawyer knew this and tried to delay the process further by petitioning to the court to postpone the court date. They argued that Mrs Lauber was in Rome and presently too unwell to travel but that she would be able to travel in May. The court dismissed the petition with the reasoning that Mrs Lauber could give a written statement.

> *Court of Appeal, March 22nd, 1891*
>
> *in the paternity suit of:*
>
> *Ramun Lauber, factory owner in Kandermatt near Frutigen represented by advocate H. Studer, Thun, defendant, appellee*
>
> *against*
>
> *Gretl Schneider factory worker, Weissbruegg near Frutigen*
>
> *Walter Schneider son of Gretl born 1889 represented by advocate, S. Steffen, Thun, and Mr A. Bertelsmann, council of Frutigen, plaintiff, respondent.*

The plaintiff worked in the packing station of the factory of the defendant. In Summer 1888 a pregnancy was ascertained. She named the defendant as father of the child. She maintained that the defendant had had sexual intercourse with her, against her will, several times in June 1888. On 5 March 1889 she gave birth, out of wedlock, to a boy, who was registered under the name Walter Schneider at the civil registry office. She demands that the defendant is convicted and ordered to pay the legal alimony and a compensation.

The defendant denies ever having had sexual intercourse with the plaintiff and demands dismissal of the case.

The defendant lays the main emphasis of his defence in the denial of having had sexual intercourse with the plaintiff. The question arises whether, through the procedure of taking evidence, as there is no direct proof of such a relationship, enough circumstantial evidence can be supplied, in order to justify, according to the practice of establishment of assumption of Art. 314 al. 1 Z.G.B. adequate high probability.

The plaintiff has not changed her testimony. She does not display any signs of unnatural sex drive that the defendant accuses her of. It is clear that the defendant, if he wanted intimate relationships with his female employees, could make arrangements to ensure he would not be disturbed either during his advances or during the sexual intercourse itself, either from his family or another third person. That the procurement of such situations was possible for the director of the factory can hardly be denied.

The defendant has portrayed the plaintiff and her family as untrustworthy and greedy. His point of view did not convince the Court of Appeal any more than it did the High Court.

The plaintiff can, however, according to the evidence and particularly the report from Dr Gutmann, be regarded as mildly disabled. As a result of her loss of hearing and speech defect, a certain helplessness attaches itself to her appearance. Her disability does not however go so far as to stop her recalling memories correctly. This is attested by her teacher Mr Stettler, her neighbour Mr Gehring, who has known her since childhood, and Dr Gutmann. We now call upon Dr Gutmann to impart to the court the findings of his examination of the plaintiff Gretl Schneider.

The psychiatrist Dr Gutmann stood up and glanced at Gretl out of benevolent eyes before facing the court.

Gretl sat in court bewildered. She knew that everyone was looking at her and it made her feel uncomfortable. She wanted to go home and be with Walter. She listened to Dr Gutmann, who had been quite nice to her and wondered what he would now say.

After the preliminaries regarding his name and status, the defendant's advocate asked: "Dr Gutmann, how would you describe the plaintiff's state of mind?"

"First of all I must emphasise that it was difficult to communicate with the patient. Her feeblemindedness is, however, only moderate and does not prevent her from carrying out, for example, household duties correctly."

"In your opinion is she capable of lying?"

"No, the plaintiff is veracious."

"Can you be certain of this? You only spent what ... a couple of hours examining her? I must remind you that you are here under oath and that a man's reputation is at stake."

"As also the reputation of a woman. Let me explain to you how we psychiatrists work to get as accurate answers as possible. I set the plaintiff a trick so that she was forced to lie to me. She lied but blushed deeply at the same time, not being able to disguise the lie. Gretl Schneider does not have a dishonest character. She did not lie because she found pleasure in doing so but out of embarrassment."

Jakob and Berta had been holding their breath, this being the defendant's major line of defence. Now they breathed out slowly again. Although they knew that Gretl was telling the truth, they had not known until this minute how the psychiatrist would judge her, or indeed whether he was in Lauber's pocket. This was obviously not the case and months of tension began to ease.

Mr Studer continued his questioning.

"Is it, in your opinion, possible that the plaintiff was influenced by her parents into naming the defendant as father?"

"I tried to answer this question by asking several suggestive questions. All without success. Gretl Schneider always adhered most adamantly to her original account of how the director had assaulted her. I could find no sign of influence. I summarise – the plaintiff is either telling the truth or standing under such powerful manipulation that she believes that she is telling the truth."

The court, consisting of three judges, conferred shortly together and were unanimous in their decision. The speaker stated the reasons for their judgement.

"It has been decided that there was no will to lie on the part of the plaintiff. That the parents Schneider are substantially interested in the outcome of this paternity suit cannot be denied. Their testimonies were valuated according to this. The question was, whether in addition to this, their characters, as according to the defendant, are untrustworthy. This is not the case, as the High Court has already confirmed.

"It remains to be mentioned, as the family are strongly dependent on the defendant, that they would hardly dare to file a suit unless they were wholly convinced that they were in the right.

"A number of circumstantial pieces of evidence indicate that the plaintiff's statement is true.

1. Her parents say that she often brought small sums of money home that she said she had received from Lauber. Together with the statements of numerous female witnesses, who also received or were offered money from the defendant for sexual intimacies, and taking into account that Gretl Schneider was not a top class worker, it may be presumed that this money was for certain sexual favours and not as a bonus for work achievements.

2. Gretl Schneider stated on 5 November 1888, at the Criminal County Court in Frutigen in the matter of extortion, that the assault had taken place 6 June 1888. That was four months before the birth.

3. It is important to note that as a result of the evidence, neither the means to carry out sexual intercourse unnoticed, nor the assessment of the defendant's character, negate the question of whether the defendant could be capable of carrying out the crime he is accused of.

"The defendant renounces any testimonies that are not in his favour because the witnesses are either related to the Schneider family or otherwise hostile towards himself. Even if the court disregards the statements of the nearest relations to the Schneider family and that of their appointee, Mr Bertelsmann, although he seemed in no way prejudiced, there are enough remaining witnesses to comprehend why the court believes that Lauber allowed himself extensive digressions with his female employees.

Among the witnesses related to the family there are a couple that cannot be ignored.

"Alice Hofstetter is a very distant relative. She may have acted wrongfully by accepting money from Mr Lauber, but alone the fact that she has admitted it, putting herself into a bad light, shows the truth of the matter. The manner of her statement, the proven testimony of the cook, the confirmation of her statement by her son, Hofstetter, do not leave any doubt to the fact that the defendant tried his luck with female servants. Whether Mr Hofstetter falsified marksman results or not, does not alter anything.

"Mrs Lauber's statement, although congenial from a human point of view in her solidarity with her accused husband, does not change anything. One might like to say that Mrs Lauber was occasionally deceived by her memory when she says that she saw the junior coachman and farmhand Lutz Bieri, taking Gretl Schneider with him on a delivery in June 1888, at the time that the sexual intercourse occurred. The senior coachman, Zumbrunn, writes down all the deliveries and transports and swears that Lutz Bieri took his last delivery in May 1888. His notebook lies here as evidence in this case. Lutz Bieri has since emigrated to America and cannot be asked himself. However, there are no other witnesses to this supposed delivery, and no witnesses have come forward who ever saw Gretl Schneider either on a delivery or talking to Bieri.

"Furthermore, Mrs Lauber states that she never had any reason to doubt her husband's fidelity. This contradicts the testimony of Agatha Stuebler who explicitly states that Mrs Lauber asked her personally, in her boudoir in 1877, whether she knew of any improper behaviour by her husband. Mrs Stuebler had denied so, not wanting to disturb the family peace.

"The defendant's arguments that the witnesses are unreliable cannot compensate for the weight of so many incriminating statements. No proof has been brought that Gretl, in the critical time, had an intimate relationship with another man.

"The court rules:

The complaint is granted and the defendant, father of the boy, Walter Schneider, born out of wedlock on 5 March 1889, is ordered to pay:

1. to the plaintiff Gretl Schneider:

   a. for the cost of childbirth eighty francs.

   b. for the loss of wages for 4 weeks before until 4 weeks after the birth two hundred and twenty-four francs.

   c. compensation of five hundred francs.

2. to the child Walter Schneider:

   a. a monthly alimony from since the birth to the completed sixth year of age sixty francs.

   b. a monthly alimony from the sixth year of age to completed twelfth year of age eighty francs.

   c. a monthly alimony from the twelfth year of age to completed eighteenth year of age one hundred francs.

The defendant's petition is rejected. The defendant is ordered to pay the court fees and the legal fees for the plaintiff. Furthermore, the defendant shall be taken from this courtroom and imprisoned for the duration of three years in the city jail of Bern."

Bern 6 May, 1891.

*****

Mr Simon Steffen, advocate in Thun, wrote to Jakob Schneider. He said that he considered the process now finally terminated as an appeal to the Swiss Federal Supreme Court would scarcely be successful. The most important declarative statement is whether the defendant had sexual intercourse with Gretl during the critical time. This a factual question, which the Appeal Court affirmed. The Federal Supreme Court is tied to the findings on Cantonal level.

Mr Steffen was mistaken. Ramun Lauber appealed to the Swiss Federal Supreme Court in Lausanne.

31

1891

The Swiss Federal Supreme Court, Lausanne.

It was unheard of. Nobody from the Kander valley had ever before appeared before the Swiss Federal Supreme Court. Journalists travelled to Weisbruegg and tried to question the Schneider family or other witnesses involved. None of the main witnesses were willing to speak but the papers were full of stories from the scandalmongers in the village. These stories had nothing to do with the case in hand but a myriad of half-true, mainly invented stories rose to the surface in print, causing part havoc, part amusement in the village.

"What? I didn't know about this!" Jakob exclaimed in the evening, poring over the newspaper. Berta and Lena came to hear what he had discovered.

"You remember that boy who sat next to Gretl at school?" Jakob asked.

"The profoundly deaf one?" Berta asked.

"We called him Young Haensel," Lena added, "I know

him, he's quite good looking actually, he's always looking out for the girls and paying them compliments."

"Well, apparently he had a crush on the widow Ruth, you know her, she lives up on the Horlauenen."

"Yes, of course. Why, she could be his mother! Carry on then, don't keep us in suspense."

"According to this article, he went to visit her every evening putting a ladder against her window and knocking to give her a bunch of flowers or a piece of cake." Jakob chuckled before continuing. "She kept telling him to go away, that she wasn't interested, but he was persistent and becoming a nuisance, waking her up every night. So, one evening she pretended to go along with him and told him to wait for her in the barn. Then she came downstairs and locked him in the barn all night until lunch time the next day."

They all laughed imagining it.

"And? Did she get her peace after that?"

"Yes, he was furious and banged on the barn doors all night. When she let him out, he told her there were plenty more maids flowering in the meadows and she told him that was fine by her and that he should bugger off."

"Oh dear," Berta said, chuckling. "Thank you for that, it took my mind off Lausanne for the second."

"Mr Steffen says Lauber can't win."

"I hope not, but still, this dragging on is tearing at my nerves and our pockets, Walter will be three soon and even if Lauber does have to repay us in the end, we still have to advance all the costs."

"It will be worth it. It will set a sign to all those other arrogant industrialists out there that we are not as helpless as we seem. It's already known all over Switzerland, and maybe Walter can get an apprenticeship. Think of it, our grandson breaking out of the poverty here."

"We may be poor but at least I'm happy. I wouldn't want to exchange places with Mrs Lauber any day."

"No, me neither."

*****

Ramun Lauber told his coachman to have the coach ready at six the next morning, hoping that no one would be around so early. He went to visit Alice Hofstetter who lived on a small farm far away from any other settlements. He brought a pouch full of money with him. He knocked at the door and went indoors.

Bert Fechtig lived on the edge of existence. Since losing his job at the matchstick factory he had only ever found odd jobs to see him and his family by, more poorly rather than well. In addition to all his other troubles, he had piles that persistently plagued him. Thanks to the doctor's secretary the whole village knew about them too, which made him a constant source of mockery. Only Alice Hofstetter had been understanding and given him a pot of homemade calendula cream. She had asked for nothing in return and said he could come as often as he liked for a refill. So occasionally he helped out on the farm, and today he arrived early for a refill of the calming cream before she left the house for the day.

He saw Marty Fuchs waiting next to a carriage, and putting two and two together, wondered what Mr Lauber was doing at Alice's place. He hid himself under the back porch and listened. He was devastated at what he heard but didn't know what to do about it.

*****

The summer dragged on and autumn arrived. Nerves were tense when, on 28 October 1891, the Swiss Federal

Supreme Court, under the presidency of the federal judge, Mr Roessel and his assisting judges Soldati, Jaeger, Lauch and Spiller, convened in Lausanne to reach a final verdict in the matter of Schneider v. Lauber.

The press had fought for places in the courtroom and artists sat in the front row with their pads and pencils busily sketching the scene.

Mr Studer, representing Lauber, stood up almost apologetically before the high judge. He knew that the chances of winning were next to nil but he hadn't been able to refuse Lauber this one last chance. He began with the revelation that Mrs Anneli Leconte was Mrs Schneider's sister and requested that her testimony be ignored.

High Judge Roessel looked down his long nose, over his glasses, sternly at Studer.

"Advocate Studer, I sincerely hope that you have better arguments than that to bring before this court. I do not regard wasting the court's time with approval."

"Y-yes, Your Honour, my apologies. I would like to call upon the witness Mrs Alice Hofstetter."

Alice took her place at the witness box and swore on the Bible to tell the truth, the whole truth and nothing but the truth. Lauber looked across to Jakob Schneider and smirked. Jakob stared straight ahead to the witness box, his countenance serious and stock still, not a muscle twitched.

"Mrs Hofstetter, at the Appeal Court you testified that Mr Lauber gave you money for sexual favours. I believe you wish to change your statement," Mr Studer prompted.

"Yes, sir," Alice spoke out boldly. She bobbed a curtsey towards the high judge and added, "Your Honour. More to the point I wish to add to my statement. On the twenty-second of July this year, the defendant visited me at my home at six o'clock in the morning and tried to bribe me to change my statement."

A gasp spread through the courtroom and reporters scribbled furiously in their notepads. The high judge looked up surprised and Lauber collapsed down in his seat. Mr Studer turned to Lauber and shrugged his shoulders helplessly. The judge hammered his gavel for silence and asked Alice Hofstetter himself.

"Mrs Hofstetter, can you prove this statement, was anyone else present at this … conversation?"

"Yes, sir, I mean, Your Honour." Alice took a pouch of money from her skirt pocket and placed it on the ledge in front of her. "This is the very pouch he offered me and Bert Fechtig heard everything. I pretended to accept because you see, Your Honour, we may not be rich but we are an honest folk and we have our pride. Just as you dislike your time wasted, Your Honour, we are an upright community, and where wrong has been done we believe in justice. So, I pretended to accept in order to bring this pouch here today and show the court what sort of person Lauber is."

A few spectators began to clap and then everyone joined in. The high judge waited until he could continue the proceedings. When all the statements had been heard, the five judges withdrew for consultation. They returned almost immediately.

A hushed silence fell over the court as High Judge Roessel announced the Supreme Court's final verdict. It was no surprise that the previous findings were confirmed. In order to pay the due alimonies, and under the presumption that Ramun Lauber would have no income in jail, he was ordered to sell his villa and the matchstick factory in Kandergrund.

*****

Düri and Jörg Gerber, Bartli Gerber's younger brothers had joined the Gold Rush in America. Contrary to the vast majority of men, they had actually found gold and had invested wisely in a cattle ranch. This had prospered well, and they decided to invest some of their fortune in their home town. They bought Lauber's villa and the matchstick factory and asked their older brother Bartli to take over the position of director. The villa was put at his disposal. Bartli and his wife couldn't be happier at their change of fortune. Some of their former begrudging town councillors asked him to join The Liberal Centre Club, but Bartli was more interested in improving the working conditions for his employees.

Epilogue

Thanks to the alimony, Gretl's son, Walter, could go to junior high school. He then left the valley and took on an apprenticeship as baker and pâtissier in Thun. In 1911 he emigrated to America. He returned over fifty years later to show his son, Herb, his motherland.

Walter suffered from a rare genetic disorder called nail patella syndrome. During the court case, the fact that his thumb nails were missing, as those of Ramun Lauber, was brought to attention. At the time medical science was not advanced enough to know that the disorder is genetic, so it was not taken into consideration.

Although the paternity suit was closed in Gretl's favour, the matter is not quite over for her descendants who have inherited the nail patella syndrome.

A Letter from Ruedi Jungen (Schneider)

Today, at the age of 73, I experience the story of the Jungens at the Horlauenen in Frutigen quite differently than when I was still a teenager.

That my father (Walter) could grow up healthy and strong under the given circumstances in a very poor family as a small child of a handicapped, unmarried, mute mother seems to me more and more like a miracle.

In these years between the world wars, born in 1924, it was common in Switzerland to tear apart families when a poverty situation emerged and to give the children to peasant families as hired helpers who were then often without rights and in parts treated very badly and thus were marked their whole lives. Only thanks to the courageous great commitment of Albert's (Walter's) grandfather, who went all the way to federal court and received justice, could such a fate be prevented.

My grandmother Elise (Gretl) who I remember as very lovable and exuberantly sweet and helpful was always a kind and grateful grandmother. Since she was very handicapped by her muteness and speech, I could unfortunately speak little with her. Father also had an intimate good and loving understanding for his mother. They communicated quite well by lip reading. Father was very anxious to help his disabled mother wherever he could.

As a student and teenager it was probably a difficult time for him to grow up in the family Jungen (Schneider) as a latecomer among the adults, always characterised by poverty and little earnings. He must have been very influenced by his school teacher. I remember that during visits to Frutigen we always visited some of his classmates and the teacher.

Despite his complaints on knees and fingers (Nail Patella Syndrome) he took part in sports; skiers, ski jumping, cross-country skiing and probably was not bad as his prizes, tin cups and small memories showed.

The more I read through old writings the clearer the picture of the poor Jungen (Schneider) family on the Horlauenenweg becomes, as a small town farmer and self-supporter with some extra income as a craftsman and day labourer on large farms or in the construction of avalanche barriers and torrents for the canton of Bern.

That my father became such a talented versatile craftsman and later in life could earn his money in all situations is certainly due to life in the Jungen (Schneider) family where he was introduced to all practices very early and had to help make a living.

I am convinced that he has also inherited some skills from his father, the match director, and I think that I still benefit from it.

Father has always "traded" something. He often spoke about his goats that he bred himself and then sold at Easter. Later he always bred and sold rabbits. Or when we lived with a butcher he worked in the store and in addition as a market driver and was a very good seller.

Much of that has remained with me as well. I have distributed and sold magazines, later sold sports equipment for mountaineering, wanted to build up a sports business, and then I became an electrician where I worked a lot on my own account.

Thus a circle closes itself from the factory director to the water barrier salesman. My father as a learned baker and confectioner occupied himself for a long time independently with a bakery and a tea and coffee restaurant.

Since my mother, as a self-employed dressmaker, also worked a lot and that was easier to do from home, she had her dressmaker's studio and father his versatile work as a baker, and Nestle worker in the printing house and warehouse. All this makes me realise only today how versatile and determined my parents worked and how this enabled the purchase of a 3 bedroom family house in Konolfingen.

I too am versatile and determined, although also handicapped by health problems (Nail Patella Syndrome). I was still able to do a lot and shape my life positively. The big setback at 46 years old was the divorce and separation from the children, which burdened me greatly for 10 years and made me experience financially uncertain times.

Thanks to good doctors, the health handicap is now largely no more and since the physical burden is less today, I am doing well.

In my whole life, however, the disability was in retrospect in many areas very hindering and burdensome and finally also a reason for divorce by my wife who could not deal well with it.

I wish you all the best and am very curious about the book.

Best regards from Switzerland,
Rudolf Jungen

The Frutigland and the Matchstick Industry

The Frutigland is located in Switzerland in the Bernese Oberland, about 60 km south of Bern. Mountains up to about 2400 m above sea level characterise the landscape. The main town is Frutigen, where the Kander from Kandersteg and the Engstlige from Adelboden flow together.

Once upon a time, the population earned its daily bread mainly from mountain farming, small-scale trade and the production of Frutig-cloth from local sheep wool. In the middle of the 19th century, lighter and more colourful fabrics replaced the sturdy Frutig-cloth and many families gradually lost their livelihoods.

After the village fire of 1827, many severe floods between 1830 and 1850 and numerous years of famine due to crop failures, poverty in the Frutigland was exceedingly great. Government governor Johann Germann wrote in his official report in 1849 that in the municipality of Frutigen an average of 800 people were supported by the poor relief association; that was almost a quarter of the population!

During this period, the newly emerging match industry spread rapidly, especially in areas without other means of earning a living. Here, enough people were found who were willing to work with the toxic phosphorus for small wages. The first factory was founded in Frutigen in 1850. Here, there were particularly large numbers of poor people without any means of earning a living.

Jobs were therefore highly welcome by the poor and the authorities, and the matchstick factories multiplied rapidly. Within 30 years, more than twenty factories were established in the district of Frutigen, and the Frutigland became a centre for matches in Switzerland: for decades, about half of Switzerland's total production came from Frutigen factories.

The original goal, the fight against poverty, was not achieved. The poor remained poor, only the poor coffers were relieved a little. Instead of prosperity, matches brought misery, child labour, disease and infirmity to Frutigland, at least during the first 50 years. Particularly bad was the so-called "phosphorus necrosis", which, triggered by the phosphorus fumes, led to the decomposition of the jaw bones.

After finally succeeding in banning phosphorus matches, the situation improved; immediately in terms of necrosis, somewhat more slowly in hygienic and economic terms. Large factories now appeared, which allowed a more rational production of matches and better wages. The number of factories decreased to ten (1900), then to only two (1936). These were modernly equipped and provided important and good jobs for the valley. Legal measures, official pressure and the economic situation, but also the influence of the Swedish Match Trust, had brought about this improvement.

The story of the Zündhölzlibueb took place around 1920.

Ruedi Egli, Frutigland Cultural Heritage Foundation

Also by Rowena Kinread

THE SCOTS OF DALRIADA

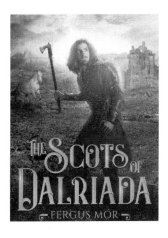

Three brothers Fergus, Loarn and Angus, Princes of the Dalriada, are forced into exile by their scheming half-brother and the druidess Birga One-tooth.

Fergus conceals himself as a stable lad on Aran and falls helplessly in love with a Scottish princess, already promised to someone else. Loarn crosses swords against the Picts. Angus designs longboats.

Together a mighty power and always on the run, the brothers must attempt to outride their adversaries by gaining power themselves. Together they achieve more than they could possibly dream of. Fergus Mór (The Great) is widely recognised as the first King of Scotland, giving Scotland its name and its language. Rulers of Scotland and England from Kenneth mac Alpín until the present time claim descent from Fergus Mór.

Full of unexpected twists and turns, this is a tale of heart-breaking love amidst treachery, deceit and murder.

Feedback from top Amazon and Goodreads' Reviewers

Intrigue, lies, dreams, treachery, romance, and brotherly bonds weave with a rich, historical setting and a create a tale to sink into... A rich weave of secrets, lies, hopes, and the desire to survive drive the tale forward as obstacles mount and every achievement seems to come with a heavy price. The relationships draw in and hit the heart, while battles rage and dangers lurk in the shadows. And all the while, the historical aspects sink in with natural finesse and create a vivid world. It's a grabbing read, and while I did find times to take a pause here and there, it was a delight to dive right back in and continue on.

Bookworm for Kids

Both thrilling and intriguing, all the way to the end. The Scots of Dalriada is a definite recommendation by Amy's Bookshelf Reviews....

Amy's Bookshelf Reviews

... an entertaining and enlightening story of a period I had previously known nothing about....

Avonna Loves Genres

Was I ever tempted to push the book aside and stop reading it? No...

Barry Litherland

... I also loved the horse: it would be worth reading the book just for that story, though it creeps in gently and takes a while to work out.
Building in the Badlands

The best kind of historical fiction is the kind that feels real, makes you feel each tragedy, each bit of passion, each gut wrenching turn. The Scots of Dalriada certainly ticks all the boxes.
David's Book Blurg

Within the narration are some lovely descriptions: 'the leather bridles...polished until they shine like dogs' noses.'...
Marian L Thorpe

... good for people interested in Historical Fiction and especially an underappreciated figure from Scottish History.
Romances of the Cross

The story reads with immense authenticity, and leaves the reader caring about this distant time, distant country and distant people. An epic achievement.
Twila's Reviews

... a rousing book of historical fiction ... A relevant and entertaining read!
Zea Perez, Author

Printed in Great Britain
by Amazon

35137812R00187